THE
500-Year
Delta

What Happens After What Comes Next

Jim Taylor and Watts Wacker
with Howard Means

HarperBusiness
A Division of HarperCollins*Publishers*

HarperCollins books may be purchased for educational, business, or sales promotional use. For information please write: Special Markets Department, HarperCollins Publishers, Inc., 10 East 53rd Street, New York, NY 10022.

FIRST EDITION

Designed by Elina D. Nudelman

Library of Congress Cataloging-in-Publication Data

Taylor, Jim.
    The 500-year delta : what happens after what comes next / Jim Taylor, and
Watts Wacker. — 1st ed.
        p.   cm.
    ISBN 0-88730-838-4
    1. Business forecasting. 2. Economic forecasting. 3. Social change.   I. Wacker, Watts.
II. Means, Howard B. III. Title.
HD30.27.W33   1997
658.4'0355—dc21   96-53069

97 98 99 00 01 ❖/RRD 10 9 8 7 6 5 4

First impressions of THE 500-YEAR DELTA

"I like [this] book. It's mind stretching and imagination expanding. While you tell us how difficult it will be to negotiate the ambient chaos if steered only by historic logic, you demonstrate that it will be eminently manageable with on-the-spot reasoning—like catching a very hot ground ball at shortstop, coming like a rocket over a rocky sandlot infield. I have a prediction—in 500 days you will have a bestseller."

—MARIO CUOMO

"If you are seriously concerned with preparing for the next 500 days, weeks, months, or years—read this book. The pages contain profound stuff and some readers may be frightened by the predictions offered by two very experienced, and respected, sages of our time. Unless we heed their advice to initiate a restructuring of nearly every aspect of our lives and embrace 'The Four New Freedoms (To Be, To Do, To Go, To Know),' our future may be bleaker than we imagine."

—DONALD C. JOHANSON, president and founder, Institute of Human Origins, author of *Lucy: The Beginnings of Humankind*

"Taylor and Wacker have assembled a wide-ranging chronicle, before the fact, of the coming century. I believe it is an accurate assessment of the challenges facing those of us who were taught to think in the twentieth century, yet find ourselves on the brink of something altogether different than what we've known. *The 500-Year Delta* deconstructs and analyzes the complexities of our uncertain future, in a simple and engaging language that even a middle-age white businessman could understand."

—DOUGLAS RUSHKOFF, author of *Ecstasy Club*, *Playing the Future*, and *Media Virus*

"This may be the most unconventional book about business ever written. In fact, it may be the most unconventional book about anything ever written.

"Taylor and Wacker have fearlessly created their own [system] for life here on earth. A grand system that takes in not only business, marketing, and advertising, but macroeconomics, government, politics, social organization, and family life. A system at the core of which is the conviction that virtually everything we believe about these institutions is a comforting myth, and that those who don't have the courage to give up these myths will be consigned to history's dustbin.

"If you want to be enlightened, startled, mystified, and infuriated—and often all on the same page—read *The 500-Year Delta*."

—BURT MANNING, chairman, J. Walter Thompson Co. Worldwide

"An absorbing book that vastly enlarges the conceptual landscape of business. These postmodern futurists share invaluable knowledge that can turbocharge how we imagine the future and locate the strategic white space within it."

—JOHN KAO, author of *Jamming: The Art and Discipline of Business Creativity*

"Taylor and Wacker have produced a dazzling array of gargantuan concepts, searing insights, and pithy observations about societal change and social values. This provocative book should be of keen interest to those whose bent of mind, quality of life, or nature of work require radical breakthrough thinking about how to live (and, incidentally, how to market) in these intellectually and morally tricky times."

—JERRY WELSH, president, Welsh Marketing Associates Inc.

To Judy and Katherine and to Betsy,
for putting up with a production many years in the making
amid great skepticism,
and to John E. Means

Only connect!

—E. M. Forster, *Howards End*

How can you connect in an age where strangers, lovers,
  landlords, your own cells betray?
Or bind the fabric together when the raging, shifting winds of
  change keep ripping away?

—Jonathan Larson, *Rent*

Contents

Acknowledgments

Every book is a collaboration of sorts—between writer and reader; between information, imagination, and audience; between past, present, and future—but some are more collaborative than others. This is one of them.

We are grateful beyond expression for the patience of our families as we worked on this and grateful as well for the many others who supported us. Raphael Sagalyn of the Sagalyn Literary Agency served as navigator on this project, always keeping us pointed in the right direction. Kim Schneider and Allison Strack juggled—and rejuggled—complex schedules to bring us together, and Kim saw to our watering and tending as we worked. Mary De Vito made us justify our speculations. Christine Griencewic searched our copy for land mines. And Gateway 2000 and SRI Consulting were generous in granting us time. In outline, a book that ranges as broadly as this requires a leap of faith, but Adrian Zackheim, the publishing director of HarperBusiness, believed in it and us wholeheartedly from the start. Harriet Rubin needs mentioning, too; without her early encouragement, this book may never have come to fruition. Thanks to them all.

And thanks to those authors, mentors, and thinkers—Alvin Toffler, the late Thomas Kuhn, Jerry Welsh, and Bradley Greenberg among them—who helped prepare this ground for us. We plant where others have plowed.

Lastly, we need to thank each other—for listening, for considering, for arguing, for amending, for enriching. We did more than collaborate; we connected. And in our own collaborator, Howard Means, we found someone who could help give voice and shape to our ideas.

JT
WW
Winter, 1996–97

Introduction

This is a book about the near-term and long-term future of business and how business leaders must reposition themselves and rethink the arenas in which they compete. It is a book about understanding every element of a business—from product through customer and marketplace—not as we wish them to be and not as they long have been assumed to operate, but as they are now becoming and as they will be over the next five hundred days, the next five hundred weeks, the next five hundred months, even the next five hundred years.

This is a book about history and the direction of the future, about the qualities and frames of mind that will sustain us and those we must jettison if we hope to cope with what lies ahead. It is a book about taking the blinders off, about seeing things whole and clear. But most of all, this is a book about change, change so rapid and so massive that by century's end it will have swept away nearly the entire underpinnings of modern life. And thus this is a book not just for businesspeople but for anyone who wants to know where society has been and where it is going.

What is this change we are talking about? It is not simply the accelerating rate of change, though that is a part of it, nor is it simply the attenuation of existing trend lines. Neither is this change just a transition writ large—from an agricultural to an industrial economy, for example, or from an Industrial Age to an Information Age. Rather, we are talking about a convergence of changes, each profound in its own right and collectively so powerful that they can be thought of only as meta-change—the change beyond which there is no more.

We have reached, in short, one of those fulcrum points in history where everything that was is tipping over into everything that will be.

The Convergence of Change

What are the elements of this convergence of change? The three most dominant forces are laid out in Part I of this book, titled "Triple-Witching Hour":

- The shift from reason-based to chaos-based logic
- The splintering of social, political, and economic organization
- The collapse of producer-controlled consumer markets

Each of these forces, in turn, is both affected and enhanced by a constellation of lesser changes that are themselves flowing together as the twentieth century draws to a close. We take those up in Part II, "Millennial Convergences":

- The waning of victimhood and the rise of authenticity and responsibility for oneself as the values of the Me Generation and Generation X yield to the values of the new Millennialists.
- A rise in principles as the driving motivational force of behavior and a simultaneous diminution in the drawing power of celebrity as the Age of Access makes celebrity self-attainable.
- An expansion of perspective as borders disappear—between nations, between peoples, between work and leisure—and governments fade into the background with them.
- The transformation of communication as the old commercial models fall to connectivity and corporate hierarchies are dissipated by e-mail, fax, and the miniaturization of time.

- The growth in the economic value of information sharing, the decline in the value of information withholding, and the rise in the value of the intellectual property people claim for themselves.
- The breakup of mass consciousness into individual realities and the emergence of situational lifestyles.
- The establishment of a new empathy, based not on historical guilt but on individual powerlessness.

Intuitively, we contend, most people understand this convergence of change is taking place. Most of us know we are straddling worlds, between what has been and what will be. We know that the old rules we learned to live by—loyalty given is loyalty received, for one—no longer apply. Our separate experiences teach us that collectively we have come to a precipice. Just as cause has come unhinged from effect, so attitudes and behaviors today are moving in different directions. Anxiety has become the dominant emotion of our times. We take this up in "Cultural Schizophrenia and the Noble Truth of Pain," the opening chapter of Part IV, "The Search for Meaning." And from there we move on to limn the outcomes of this flood tide of transitions:

- The fusion, *not* fission, of these swirling particles of change to create, through the dislocation of our own times, both consensus materialism and an epoch of extraordinary vitality.
- The creation of demand-based markets.
- The rise of tribalism and the need for tribal marketing as society reorganizes itself to fit the new realities.
- The movement away from conspicuous consumption to stealth wealth and "downward nobility," with its demand not for many things but a few good things.
- The absolute necessity in a chaos-driven world for companies to effectively manage the risk of their customers.
- The emergence of privacy management as one of the great growth industries of the next decade.
- The rising currency value of personal energy as time compresses and intersects with stress, and the imperative on corporations to preserve their human-energy resources.

- Thrival srategies and skills that can help position you and your company for the world that lies beyond.

Along the way, we simply have fun because we mean for this book to be that, too: entertaining as well as illuminating, useful in the short term as well as thought-provoking in the long term.

Part III, "Unreal Realities," is a catalogue of both the acceleration and massive accumulation of change—a catalogue, we should add, that surprised even us—as well as an overview of the sustaining myths of our times. Part V, "New Rules for a Chaos World," is a distillation in practical terms of the larger argument of the book. In Part VI, "The 500-Year Delta," we take the gloves off and begin to detail the world as it will be in five hundred days, five hundred weeks, five hundred months, even briefly in the next five hundred years. Happily for us, we won't be around in the year 2500 to live with our predictions if they are wrong, but we fully expect someone born in the year 2500 to have a perfectly valid expectation of living to the year 3000 and beyond. And in all honesty, we don't expect our predictions to be wrong in any event.

Happily, too, we do expect to be around to see much of what we foresee come true, not because we want to gloat over our accuracy, but because we foresee an epoch of pure possibility that we want to be a part of. More about that in the penultimate section of this book, "The Age of Possibility."

Finally, we end the book with "A New Vocabulary of Change"—a glossary for the new age rising: "disharmonious conjunctions," "eco-magnetics," "endotruths," "latent personalization," "nulture," "oxymoronic future," "pagan capital," "sisbertize," "wrebel," and many more. Without the words to talk about this world that is forming, it will always float just ahead in the mists.

Who We Are

Who are we? How do we claim such powers of divination? How do we purport to see through the fog and murk of time to come? In fact, we claim no special powers whatsoever. Everything we know about today, everything we know about where business and society have been and where they are going, has been learned in the trenches.

We'll come later to more details of our life stories, including some of the rough stuff. For the moment, let this introduction suffice: We are both former editors—and in one case a former majority owner—of the *Yankelovich Monitor*, the nation's premier predicting tool. Watts Wacker today is the resident futurist for SRI (formerly, the Stanford Research Institute), one of the nation's leading think tanks. Until recently, Jim Taylor was managing director of Hill & Knowlton, among the leading public-relations firms in the world. Today he is worldwide marketing director for Gateway 2000, a company that understood demand-based markets long before anyone knew what they were.

We are number crunchers and content analysts. We have pored over survey data and created hundreds of surveys of our own. We have also been given an extraordinary opportunity to see the world of affairs from deep inside the beast. Working separately and together, we have advised top executives of nearly every Fortune 100 company in America—as well as a vast number of leading international corporations—on how to position themselves for the world that lies ahead. Our client list runs from Volvo to MCI and Radio Shack; from Tambrands to Sears and the Canyon Ranch health spas; from Ralston Purina to Bacardi and Charles Schwab; from Pepsi to the U.S. government, the U.S. Olympic Committee, Mont Blanc Pens, the DreamWorks movie studio, and Nike athletic wear.

Just as important, we have been given an extraordinary opportunity to see the world of affairs from its farthest fringes. We have panhandled on the streets of Manhattan, sat with Rastafarian prophets on a Jamaican mountaintop, wrangled mustangs in the wild hills of southern Montana. Why? Because often it is only from the edge that you can truly comprehend the dance at the center.

We have both had gifted lives. But maybe the greatest gift of all has been this: We have been allowed to immerse ourselves in the tumult of our times, have been allowed to dance with chaos, and we still have been able to see hope shining clear as a freshly risen sun on the horizon.

The Four New Freedoms

Lamenting the world this steadily accelerating, steadily accumulating change has presented us with has become a popular parlor sport these days. There's no more shared reality, people say. Loyalty has disappeared;

trust is on the wane. Through connectivity, so much information pours in on us that it all turns into static. If the kids get their information off the World Wide Web, they'll never learn basic research. If the grown-ups move from job to job, from marriage to marriage, from town to town, they'll never put down roots. If we can't cut through the white noise of information, we'll become trapped in it, immobilized by input.

Alvin Toffler was the first writer to identify the accelerating rate of change, in his 1970 best-seller *Future Shock*, but by the time he got to his most recent book—*The Third Wave*, published in 1980—Toffler was openly despairing about where this change was leading us. For our part, we look out on the same landscape, see the same phenomena, the same rising distrust in our institutions, corporations, and social structures. And yet we draw precisely the opposite conclusion.

We look at the World Wide Web, the Internet technologies, the massive mountains of data waiting for electronic retrieval, and we see not a rising tide of casual information-mongering but rather a global "freedom to know"—a world in which for the first time in human history caste or schooling or economic circumstance no longer limits access to knowledge, a world in which knowledge itself is less important than the skill to access it.

We look at the dissolution of borders, the collapse of national identity, the disempowering of governments, and we see not a world order in peril but rather the rise of a global "freedom to go"—a world in which for the first time true global citizens will have true global mobility.

We look out on the collapse of corporate loyalty and see the rise of deal-making—a global "freedom to do" in accord not with professional processes or bureaucratic structures but with one's own intuition and entrepreneurial zeal.

And we look out on a splintering reality and see the opportunity to create one's own reality, a global "freedom to be" whatever one wants to be *and* the obligation to exercise that freedom.

We look out, in short, on this landscape of the present and see not the abrogation of old freedoms but the rise of four new ones: to know, to go, to do, to be. And we see just ahead of us, just beyond the coming millennium, an Age of Possibility such as the world has never known. The terror, we contend, lies only in getting there.

Triple-Witching Hour

PART I

Find yourself in this story:

It is 3:00 A.M. on a weekday morning and, as so often happens in this formless, voidless middle of the night, sleep drifts just beyond your grasp. You've awakened from a dream of which you can capture only the thinnest edges. And it is between the specter of the dream and the annoyance of wakefulness—the fear of being tired at the office—that you hover. Everyone has an internalized balance sheet of life, and to occupy your mind, to draw it away from the dream into the real world, you begin to run through both sides of the ledger.

Work first: One of your employees came to you twelve hours ago with an interesting proposition. She could deliver $1 million worth of business, she said. She had it in her pocket, signed and sealed. But there was one hitch: She wanted a 10 percent commission before she delivered—$100,000, off the top. You pointed out that this was not the way things were done in your company; she was paid well to do just what she had done. "Tough," she said. "No commission, no deal." You sit on top of a decision pyramid. You run a department, a division, a

1

company. Yet who has the greater power—you or this person who works for you? You or your most unstable variable?

You check the digital clock on your night table.

3:05.

To escape work, you turn your mind to the house or the condo you are lying awake in, or the one you hope soon to buy. It is large, comfortable, and tastefully furnished. A lawn stretches majestically in front of the house. There's a view of midtown, the ocean, or mountains from the condo balcony and the mortgage is crushing: twice your annual salary, monthly payments that attack your paycheck like a school of piranha and stretch until the threshold of retirement. Worse, the house or condo may be a diminishing asset. The one two doors down is on the market for $50,000 less than you paid for yours four years ago. What is so different about the two of them?

3:13.

Work again: You've had feelers. Or you haven't had them. Inquiries have been made about your availability, your willingness to jump, your salary demands. Or they haven't been made. Either way, you worry—worry that if you leave now, the career ladder you have been carefully building these past two, five, ten years will collapse beneath you; worry that if you don't jump now, there will be no ladder left to climb; worry that you will be leaping into the unknown, that you have no market value, that in your chosen career, you have suddenly become invisible.

3:21.

Your spouse or significant other: He or she is lying beside you, a regular breathing that could be sleep or could be its pantomime. You would like to nudge your significant other and ask about these things—about your career, about the possibly diminishing value of your greatest asset, about the $100,000 you have been asked to pay. Truth told, you would like to nudge your significant other and suggest something more intimate. He or she still arouses you. Even in the unalluring first light of day, you rarely fail to be struck by her beauty, his profile. Better still, you sleep like a log after sex. But middle-of-the-night protocols won't allow this. Your significant other has just as much need of sleep as you do, assuming he or she is asleep and not playing possum beside you. And, truth told again, there have been problems. You work too long; he or she works too long. Your moments of intersection have been too few in recent months and too crusted with tension, and you are not the only one with career-ladder concerns. If your significant other does take the new job that has been offered, what will that mean for the dynamics of your relationship? How much change can one relationship, one life, absorb?

3:30.

Work: The directive you received last week sits like a rock in your stomach. You are to come up with five-year goals for your division, a five-year plan for achieving them. The goals are easy: greater profits, greater efficiency, larger market share, better communication. But every time you try to map a route to get there, the variables seem overwhelming. Is it make-work that you can kiss off? If it isn't make-work, how can you defend a chain of causality that is as fragile as a butterfly's wing?

3:43.

Your daughter, your son, a stepchild, a younger brother or sister: Love is not adequate to describe your feelings, nor fear adequate to describe your concerns. She is beautiful, and she is careless—with her clothes, her room, her words, maybe her body. He is smart, gifted, and talented—who isn't these days, you remind yourself—and careless with his intelligence, too. If he doesn't get into the right school, what claim will he be able to make on the future? If she doesn't begin to make better choices, what claim can she hope to have on life? There is a lack of direction, a casual recklessness, a fear of engagement—with work, school, friends, family. There seems to be no anchor, only drift. This is no world for anomie. It is a jungle out there.

3:50.

Work once more: You know something about that jungle at least. A proposal for a $15 million contract was sitting on your desk when you finally left the office past seven o'clock last evening. Lying in bed now, you subject it to a systematic scrutiny. Has the planning procedure been adequate? Has every contingency been taken into consideration? Every possible source of information consulted? Every relevant data bank crunched? Are the cost projections adequate? Has the contract been priced out right? Has the team you put in place to work on it been up to the challenge? A team, you tell yourself, is only as strong as its weakest link. Who's the weakest link on this team? And who is responsible for the weakest link being there? You? Everyone needs $15 million, but your division specifically needs *this* $15 million contract. It has a multiplier effect built into it. From this one job many more will flow. A rising tide lifts all ships . . . and a falling tide drops them. If you don't win the contract, who will you keep? And who let go? And the contract is only one of your worries. Your chief planner is leaving unless you double his salary to keep him, and if you double his salary, you won't have enough left over in the salary pool to keep your management information director or your brilliant thirty-three-year-old systems analyst. Assuming there will be any systems to analyze. Assuming the ground has not already shifted so far under your feet that you are directing a department, a division, a company that has no marketplace left to pursue. Not to mention the $100,000 bribe you were asked to pony up this afternoon.

4:05.

Maybe there's something in the medicine cabinet that will help you get back to sleep.

If you cannot find yourself in the story we have just told, congratulations. You are leading a charmed life. We believe, though, that most readers will find themselves in it multiple times because the dis-ease, the discontentment and anxiety it describes, is precisely where history has brought us: to the end of a five-hundred-year experiment with reason as the controlling force of logic, to the breakup of consumer markets and economic relationships as we have known them, to the collapse of patterns of social organization far older than consumer markets or the regency of reason, to a time when attitudes and behaviors are disconnected—a pervasive social condition we call "cultural schizophrenia."

We long for order in this world. We long for clear lines of causality, for stable relationships, for predictability in our work and personal lives. But the order we keep finding is best expressed in the two-ball metaphor advanced by the great philosopher of science Hans Reichenbach earlier in this century to explain the workings of fusion and quantum mechanics.

Imagine, Reichenbach said, two balls traveling through space. Imagine them moving through the three vectors of space—longitude, latitude, and depth—in such a way, along such predictable paths, at so precisely the same rate of acceleration, that we can predict with absolute certainty where and when they will collide. Then imagine that at each instantaneous moment the balls travel through space, they change color. If the balls are the same color when they collide, they will fuse, but if they are not the same color when they collide, they cannot be in the same place.

Whether or not we fully understand Reichenbach's fourth dimension, most of us intuitively know it to be a true picture of the modern condition. Cause has come unhinged from effect. The balls not only change color constantly, they arrive along vectors and in sequences that only the insane could translate. Loyalty has disappeared, in business, in marriage, in life itself. The rules we learned to live by no longer explain our successes or failures. Nor do the old rules of corporate life apply. Coherence has turned into incoherence. There is no stability anywhere. To comfort ourselves, we keep grasping for new explanations—reengineering, Edward Demming's finely tuned theories of Japanese management practices, the Third Wave—only to find each of them poor guides to problem solving.

Why?

Try another exercise in imagination. Think of time as a river that has been flowing for five centuries now out of the earliest years of the Renaissance, and think of yourself as bobbing in the flow.

At the beginning of the journey, titans stand along the shore: Copernicus, Kepler, Galileo; Descartes and Locke; Petrarch, da Vinci, Michelangelo; Shakespeare—all those who helped free science, logic, and art from the hegemony of the Church, all those who helped established the primacy of man as a reasoning creature, what came to be known as humanism. As Descartes put it so famously in his first certitude: *Cogito ergo sum.* I think, therefore I am.

Our ride down this river of time takes us past great art, literature, and music; the rise of the novel, the modern university, mass education, and mass media. There was no such thing as a corporation at the outset of our journey, no such thing as an organized marketplace except in the village square. The state as we understand it today didn't exist until Columbus opened up the New World to resource exploitation. Before Columbus, there was no need for the "state" because the state didn't have any resources worth keeping except land and precious stones. After Columbus and the conquistadors who followed him, there was gold.

At our outset, science and medicine were still emerging from the Middle Ages. In the fourteenth century, the lifespan of an average European was about thirty-eight years. By the seventeenth century the average lifespan had grown to fifty-one years, and today it is seventy-six years. When we began our trip, self-government—true democracy—was almost unthinkable. Today, true democracy has almost arrived. Slaves have been freed, mostly. Wealth has been shared, somewhat. And all of this—from the elegantly crafted musical meters of Bach to the elegantly crafted monitors of the modern hospital delivery room, from the right to vote to freedom of speech and assembly—can claim at least partial descendance from the regency of reason.

Toward its end, though, our journey began to accelerate. As time accumulated in this flow of logic and time—as our river reached flood tide—the sights on the shore rolled by faster and faster, the navigatory givens grew less certain, change compounded on change until finally we are now being swept in a blur into what great rivers often arrive at when they reach their end: a delta, built of the swirling silt and accumulated debris that has been pushed in front of us. As with all deltas, there are safe passages and false channels through, sure footing and quicksand.

This is the world we have arrived at today: one in which the principles driving change are no longer reason but chaos, no longer causal relationships but disharmonious conjunctions. And yet, because we inevitably remain living in the past while we are carried into the future, we keep using reasonable explanations to account for unreasonable feelings and actions. That is the modern condition, a source of our contemporary, pervasive anxiety. But it is only one source, because as we drive toward the century's end, drive toward the millennium, reason is only one of three great rivers converging at the same delta.

Simultaneously, another five-hundred-year experiment—this one with the creation of consumer markets as the fundamental organizing principle of economics—is coming to an end. At the same time, a two-thousand-year-old experiment in social organization—a model of the family and society as old as Christianity—is racing to its close. And like the river of reason, both these rivers, too, flow at flood tide.

The delta that we face is composed of the commingled silt of all three forces, and it is this joined loss of social, economic, political, and logical certainty that fully feeds the beast of anxiety—that has us stark awake in our beds at three in the morning, toting up the balance sheets of our lives. If the rivers that have formed the delta are all the same color when they converge, they will fuse and produce a future of enormous energy. If they are not, they cannot be in the same place, and social dislocation at an unprecedented scale will follow. Either way, we cannot turn back. We have no choice but to move forward with the flow.

In his 1962 monograph "The Structure of Scientific Revolution," the physicist Thomas Kuhn, who died as we were writing this book, argued that the natural sciences proceed not by steady evolution but by "a series of peaceful interludes punctuated by intellectually violent revolutions." It is at those moments of revolution that the intellectual order is overthrown and new explanatory models arise—new "paradigms" as Kuhn put it, a word he would live to deeply regret the abuse of.

As it is with the natural sciences, so it is with history as a whole. For whatever purposes in history's grand scheme, the vectors of society tip along five-hundred-year intervals—the birth of Christianity, the fall of Rome, the collapse of feudalism, the rise of the Renaissance—and something wholly new is born. That, too, is where we have arrived: at a period of truncated equilibrium when the long plateau of history is poised for a huge forward leap; at a social triple-witching hour; at a delta in both its senses—as a geological formation and as the mathematical symbol of the function of change; at one of those rare fulcrum points in the long history of the planet when logical, social, and economic assumptions are being simultaneously overthrown and nothing afterward will be the same as it was before.

It is right to be afraid in such times, right to be anxious. It is even smart to be so, and smartest of all for those who need to learn to do business in this forming world. But the bet of this book is that the rivers will be the same color when they converge. The bet of this book is that enormous possibility—true democracy, true equality of opportunity, true individualism, true freedom—lies just on the other side of the delta for those prepared to take advantage of it. The purpose of this book is quite simple: to provide safe passage there.

1

The Disposition of Reason

In a truly reasonable world, you could plan your way to a reasonable end.
Cause would be discernible, effect would be predictable. There would
be rewards for rules followed, for loyalty given. Social organization
would hold. Economic and political decisions would be binding over
the long haul, because the ends they were meant to achieve would be
discernible at their birth. In a truly reasonable world, the concept of a
single career pursued over a lifetime would still make sense. That it
doesn't—that virtually every young person coming out of college
today at least senses the need to be prepared to pursue multiple
careers in multiple fields—tells us a great deal about the world as it is,
not the world as nostalgia wants it to be.

How reasonable is the world we find ourselves in today?

Reason would say that for Jim McCann to become the greatest
florist in the world, he would have had to strategize his way there. In
fact, McCann's company—1-800-FLOWERS—became the world's
leading florist by exactly the opposite route. Instead of focusing on
the strategy necessary to achieve his goal, McCann focused on being

the very best, and in the process of focusing on that outcome—of focusing on being the very best—he discovered every single day through trial and error what he was doing wrong, what he needed to improve. If he had sat down at the beginning and said, "I'm going to be the greatest florist in the world and these twelve factors will lead to my being the greatest florist in the world," he would have been wrong on all twelve of them.

In effect, Gateway 2000 founder Ted Waitt did the same thing. From the outset, he was determined to build a company that people would trust so much that they would pick up the telephone and agree to an average credit-card charge of $2,500 for a computer they could not see, touch, or hold. Every adjustment that has been made since at Gateway has been made in the service of that end, and in the process Waitt has built a business worth more than $5 billion.

Reason teaches that to achieve an end we have to proceed inductively: If I do a, then b, I will eventually arrive at z. The new logic teaches that it is only by proceeding deductively—by working backward from the outcome—that you can manage the storm of variables that will assault any business strategy. And what is true of companies, by the way, is equally true of individuals.

How reasonable is this "reasonable" world?

A friend of ours works for a privately funded sex-education council in Midtown Manhattan. Not long ago, she was attending a board meeting of the council and met a new member—a Native American. The new member's hair was, of course, jet black, long and flowing; the new member wore a great deal of makeup and beautiful pieces of native jewelry. Our friend is sophisticated and urbane, but she has spent a good deal of time in the West, among the Crow and the Blackfoot. Getting along famously with the new member should have been no problem with her, but there was one thing she couldn't get around during the first part of the board meeting: She could not determine the sex of the new board member. Because of this, she says, she was paralyzed with anxiety the whole time she was trying to interact.

If the new board member were a male, would she say something inappropriate and permanently offend him, perhaps even jeopardize her own job? If she were a female, would she violate the canons of sisterhood? Every attempt at conversation was stilted by this fear, by her inability to make the cognitive jump, and because it was, every attempt failed. And then finally, our friend says, she saw the new board member coming out of the men's room during a break in the board meeting and all the problems of acceptance disappeared in, well, a New York second.

It is an extreme example, naturally, but a useful one. Reason depends on the constancy of those things we perceive to be givens. We live increasingly in a world where the givens not only don't hold, but can be impossible to determine.

How reasonable is our world today?

Of all places, the one most desperately in need of tight control, of a carefully defined hierarchy, would seem to be an emergency medical center. But the R Adams Cowley Shock Trauma Center at the University of Maryland Medical Center succeeded not because it imposed hierarchical controls, but because it abandoned them.

R Adams Cowley was the emergency room physician who invented the concept of the Golden Hour—the critical first hour in the care of victims of serious injury, the time frame that holds the greatest opportunity to limit the long-term damage they suffer. To test Cowley's concept, the National Institutes of Health provided him with funds in the mid–1980s to construct a trauma center. All the latest technology was installed, including a helicopter pad on the roof and ambulance bays at every door. Patients—primarily the victims of blunt trauma wounds—were brought to the middle of the building, where they were immobilized with drugs and placed in bed spaces. Instead of wheeling beds through the stations of the emergency room cross—those dramatic *ER* shots—all services were brought to the patient. X-ray machines circulated overhead. Each bed was broken into hundreds of micropods so that the body could be physically evaluated without risking further damage to broken bones or traumatized spinal cords. Beside each bed, four large computer screens provided information in real time to physicians and labs located in other departments throughout the hospital.

The genius of Cowley's center, however, wasn't its technology. The genius was that Cowley eliminated the caste differences that characterize traditional organizations: Emergency room nurses and doctors regarded themselves as part of a team of equals serving the patient at the point of entry, and because they did—because bureaucratic control was surrendered in the interest of accomplishing a common objective—that objective, the chaotic business of evaluating and beginning to mend a desperately broken body within the critical Golden Hour, became accomplishable.

R Adams Cowley has since died, and without him the center has sunk into bureaucratic haggling. Nurses have to report through the line to a head nurse; doctors have to work up the line to senior medical staff. The billing and material-controls department have gotten into the act. All of it has brought a degradation of teamwork and a substantial decline in reputation. But while it worked in its purest form, Dr. Cowley's creation was a spectacular success and pure beauty to watch in action. To see it was to see chaos in the form of a dance, and hundreds of patients have that dance to be thankful for every day of their lives.

Reason says that it is only through the implementation of a hierarchy that control can be maintained. The Cowley Shock Trauma Center says that surrendering control creates control.

One more example of this "reasonable" world:

Some years back, in the midst of the Cold War, the United States government assembled a consulting team for one of the most macabre tasks imaginable: to figure out how to announce nuclear war to the American people—what the communication strategy would be, what the actual words would be, and who would do it.

The fantasy is that there is no time for such things. Submarines are waiting somewhere in the deep troughs of the Atlantic and Pacific oceans, and we have fourteen minutes from the time the first nuclear-warhead missiles break the water's surface to get our affairs in order and make peace with our Maker. The reality is that all governments, even enemy ones, are bureaucracies; Mutually Assured Destruction also meant mutually assured channels and procedures. In the United States, those procedures get formalized under what are known as DEFCONs, or defense conditions. At DEFCON 5, the world is at peace. DEFCON 4 calls for heightened readiness. At DEFCON 3, we have reached crisis. In those days, DEFCON 2 meant that conventional warfare was literally under way; figuratively, it indicated that, while nuclear attack was more imminent, lines of satellite communication were still open between Washington and Moscow or Beijing so that both sides could stand down their warheads. Because the first phase of attack from either side was expected to be high-altitude blasts to destroy communication, we and our enemies would move to DEFCON 1 when the other side switched to ground communication. Only at that point would mutually assured destruction be truly mutually assured. With lines of contact shut down, there would be no way to call the war off.

Because the Soviets had developed a massive evacuation plan—and because it was assumed that both sides would launch highly targeted attacks to keep as much of the physical assets of the enemy intact as possible—the consulting team was given a window of three days to, in effect, tell Americans in target zones, which mostly meant large cities, to get in their cars and get the hell out of town. But how to do it? How to keep the streets from filling up with frenzied people screaming, "Don't do it! Don't do it!"?

The plan that was developed was, in fact, the very essence of reason. It called for a famous personality—then and still one of the most trusted people in America—to appear in a preemptive television broadcast near the beginning of the crisis. The script would have had him say, "I'm speaking to the American people on behalf of the government of the United States in Washington, D.C. The President will speak with you in ten minutes, but he has asked me to confirm the following: A nuclear state of war exists between the United States of America and the [Union of Soviet Socialist Republics, People's Republic of China, etc.], and it is impossible to stand down from this state of war. We expect to be carrying out an attack within the next forty-eight hours, and we expect to be similarly attacked in the next forty-eight hours. It is incumbent upon every American in targeted zones to take precautions to protect himself or herself. . . ."

Meanwhile, various government agencies were to be preparing citizens to take such precautions. Comic books would be parachuted into targeted areas, showing people in the simplest of terms what they could carry with them. Policemen and soldiers would go door-to-door in targeted areas to alert the populace and issue travel passes. Other policemen, soldiers, and public officials would prepare to reverse the traffic flow so everyone could get out of Dodge. And all the time, this most-trusted American would be on television nonstop, between presidential cameo appearances, assuring the public that everything was in place, everything was working, life would go on.

As we say, it was the essence of reason. But there were problems. Some parts of most large cities were deemed unable to be evacuated. If you lived in Manhattan, for example, you could leave—assuming you had access to a vehicle—because the traffic flow could be reversed sufficiently to get you across the George Washington Bridge. If you lived in Queens, you couldn't leave. Had you shown up at one of the evacuation-route bridges or tunnels without exit approval, you would have been turned away. No exit visa, either, if you lived in the ghetto. Ghetto dwellers were assumed not to have cars. Not to mention, of course, the reception these urban sophisticates were likely to get when they showed up in Grover's Corner expecting sanctuary. Rural people tend to be heavily armed and fiercely protective of their own. Not to mention the strains on a sense of duty that might be felt by a block captain or bridge guard desperately anxious to assure the safety of himself and his family, or the sheer animal instinct for survival that would have turned every targeted area into sheer management hell.

So much, in short, for a reasonable world.

The Multiplicity of Change

An old rule of thumb holds that you cannot change your job, your marital status, and your address at the same time. One is doable, if hardly fun. Two is possible. Move up to three, and the stress circuits overload—the whole system crashes and traumatic stress disorder sets in. It is just that: an old rule, overwhelmed by the acceleration of the rate of change, buried under the sheer tonnage of change that has accumulated over recent decades.

Each year, about 26 million Americans change jobs. That figure will only rise, broadly across the job spectrum, not just at the traditionally vulnerable bottom of the job pyramid, because job stability has disappeared along with job loyalty. They have been replaced by deal-based employment relations. How about marital status? About one in every seven American women and one in eight American men ages thirty-five to fifty-four is currently divorced. There are fewer than two marriages annually in the United States for every one divorce. Compare that to 1950 when there were more than four marriages for every divorce. Address stability? About 42 million Americans move each year, and a third of those move at least across county lines.

In two generations, we have shifted from a society that nearly sanctified stability—in the workplace and at home—to one that can barely sit still for a half-hour sitcom, and then only with channel-grazer in hand. The jangling images and quick cuts of an MTV video are nothing more than the reflection of the jangling, quick-cut internal rhythms of our lives today. Been there. Done that. See you around. Gotta move on.

An old rule of employment held that you looked before you leaped. You hired a consultant who would tell you how much the prospective employee was worth based on experience, age, prior position, the intended position, industry comparables, and the like—all worked out on what were known as "payroll bicompetency grids." You then sat down with the would-be employee and made a personal assessment. The consultants still get hired; the process still has the trappings of order. We part painfully with the old structures. But today, you cannot even ask the questions you need to ask, let alone demand the answers you need to know. Is the prospective employee in a dissolving marriage? Does he have a serious career problem? Does she somehow have leverage over you? Don't even think about it. And absolutely don't think about asking if he or she has AIDS or a child with a medical problem so severe that it will drive HMO rates up for the entire workforce. That way lies the in-house counsel's office.

Change is overwhelming workers as much as it is overwhelming the workplace, yet legislation and the threat of litigation hang over personnel decisions like a sword of Damocles, suspended by a single hair, ready to drop at the least inquiry about the most significant variables. Personnel decisions today aren't rational; they are for the most part irrational in the extreme—leaps of faith. The saving grace is that the work relationship is likely to be of such brief duration.

An old rule of logic held that if *a* equaled *b* and *b* equaled *c*, then *a* was equal to *c*. Today, to borrow again from Hans Reichenbach, it is true only if *a* and *c* are the same color when they collide. Linear reason has died, squeezed out of existence by the compression of time, by the narrowing of the window in which any decision must be rendered. A might have equaled *b* when the formulation was made, and *b* might have equaled *c*, but in the space of time it takes to join *a* and *c*, *b* will have fallen entirely out of the equation or a new flood of information will have altered the meaning of *a* or *c*. To assume today that *a* equals *c* is to invite disaster. Givens don't hold. Linearity has yielded to circularity, just as point-to-point communication is yielding to the World Wide Web. Rational theory has been replaced by chaos theory. And in Chaos, as John Milton taught us more than three hundred years ago, matter is formless and space infinite. In Chaos you cannot do, you cannot plan, you cannot reason to an end point. In Chaos, you can only be.

If graduate schools really wanted to measure the practical intelligence of their applicants, they would stop asking them to complete analogies and begin testing them in their facility with game theory. Analogies link relationships over a rational linear spectrum—hot is to touch as sweet is to smell. They assume, because they must to exist, that givens hold. Game theory invokes the ability to use irrational means to achieve concrete ends. The only given it assumes is the treachery of relying on any given. *That* is the world as it is. Remember Lily Tomlin and Jane Wagner's wonderful line: "Reality is a collective hunch."

A final rule: Experience is the best teacher. When a paradigm shifts as is now happening, experience is quite possibly the worst teacher in town. Why? Because in the reason age now ending, experience has been built on a knowledge of causal relationships—if *a*, then *b*; if sales spiked, the reason is that prices rose; if productivity increased, the reason is that flex-time was instituted; if 1.2 million people showed up at major-league ballparks last Sunday, 1.2 million will show up this Sunday. In a reason-based world, the relationship is as plain as the nose on your face. But in the Chaos Age now forming, causality, like linear logic, has been summarily deposed. Those 1.2 million people may or may not show up at ballparks on Sunday, but chaos theory says that we cannot predict a single one of them will arrive without knowing he or she has bought a ticket and is moving through the turnstile.

Change moves too fast, time is too compressed to draw any link with experience. Rational connections have been routed by connectivity. In the world as it now is, you can no longer discern the cause or the effect of any action. You cannot control the relationship or even the moment when the relationship might be valid. All you can know about any action, any effect, is that it happened. The more you search for causality, the further behind you will fall. The more successful you have been in the reason-based world, the harder it will be for you to leave it.

Grim as it is, that is one of the grim ironies of paradigm shifts: Past success breeds future failure. Rationally, it is entirely wrong. Evolutionarily, it is simply what is. Evolution is neither right nor wrong. Ask the *Australopithecines*, the dodo, *Tyrannosaurus rex*, or the passenger pigeon: Evolution is absolutely amoral.

In fact, we have built an entire world on rational relationships. If we give love, we will receive love in return. If we give loyalty to our employer, we will receive loyalty in return. If we planned, if we labored in fulfillment of our plan, in time we would be rewarded. In accord with biblical injunction, we built our castles on rock, not on the shifting sands. A yields *b*; *b* yields *c*. And finally, if we truly look around, we find that in the delta of the river of reason, shifting sands are precisely the geological condition that applies. Love? Please. We still need it; we still value it deeply and turn ourselves inside out to find it. But see the divorce statistics above. Loyalty? Please, again. Ask the 30,000 ever-loyal middle managers of ever-loyal IBM who were laid off in a single swipe of the pen.

In this waning of the age of reason, we find ourselves finally in the decade of denial. We invoke the "reasonable" workings of the marketplace to disguise the fact that we are creating a dangerously bifurcated society. In a single generation, we have virtually eradicated the middle class. In a single generation, we have so reconcentrated wealth in America that today 4 percent of the populace collectively controls $1.3 trillion. In a single generation, we have moved from the war on poverty to waging war on the impoverished. In the name of "reason," we impose on ourselves a political correctness that denies us access to a language that would even let us talk about the problems we face as a nation. In the name of reason, we plan and labor in fulfillment of our plans, we give loyalty and love. And then one day we happen to find ourselves, like Tom Wolfe's Sherman McCoy, with a flat tire in a part of town we would never willingly visit with a sixteen-year-old waving a .38 in our face. "Wait a minute," we say. "This isn't reasonable. You could spend the rest of your life in jail." And he says, "Fuck reason, I'm going to shoot you." It's not a reasonable answer, Lord knows, but it's good enough for us. Evolution, as we said, is absolutely amoral. Any successful corporate manager will know exactly what we are talking about. Success can no longer be built on appeals to reason; success lies in appeals to self.

The Rise of Intuition

What is the true condition of the modern corporate manager? Most of you don't need us to tell you that, but it is worth limning all the same.

In storybooks—and undoubtedly still in some graduate courses in basic management practices—the "true" condition is easy to describe. Challenges arrive sequentially. Information is gathered. Wise heads are consulted. A plan is formed. Contingencies are pondered and provided for. Ducks are lined up. The big guns are pulled out. And finally a solution is executed.

In the real world, nothing like that happens. In the real world, billions of variables interact continuously. In the real world, if you study all the information available to you that might help illuminate a single decision, you will go blind from reading. There is too much of it, and thanks to connectivity, it is too instantaneously accessible. In the real world, if you ponder all the contingencies that might bear on a single decision, you will go mad from planning. The process is too compressed. The variables could fill the Milky Way. In the real world, things might arrive sequentially, but the space between the sequences is too thin to discern, too infinitely small to be meaningful. In the real world, it is not reason-based logic a corporate manager is dealing with, it is particle logic. All the elements that weigh on any decision have been reduced to the subatomic level, and they exist in a constant swirl. Perhaps the ducks are lined up in a row, perhaps they are not. In any event, you couldn't see them without an electronic spectrograph, and by the time your optic nerve registers the configuration and passes it up the neural chain, the configuration will have changed.

Finally, if you are going to succeed in this real world, you cannot act on assumptions. Assumptions disappear. You cannot act on the predicted fulfillment of some causal chain. The path coefficients that would fulfill that prediction are subject to too many random variations and mutations. You cannot act because the last time you made such a choice, it produced such a consequence.

Just as cause has come unhinged from effect, experience has come unhinged from outcome. If you are going to succeed in chaos, you must connect with chaos. You must act in concert with chaos. What does that mean? It means that you must trust in intuition, trust in self. One of the true beauties of the age now forming is that, finally, you will have to make choices on purely arbitrary bases—because they feel right. It is the ultimate democratization of logic.

"What I must do is all that concerns me, not what the people think," Ralph Waldo Emerson wrote in that seminal American essay, "Self-Reliance." "This rule, equally arduous in actual and in intellectual life, may serve for the whole distinction between greatness and meanness. It is the harder because you will always find those who think they know what is your duty better than you know it. It is easy in the world to live after the world's opinion; it is easy in solitude to live after our own; but the great man is he who in the midst of the crowd keeps with perfect sweetness the independence of solitude."

We would alter that slightly: "What I must be is all that concerns me. . . ." But as he was on so many things, Emerson was right on this. True self-reliance is true freedom.

Such a rising world should be terrifying—indeed it is to many—and it should be most terrifying to the highest animals on the corporate food chain: chief executive officers. CEOs not only must operate in a chaos environment like any other manager, they must also nurture the asset, preserve it, make it grow. That is what they are employed to do, what they are paid often great sums to accomplish. Precisely because they are paid those great sums, have been made the stewards of such great assets, are the princes of the New World Order, and can raise or topple governments simply by where they choose to place a factory, CEOs also have a very particular responsibility. They are the ones whose eyes must never be shut. They more than anyone else cannot afford to be blinded by reason from seeing the chaos that surrounds them, because they more than anyone else have the power to deflect the assets in ways that are compatible with change.

The story is much told of the African prince who couldn't lie down for fear that the winds would sweep his village away. That is the condition of modern CEOs: They can't shut their eyes for fear that the winds will sweep their businesses away.

2   The Disorganization of Organization

The model for the organization of the family is rooted in 2,000 years of Judeo-Christian thought and practice: loving parents and dutiful children mutually obliged to one another by bonds of blood and custom, together "until death do us part." This is the family of Mary, Joseph, and the baby Jesus, the family of the clustered ancestral groupings found in Heaven as taught by the Church of Jesus Christ of the Latter-Day Saints. It is the family that the Christian Coalition and Pat Buchanan have in mind when they talk about "family values," the family enshrined in such television series as *Father Knows Best* and *Ozzie and Harriet,* and in Laura Ingalls Wilder's collection of *Little House on the Prairie* novels. Love and respect are given upward in this family; love and direction, love and control are given downward. Everyone sits down together at six every evening for two vegetables, a roasted chicken, and a steaming fruit pie for dessert.

The reality, measured by the statistical mean, is that this "typical American family" no longer exists. The reality is that off-screen Robert Young, the father of *Father Knows Best,* nearly drank himself to death, and Ozzie Nelson was chasing women while his youngest son developed a dependence on cocaine. The reality of the family, indeed, is far closer to the *Little House on the Prairie* TV series than it is to the novels that inspired the series: Holding the family together is a constant fight against forces that would rip it apart. The reality is that even the Virgin Mary was an unwed mother whose grown son was put to death.

There is a model, too, for the organization of the corporation, quite like the family model. Respect goes upward, control falls downward, and the greatest power always rests on the highest floor. The hierarchy goes unquestioned because it is so clearly discernible and so easily enforced. Once a year, everyone gets together at the company picnic to renew old acquaintances up and down the corporate food chain. Statistically, judged by the mean, this model does still exist. In practice, it is fast becoming a paper shell.

There is a model, as well, for the organization of governance, both quite like and quite different from the previous two. Control still flows down, although in the United States the reins of control can be snatched away on a single first Tuesday after the first Monday in November. Respect still flows upward, if not (and rarely of late) to the governors themselves then at least to the institution being governed. Rules are followed, discipline is exacted. There is a mutual sacrifice—taxes, military service, jury duty—for the common good. What binds it all together is what we call patriotism—from the Greek *patris*, fatherland—and a common set of symbols and rituals that encapsulate that sense of national family: "I pledge allegiance to the flag of the United States of America. . . ." Today in most public schools the "Pledge of Allegiance" is rarely recited beyond elementary school. Children simply won't stand still for it. Today, most teenagers, boys and girls, are far more likely to have American-flag boxer shorts in their dresser drawers than they are to have an American flag displayed anywhere in their room or homes.

And, there is a model for the organization of decision making, rooted in the dictates of reason. The problem is identified, wise heads are consulted, channels are worked, causality is established, and by the time a strategy is launched, the battle has moved to another killing field and the combatants are barely recognizable. It is all as quaint as a horse and buckboard, and just about as useful for getting you from L.A. to London for a 10 A.M. conference.

• • •

Historically, the defining organizations of our society have resembled amoebas. Their membranes were semipermeable—fluids could seep in or out of them—but they contained within themselves all the requirements for survival. Today, our defining organizations are far closer to hosts inhabited by colonies of viruses.

Like viruses, we live off organizations without particularly respecting them or even believing in them. Like viruses, we move freely from one organization to another, and as we move, we replicate and even eat the replicants. To survive, we do, in short, whatever circumstances require us to do at whatever time they require it. It is the one clear lesson that contemporary history has taught us.

Social Organization: The Real Family Values

What do Americans truly value in their family relations? Statistics would tell us that what they truly value are mobility, short-term unions, and ever-shifting configurations; not loyalty, but disloyalty; not mutual obligation, but mutual disobligation. Statistics, of course, mislead—and never more so than when they are invoked to explain sweeping social trends—but they at least point to the true landscape of the American family.

Statistics, for example, tell us that slightly more than half of all marriages end in divorce and that that figure has largely leveled off in the past decade. But even those figures are masking deeper ones. Divorce rates have always been skewed by the tendency of divorced people to remarry, divorce, and repeat the cycle again—to become repeat offenders. Today, however, the remarriage rate of divorced people is falling while the divorce rate of younger married couples is rising. "Generation X'ers," those in the sixteen-to-thirty age group, talk openly about what they call the "divorce assumption"—the assumption, in effect, that marriage is an experiment that can always be terminated, that a spouse is a housemate who may or may not work out. As we'll discuss later, that's part of the risk aversion of Generation X'ers, their propensity to establish an exit before ever entering.

What does this mean in the aggregate? That of any 1,000 American marriages in a single year, a little more than 350 will terminate within seven years, and another 150-plus will disappear within fourteen years. What about the children of these shifting alliances? Each year, a million American children watch their parents divorce. In toto, about 75 percent of all children will come under new management—stepfathers, stepmothers, foster parents, wards of the state—during the course of their childhoods.

One of the odder ironies of the collapse of the family is that it has led to a wholesale increase in the number of "fathers" and "mothers." That's why we recommended to Hallmark Cards that it create a "step-grandparents" day and to Jim McCann's 1-800-FLOWERS that it create an "all-occasion" calendar. In fact, we do need a new holiday in America, an All-Family Day, so that everyone involved in these infinitely complicated, blended relationships—stepparents, stepcousins, half-siblings—can feel good about their relationships.

Just as we have entered the age of particle logic, so have we entered the age of particle families, not nuclear ones. To capture the full range of an average American family's relationships, to fully penetrate its dimensionality, we have to search at the subatomic level.

Marriage persists and always will because love persists and always will. It persists despite all its multiple failures because no one has ever thought up a better arrangement in law for the sharing and division of property. It persists because, for many people, a slightly angry warm body beside them in the bed is better than no body at all. It persists because it is a convenient vehicle for begetting and raising children and because the begetting and raising of children will persist so long as the capacity to give and feel love exists, and that will be forever. But such reasoning cannot blind us to the reality of family life today.

To preserve the myth that "families" still exist in any traditional form in America, we have had to broaden the umbrella of the word to include in undifferentiated fashion what were once called "broken families" and what were once considered barely families at all—a child or children and a single, never-married mother.

To preserve the myth that the "family values" of the 1990s can be anything like the family values of the 1950s, we have had to willfully ignore the fact that 65 percent of mothers of children under eighteen years of age now work full- or part-time outside the household. We have had to willfully close our eyes to the reality that there are more than 1.6 million official "latch-key" children in the United States, and many more than that who come home from school to an empty house or live virtually isolated existences within the confines of the family unit. A 1985 California study found that the average father spent thirty-seven seconds a day in "meaningful interaction" with his children. A subsequent study was more positive, but only because it broadened the base: That one found that the average father spent six minutes a day with his children in interactions of all sorts, while mothers spent only a few minutes more.

The "family" that Ronald Reagan rhapsodized on, the one that many fundamentalists want to reinstate—this nuclear social organization that will make America once again the shining city on the hill—is fabulism, another of those short-term reasons that appear in times of radical change to explain long-term transitions. Such families exist in their pure form in any abundance in precisely two places on the planet: the Third World and the most affluent suburbs. Among Americans, only the very upper-middle class and beyond can afford its luxury—its clothing, its doctors' (and all too often its therapists') bills, the education costs, the incredible connectivity costs in money and energy that allow it to reassemble for holidays and reinforce its binding rituals once the children are grown and gone.

The humor taken at Bill and Hillary Clinton's expense—his alleged philandering, her alleged temper tantrums—is based on the idealized family, not the actual one. In the real world, the Clintons focused on a goal—to be the First Family—and stuck to it through thick and thin. They are intact, blessed with a seemingly happy and well-adjusted daughter. Mark them down not as a failed marriage but as one of conjugality's increasingly rare successes.

If not families, what then is the engine behind the new social agenda? Society will always be driven to organize, but what is it organizing around as we drift into this millennial delta? Neo-tribes. Cohabiting affinity groups. Fraternities of strangers.

Ask any one hundred people who their best friend is, and the majority are likely to name the person they share the most meaningful personal secrets with, not the person they have known the longest, the one who has the most details about their lives. Why? Because in a hypermobile society, a society that is constantly reconfiguring its family groupings, longitudinal friends—deep friends—get relocated out of our lives.

Ask the same one hundred people if their best friend is someone they met through a country club, a lunch club, or the neighborhood, and the answer is again likely to be no. Clubs are for the fulfillment of social and professional obligations. More and more neighborhoods are for the fulfillment of sleep. The fiction that they are anything more— that they are places for forming deep attachments—only heightens the anxiety of members or neighbors who wonder if they're the only ones in the setting with no friends. We belong to such organizations and live in such places without being defined by them.

Where do we make our friends? Where mobility takes us, where we find ourselves, which for most people means work. But the workplace is no longer organized around loyalty and long association. Rather, it is driven by fleeting relationships that are at once competitive, symbiotic, parasitic, and predatory. Relationships in the workplace serve to get the deal done, one deal at a time. Friendship only clouds the issue; it can rarely drive to the questions that establish true intimacy: How much do you make? How do you feel about your partner in love?

What then are we defined by? Where do we find real friends in an age so overwhelmed by change? How do we group ourselves? For once, television has it pretty much right. *Friends*, *Melrose Place*, *Baywatch*— they are all about cohabiting affinity groups, people with little previous knowledge of one another who are drawn together into ad hoc relationships, often by economic necessity.

Yes, the shows are funny in the former case, and bathetically funny in the other two. Yes, the shows themselves are propelled by minor, often altogether unbelievable crises. Yes, happily, in the latter show, handsome men and well-developed women manage to wear only a bare necessity of clothing. That is the surface appeal of the shows, why they survive so handsomely in prime time and syndication. But at a deeper level, all three shows tap into a fundamental change in social organization. Families had been created to protect each other from danger, to keep each other safe and fed through mutual reliance, to—in the most idealized form—nurture and grow the young. Today "families" are fraternities of strangers drawn together largely as protection against loneliness.

No show, in fact, had that more right than the long-running *Cheers*. The "Norm" that rang out when actor George Wendt walked into the bar was nothing more than "Welcome home," updated for an age without families. Just as important to the success of the show, the "family" of *Cheers* is all that kept the postman Cliff Claven from going postal.

It was precisely this shift in social organization that MCI took advantage of when it organized its "Family & Friends" phone networks. Most Americans today don't have enough intact family to fill a dining-room table, much less a dance card or phone menu. But broaden the umbrella of "family" to include friends, provide a mechanism for all those half-siblings and stepparents to reach out to each other, and you have an instant marketing success.

How else do we organize ourselves? Through symbols, icons, and totems. Through the logos we wear on our clothing. Through the social signs we broadcast.

A San Francisco 49ers jacket worn on Chicago's North Michigan Avenue is more than protection against the winter winds—and perhaps an invitation to mayhem at the hands of an enraged Bears fan. It's an invitation to familiarity, a way of positioning yourself socially among all those people on the Magnificent Mile huddled against the cold.

The motorcycle company Harley-Davidson has been absolutely ingenious in creating an entire social organization around its product—from the chrome-rich hogs themselves to the symbol-ridden clothing that riders don and the weekend riding clubs that assuage the riders' weekday loneliness. In effect, Harley has taken its customer base, expanded it into a tribe, and provided the tribe the means to constantly reinforce its rituals. All those riding clubs lack is warpaint to complete the effect.

Decorative house flags—tulip flags for the spring, corn flags for summer, turkey flags for the Thanksgiving season, and so on around the calendar—are more than ornamentation. They, too, are a form of communalism, icons of tribalism, a way of announcing a set of tastes, an invitation to fraternity. Herd crimes—crimes that define someone as a member of the group—are a form of tribalism, too, whether it is pot smoking for the countercultural tribe, petty shoplifting for the early-teenage-girl tribe, or expense-account padding for the junior-executive tribe. Herd crimes mean you belong.

Most broadly—and of most interest to merchandisers and advertisers—we organize ourselves socially into media communes. Part of that lies in our proclivity to use the media and our skill set at doing so. Cybergeeks have far more to say to each other at a first meeting than do members of corresponding downtown clubs or half-brothers and half-sisters. So, for that matter, do media recluses, those who make a personal choice to divorce themselves from the media world. Consciously avoiding the media provides them with a common language.

A larger part of this organizing, though, lies in the consistent selections we make from the universe of media choices, especially from the universe of magazine choices, because magazines are both relatively enduring and for the most part relatively fine-bore in their subject matter. We have identified seven of these media communes—seven major reading tribes that collectively account for about 45 percent of the U.S. population. Each is a fraternity of strangers, yet within each, media habits are so much alike that attitudes about social, political, and economic phenomena can be predicted with remarkable precision.

- **The Seven Sisters.**
  A commune defined by magazines such as *Cosmopolitan, Ladies' Home Journal, Redbook, Good Housekeeping,* and *McCall's.* Its primary media choices are, in effect, management guidebooks for women seeking to adjust to their fourfold roles as workers, mothers, women, and CEOs of their own households. The media choices, in turn, collectively express an appreciation for the roles these women have undertaken.

- **Real Guys.**
  Periodicals that exist mostly to sell and manage the fantasies of deskbound males aged thirty-five to fifty, from kayaking the upper Amazon to winning Wimbledon to undressing Claudia Schiffer and

playing wargames. Some of the titles: *Playboy, Field & Stream, Guns & Ammo,* as well as the whole gamut of "warrior" magazines.

- **Intelligentsia.**

  A sexually neutral group that spends most of its magazine time inter-acting with publications that tell them how to get ahead in their jobs, how to get along on their career tracks, how to improve the quality of their experience in the work- and marketplace, how to interpret the business theory *du jour,* and how to live in a manner commensurate with their success. Not surprisingly, the media choices of the Intelligentsia serve to reinforce the members' sense of intellectual superiority. The titles: *Inc., Smart Money, Fortune, Forbes,* as well as such periodicals of the affluent lifestyle as *Architectural Digest, Gourmet, Martha Stewart Living,* and *Town & Country. People* is the bonbon magazine of the Intelligentsia.

- **Girl Talk.**

  Periodicals—*Savvy, Friends,* etc.—that communicate almost exclu-sively with younger women, frequently younger women with rela-tively low self-esteem, about how to be a successful female in the new age and, just as important, how to look good, not to men, but to their friends. *Cosmopolitan* serves as a crossover media choice between Girl Talkers and the Seven Sisters.

- **Armchair Adventurers.**

  National Geographic. Modern Maturity. Reader's Digest. Magazines for senior citizens who travel largely through the stories they read. This commune, by the way, extends into the Arts & Entertainment and Discovery cable channels. Had the senior executives of the National Geographic Society fully understood that, they would have taken over the Discovery Channel nearly a decade ago, back when it was struggling through its infancy, desperate for a cash infusion, and offered to the Society almost for free.

- **Mother Jones.**

  Named for the lefty San Francisco–based monthly and composed of periodicals—including Jan Wenner's *Rolling Stone, Wired,* and the *Utne Reader*—that advocate liberal social policies and take a highly critical stance toward authority of all sorts. The high computer literacy of this commune had a powerful influence on the antiestablishment orientation evident especially in the early days of the Internet and World Wide Web.

• **God Talk.**
The newest of the media communes. Often reactionary politics are justified in scripture and disseminated through *Christian Life* and myriad small publications, as well as through Pat Robertson's Christian Broadcasting Network. Intriguingly, this is both the most tightly bound of all the media communes—the one most informed by an us-against-them mentality—and the most diffuse. Despite strong advocacy of "family values," members tend to come from isolated households and are widely scattered across the economic spectrum.

In effect, these media communes are America's new extended families, the seven groups of people who most readily understand each other's experience of life and thus most easily bond. Like tightly knit families, these media communes thrive on cryptocentrism; they build up private languages that allow them to communicate in code with one another and to identify who is in and out of the group. Through a process we call "evilution," media communes create their own constantly evolving definitions of who is evil and who is good in our society—Richard Nixon, O. J. Simpson, Hillary Clinton; trial lawyers, big business, meat-eaters.

Media communes not only have their own hierarchies, they determine the hierarchies and create the mediocrats of the microcultures that fall within their purview. Increasingly, it is through these media-anointed mediocrats—Reverend Al Sharpton for New York's black dispossessed microculture, to cite one example—that microcultures talk to one another. Increasingly, too, it is through media communes that people remake themselves whenever and in whatever ways they choose. Think of doing so as the Madonna syndrome, after the constantly reborn singer and actress, and think of Bill Clinton as the foremost practitioner of the Madonna syndrome in the political arena.

As social organization continues to "particalize"—as it breaks down into ever smaller, autonomous units— the lines of these media communes will be ever more tightly drawn, and the communes themselves will become ever more fragmented. And as that happens, new media choices will emerge to claim subcommunes of the gross communes that now exist.

Leaders magazine, in fact, already does that. Published by Henry Doorman, who came up with the idea of putting the *National Enquirer* next to every supermarket checkout line in America, *Leaders* is given free to 35,000 corporate, government, military, and religious leaders around the world, and it is for them and by them alone. Leaders write the articles for *Leaders*. What's more, they aren't paid for this work; they buy their way onto the editorial pages by purchasing an advertisement for whatever enterprise they happen to lead. By the standards of the Magazine Publishers of America, *Leaders* is hardly a magazine at all—its content can't even qualify for the National Magazine Awards, the MPA's Pulitzers. Yet *Leaders* is enormously successful. A typical issue might have 170 pages of advertising, sold at more than $20,000 a page, and all this for a circulation less than one-fiftieth the size of *Time* or *Newsweek*. Why such success? Because Doorman has created a media subcommune; he has carved out a chunk of the Intelligentsia commune and provided it with an intermediary for increasing the dialogue between people otherwise too busy to communicate with one another directly.

The media today is not only the message—it is the message discriminator. And increasingly it is around those finely discriminated messages that we organize our social lives.

Corporate Organization: The Rise of Free Agency

The woman we used to help introduce this section—the employee who went to her boss and demanded a $100,000 commission before turning over $1 million worth of business—wasn't made up. She was real. The only thing fictional about the story were the sums involved. The piece of business she held in her pocket was worth $15 million, not $1 million; she wanted a far bigger piece of change than $100,000 for delivering it; and in fact she got every penny of what she demanded, over the strident objections of the head of accounting.

Was it a good deal that this employee was structuring for herself? Not if we judge it by the traditional norms of corporate life. Great as it was, the present value of the commission she received was still worth far less than the future value of her employment guarantee, which she had fatally jeopardized by her behavior. But this woman knew what too many middle- and upper-level managers have had to learn the hard way—that there is no employment guarantee any longer and that, because there is none, an employment guarantee has no value beyond the moment. When she walked into her boss's office demanding a commission, this woman was declaring her free agency. She was already crossing the delta, already seeing the world for what it is, not what it was.

What is the rational structure of a corporate organization? The rational structure is rules-driven. It seeks to minimize the amount of time employees spend during any eight-hour workday on extraneous matters. It seeks to maximize the amount of time they spend on task, whatever the task may be. The rational structure assures that an employee communicates only with his or her immediate subordinates or his or her immediate boss, and it provides penalties for going outside those channels. A rational structure rewards loyalty and demands loyalty be given in return. A rational structure has a rational pecking order. It has a rational flow of power from the mail room to the CEO's office. Time-motion studies work in rational organizations because the entire organization has been structured to assure that they work.

We could point to dozens of companies that maintain such a rational structure, dozens upon dozens of companies where the old rules still hold sway. And in doing so, we could almost assure you that unless they change their ways radically and quickly, they will cease to exist in any meaningful form within ten years.

Why? Because reason has been deposed.

The woman we mentioned above is not the first employee to figure out that loyalty is neither to be given nor received in the modern business world. Increasingly, corporations are coming to resemble National Football League teams. There are franchise employees whom you can't lure away for love or money, employees who are so central to the purpose that you will give them anything to keep them on—but can, of course, fire. Just as in the NFL, there are a few employees beneath the franchise employee who are considered so valuable that you will rob the till to keep them on—but can, of course, fire, too. And everyone else? They are journeymen and free agents, whom you can fire as well, but who can just as easily fire you. And the better they are at their jobs, the more survival skills they have in the corporate world, the more free-agent minded they will be. See you later, alligator.

Why do the traditional rational structures no longer work? Because connectivity has made lines of communication impossible to protect.

The locus of power floats all through an organization in a chaos world. The woman who demanded the commission had no power in the traditional sense: Her pay could have been docked. She could have been fired on the spot. But this woman wasn't dealing in that kind of power. She held the critical variable that would determine not just whether her employer got a $15 million contract but whether that contract would open other doors for the business. In a particle corporate structure, power is diffuse. It's the critical variables that have muscle.

Why do rational corporations no longer work? Because what Elliot Jacques called the "time span of discretion" has been so miniaturized by the accelerating rate of change as to become nearly immeasurable.

Jacques's theory, which he first advanced in 1956, was—and is—an elegant one. What he noted was that what really mattered in any organization was not how many people you managed, not how much money you had under your control, but how binding your decision was on the life span of the organization.

Most decisions made by most employees, whether they are clerks or on the production line, have a binding consequence on the organization that can be measured in seconds: In the time it takes to decide to put the screw in place or enter the fulfillment code, the act itself has faded from corporate memory. Find a better, cheaper supplier for the screw guns the production line crew is assigned or for the keyboards employees are using to enter fulfillment codes, and your act begins to have a discernible time span of discretion. Come up with a strategic model for investing in $5 billion worth of bonds, and in theory you have an impact stretching into many years, and thus, by Jacques's model, you matter more to the organization than someone making less durable decisions, even if that person has a grander title and more human and capital assets at his or her disposal.

So far, so good. But as change accelerates, the time span of discretion shrinks. In a thoroughly rational world, a decision could have a binding impact lasting many years, presumably into decades. Plans held, givens had staying power. That was the long-view world that the Japanese were supposedly opening our eyes to during their miracle years of the 1980s—before their cheap labor and Western core industries woke up, before the Tokyo financial crisis and the global real-estate collapse.

In a chaos world—the real world—the time span of discretion grows shorter and shorter, and the long term always turns out different from what we expected it to be. Five-year plans are death, givens are fluid. In practical terms, all decisions now—however grandly meant—hit the wall in months, not years. And thus it becomes nearly impossible to measure which of them has the greater impact.

Why do rationally structured corporations no longer work? Because in a world driven by variables, not by givens, workers need the flexibility to respond to variation as it arises. That is the new logic of organization.

The bottom line? Rationally structured corporations don't recognize that the paradigm for success has shifted. It is not just that employees are disloyal to their corporations. Increasingly, to achieve the greatest possible success employees have to be first of all loyal to themselves.

The historic paradigm for personal success also depended on a rational structure, on a graduated rising through the ranks. In the professions, you would enter a major accounting firm first as an assistant or junior staffer. After three years of nearly endless nose-to-the-grindstone work, you would be promoted to the senior level, which meant you managed a group of assistants carrying out a common task. In another three years, you would become a manager in charge of seniors who were in turn in charge of assistants, and then after still another three years—nine years in all—you would be elevated to senior manager and eventually, so the hope went, promoted to partner.

Law firms, large architectural firms, even medicine in its own slightly skewed way followed the same procedure, and there was pure predictability to the process. So long as you performed at or near the top of your peer group, you would move on to the next level.

Meanwhile, the partnership held all the capital and divided up all the profits, and thus had a significant vested interest in keeping the bottom of the pyramid large and the top small. Over all that was the glue of collegiality, of mutual respect, of tradition. Everyone at the top had been through what everyone beneath them was experiencing. The partners were the promise of what hard work would achieve, and it was only through the established process that you could get there.

That carefully structured process began to unravel as far back as the late 1970s. Today, although flow charts still pay homage to the principles of partnership progression, it is largely a myth. Employees below the partnership level discovered their specialized skills had a high economic valuation and that they could trade that valuation for more rapid advancement toward the partnership level or could carry their skills to another firm. Intellectual property, it turned out, had worth, and that worth belonged to the holder, not to the larger entity. Rainmakers, too, arose—individuals who simply by virtue of their existence, their contacts, and their reputations could cause large pieces of business to move with them. How to maximize that value? By giving it free expression; by moving from firm to firm, always exacting ever higher shares of the partnership profits.

Suddenly, firms that had existed essentially as guilds for hundreds of years found themselves destabilized. War broke out between younger and older members of the firm; collegiality vanished as partners battled over whether to bring rainmakers in and what percentage of the profits to pay them. And as destabilization heightened, the value of the most critical human variables—the rainmakers, the narrowly but highly skilled seniors and managers—heightened proportionally.

In the corporate world, the historic success paradigm was much the same. You entered as a junior, worked like a dog, and moved through the chairs by performing combat in the interest of the corporation. The progression wasn't as lock-step as it was in the professions; the signals of success—or failure—were more mixed. But if you gave, you got. In essence, the model still holds at many blue-chip companies. At IBM or DuPont, compensation rises about 4 percent annually on the average; if you're performing well, you can look forward to a promotion and perhaps relocation on a three-year cycle.

The problem is that this rational success paradigm no longer yields the greatest success. Just as in the professions, the greatest resources now go to the most significant human variables—entrepreneurs brought in to run incubator divisions meant to spawn new products. Just as in the professions, dis-ease rakes the senior ranks when diversification imports executives who haven't been through the chairs—a process that has, in fact, been going on since the 1960s. Unlike in many of the professions, the threat of downsizing—of spinning off or dismantling large corporate chunks that have little potential for growth—sows a sense of organizational injustice up and down the corporate ladder.

Who wins in both instances? The island-hopping executive. The professional who is most willing to make life changes not in pursuit of the group mission but in pursuit of his or her own ambition. The employee who recognizes that power in a chaos organization migrates to the greatest variable, that the new success paradigm frees the individual.

The myth is that organizations can be organized in a chaos environment. The reality is that they have to disorganize the given world in order to survive in it.

No business is more scheduled than the U.S. Postal Service, down to its every sorter and route person, and no business is more doomed to lag behind the competition as a result. How, meanwhile, did Federal Express become the most respected company in America? By doing what the U.S. Postal Service could never in a million years bring itself to do—by rethinking express delivery from the ground floor up, by breaking every rule of common sense, by coming up with the utterly screwball proposition of flying every package it delivers into Memphis, Tennessee, of all places, so that it could take advantage of intercity exchange rates and never, ever let a delivery plane fly out of Memphis empty again. The answer, in fact, was sitting there all along, just waiting for FedEx founder Fred Smith to find it.

How, then, do you organize a business in a chaos world? Precisely by *disorganizing* it. By embracing chaos. By seeking to understand chaos's true nature.

Governmental Organization: A Borderless World

We have friends who think they have lost their teenage son. No one comes to the house to visit him, and he almost never leaves the house willingly, not even for high school, where his more-than-spotty attendance record has placed him in danger of failing.

Our friends can't go away for weekends, they say, because their son will barely eat or sleep if they are not there to remind him to do both. Although he passed his sixteenth birthday a year ago, they can't get him to apply for a driver's license, can't get him to even begin to learn to drive. He has absolutely no interest in internal-combustion mobility. When the family is at home, he rarely leaves his bedroom to socialize with its other members. Should guests come—a grandparent, an aunt or uncle, neighbors—he has to be forced to come downstairs, and even then the exchange is always painful, for both sides. Their son, our friends say, has no social graces, no experience with personal interaction, no survival skills.

In fact, their son has become a citizen—albeit perhaps a poor one—of the New World. People come to visit him and he visits other people all the time, on the Internet. His friends, it turns out, are mostly in Finland. For whatever reasons, he has tapped into a number of international teen chat lines heavily visited by Finns, and it is there that he spends his time, always in English, because English is the universal language of the Net just as it is the universal language of commerce.

Our friends' son has enormous experience with personal interaction. He can coax responses from utter strangers. Like the classic teenage girl on the telephone, he shares his innermost feelings daily, but instead of doing it with a classmate, he does it with a Netmate, and not just one but dozens each night. Our friends' son has plenty of graces; they are simply cybergraces—Netiquette. He has plenty of skills; they are simply cyberskills. He has almost infinite mobility, and it is entirely free of charge. (Happily for his parents, his father works for the U.S. government; an Internet link comes with the job. Thanks to the generosity of America's taxpayers, there is no limit on monthly hours.)

Beyond doubt, our friends' son is a cybergeek, which is likely to make him a drudge of the New World, not one of its princes. But the larger question about our friends' son is this: Is he a citizen of the United States of America, where he was born and lives, or is he in effect a citizen of Finland, where he spends all his time? (Real time, we hasten to add.) Or is he a citizen of some new virtual nation, some place defined not by borders and border guards, not by currency, not by language or ethnicity, not by flags or oaths of allegiance, but rather simply by interstices on the World Wide Web? Arguably, at least, the latter comes closest to describing his true perception of his own citizenship, and in the chaos world the only passport that really matters is the one you think you hold. That, in a nutshell, is the potentially calamitous challenge faced by governmental organizations today.

Ever since there have been governments, they have ruled by exclusion and defined themselves by their borders and all the apparatus necessary to secure those borders—guards, immigration quotas and the requirements of work permits, tariffs and other barriers to trade. And the more totalitarian the governments were, the tighter they fixed the screws.

But as the collapse of the Soviet Union so dramatically proved, access recognizes no borders. For decades, the Soviets looked east for their enemies, to the ICBMs buried in silos in the Dakota plains. They looked west across Eastern Europe to the massed forces of NATO. But as Scott Shane, the former Moscow correspondent for the *Baltimore Sun*, showed in his book *Dismantling Utopia*, the true enemies of the state were basic electronics: CD players, televisions, VCRs, fax machines, Xerox machines, computers, communication satellites.

What mutually assured destruction couldn't destroy, pirated tapes of the Beatles and *Die Hard* cassettes destroyed in an historical blink of the eye. While the state was looking for signs of a preemptive nuclear strike, while it was scouring the back alleys of the Arbat for espionage activity, the people were joining global media communes. They were redefining their citizenship based not on their place of birth, but on a mutuality of interests. And once they had done that, there was no turning back. Access frees not only individuals, access frees whole peoples. And it connects them.

MTV is more than a purveyor of music videos—and a promotional tool of the recording industry. It's the first truly global network, the first network to deliver a single stream of programming in virtually every country in the world. In the process, MTV is creating a single sense of shared global reality for its viewers, children and young adults. Recent research has found that young people around the planet more and more share not just common pop icons and common tastes, but common expectations for their careers, common sets of values about what is meaningful in life and what there is to be afraid of, a common sense that politics is less important than their own abilities in shaping their futures.

In effect, MTV is helping to create a global persona and global citizens. In a massive survey of 25,000 middle-class high school students on five continents—conducted during the 1995–1996 school year by the Brainwaves Group, a New York–based consumer-research firm—nine in ten students agreed that "It's up to me to get what I want out of life" and almost half the teens said they expected to leave the country of their birth in pursuit of their goals.

Which is the more powerful force, the United Nations or MTV, NATO or MTV, the U.S. Navy's Pacific fleet or MTV? The question is not as silly as it sounds. Bill Clinton was playing pure politics when he took his presidential campaign to the music-video channel in 1992, but he was connecting with the future in a fundamental way, too.

And, of course, "access" also works in other, darker ways to break down borders. Foreign governments have spent billions of dollars and millions of hours trying to penetrate U.S. defense systems and planning, generally to a remarkable lack of success. Meanwhile, according to court documents, sixteen-year-old Richard Pryce sat at a computer in his north London bedroom for some seven months, touring through U.S. Defense Department weapons-research files and reading "secure" messages from U.S. intelligence agents in North Korea during the 1994 showdown over access to nuclear facilities there. Which is the more powerful force, the modem or the FBI? The modem or the CIA? Those questions are not as silly as they sound, either.

Even the great "unalienable Rights" set forth in the Declaration of Independence—the rights of "Life, Liberty, and the Pursuit of Happiness"—never assumed the world that is already here. The Declaration was itself a declaration of war. The Articles of Confederation and the Constitution that followed the successful completion of that war both assumed a world in which nation states would be engaged in constant struggles with one another, constantly colliding with one another—a world defined, in short, by physical borders, by geographic boundaries, by nationhood. The particular genius of the American Founding Fathers was to add to the articles of incorporation an obligation to maximize the personal freedom of people living within the American borders. Yet to qualify for that obligation—to have your freedoms protected—you had to surrender them in the purest sense.

With the now nearly global triumph of American-style self-rule, governments govern more and more by the consent of the governed. But if the governed no longer define themselves as members of the state—if access has made them global citizens, not national ones; if they group themselves in affinity communes, not national ones—then how is self-rule to work? And on what basis will governments be able to demand the sacrifice of individual freedoms in the name of the common, national good?

The self-styled "Freemen" who holed up in their Montana compound for three months in the late winter and early spring of 1996 surrounded by the Federal Bureau of Investigation were many things—wacky perhaps, allegedly criminal-minded, and perhaps con artists, too—but at heart they were an affinity commune. They defined themselves not by their nationhood but by the particular worldview that a peculiar mix of media input had created for them. And as nations particalize, the Freemen are only the beginning of the problems that all governments face.

Why? Because access creates globalism, and globalism disrupts political systems by making the concept of borders obsolete. As borders disappear, the concept of taxation, which supports governments, becomes increasingly fragile. Witness, again, the Freemen, whose primary point of the contention with federal authorities was their refusal to pay taxes to a government they no longer recognized. As borders disappear, the concept of entitlement—the belief that because you were born in a particular place, you are entitled to the economic advantages associated with that place—falls apart, and as it falls apart, the perks of nationhood fall apart with it. And as all that happens, the ideals that underlie nationhood—patriotism, democracy, the state, the melting pot, unification, responsible participation, whatever they happen to be in whatever nation one is living in—get relegated to the junk heap of history.

A patriot? For most Americans in their twenties, thirties, and forties, the most common use of the word "patriot" today is to describe a ground-fired antimissile system developed by the Raytheon Corporation that rose to prominence doing battle against Iraqi SCUDs in the 1992 Gulf War. The simple fact is that the larger sense of patriotism—a love of nation, a sense of filial duty to it—is not a particularly useful predisposition to have any longer.

Governments and, through them, nations restrict. It is through the dictates of government that an American businessman is not free to build a shopping center in Havana or open an auto-assembly plant in Pyongyang, North Korea; through the dictates of government that an American oil wholesaler cannot buy Iraqi crude; through the dictates of government that an American textile manufacturer cannot have her apparel pieced together in the discount factories of Southeast Asia.

In the service of nationhood, passports and visas are required. In theory, you could live in New York, because it is the world's sacred financial spot, and work in Sydney, because as East and West merge, it is one of the places they are merging most interestingly. Distance is no barrier: There are plenty of direct flights to Sydney, plenty of first-class cabins to relax in while you travel. But there are those work permits to worry about and, should you choose to redefine your citizenship, immigration quotas to worry about.

Such restrictions presumably serve the larger interests of nationhood. In the case of Iraqi crude and the piecing sweatshops of Thailand, the restrictions may even serve legitimate humanitarian ends. But when the dictates of government lose congruency with the desire or experience of the governed, the foundations of nationhood begin to crumble. Myths are public dreams, broadly shared, which is why the myth of nationhood persists. But myths without perspective, myths without authenticity, are fairy tales. That is what nationhood is becoming.

The citizenship ethos of the Age of Access is both clear and inevitable because the momentum of connectivity leads in only one direction. Citizens who thrive in this global society will identify themselves globally. They will make political, social, and economic choices based not on national identity, but on how those choices relate to themselves directly and to people like them around the world. They will be less citizens than cityzens, grouped into the 560 megacities that already dominate the world's population, and they will think of themselves more as living in those cities than as living in whatever national configuration their city happens to fall into. (It is only futopists, we should add, who attempt to predict the future without accounting for the rock-hard reality of these megacities. They are the new eight-hundred-pound gorillas of social mega-organization, not nations.)

Nations and corporations who thrive will organize themselves accordingly. They will maximize the freedom to know, to go, to do, to be. Nations and corporations that don't, that continue to fight rear-guard actions based on nostalgia, will atrophy. The immigration battle now raging in the United States—a nostalgia trip that has transmogrified itself into an ugly moral battleground—is the past. A Europe without passports is the beginning of the future.

Accounting firms are the ugly sisters of the professional service industry, congenitally gray because that is what is expected of a business that helps count the money. A movie will never be made about the Arthur Andersen accounting firm. Sean Connery will never be asked to play Leonard Spacek, who used to be the Andersen vice president in charge of operations. But it was Spacek who came up with the single most revolutionary idea in corporate compensation in this century, an idea so perfectly attuned to the world as it was then becoming as to be almost frighteningly prescient. Spacek's idea was this: Arthur Andersen, which was already spread around the globe, would henceforth have a single global compensation structure. Partners would be paid out of a common kitty according to the level they occupied in the company, not according to the income their office generated.

With that single innovation, Spacek truly globalized a global company, and globalized it over the long term. Suddenly, there was no disincentive to running the Bombay office because the Bombay office generated less cash flow than the Tokyo office, and no disincentive to running Tokyo because it was less of a cash pig than New York. Suddenly, it was possible for Arthur Andersen to swap its people all over the world because there were no compensatory consequences to doing so, and after twenty years of swapping, there were no psychological or sociological consequences to moving either. An American company with worldwide interests became a worldwide company period. Andersen's "citizens" in consequence became global citizens, and its corporate ethos became what every corporate and government ethos will have to become to prosper beyond the millennium, on the other side of the delta: a global ethos.

The Deconstruction of Economics

In a rational economy, rational forces hold sway. Tendencies are consistent. Patterns are discernible. Adam Smith's "invisible hand"—a harmony of interests—guides all. In a rational economy, long-range planning is rewarded with long-term growth. Ownership of physical assets is desirable. Economic relationships can be classified: You know who your competitors and your parasites are. Business typologies are easily drawn up: You know which industry sector you fall into. The flow of goods between manufacturers, retailers, and customers is stable: Manufacturers make the product and create a market for it, retailers transfer the product and further enhance the market, and customers consume what is made for them. In an economy built on the logic of reason, cause and effect are linked and discernible.

This, essentially, is the economy that has been building for the last five hundred years, since the collapse of feudal states, the rise of nations, and the discovery of the New World. Exactly what was in the best interests of that economy, how wealth was to be defined, how much control the nation was to exert over the workings of the economy, and to what extent economic activity drove all other activity

44

has been the subject of almost constant debate across all five centuries—from the mercantilists through the French Physiocrats and Adam Smith to Karl Marx, the social economists, and John Maynard Keynes—but at the heart of all this furious theorizing lay a simple premise and a single goal. The premise was that the chaos of competition could somehow be transformed into an orderly mechanism, whether by a benign Providence or by the reasonable formulations of the dismal scientists of economics. The goal was the creation of mass consumer markets.

At the end of the twentieth century, the new reality of economic organization has become obvious to anyone willing to see it: The chaos of competition is just that: the chaos of competition. The only way to survive and prosper in this chaos is not to pursue mass consumer markets, but to satisfy individual consumer demands.

Judged reasonably, almost nothing about the real workings of the economy, the marketplace, corporate life, and even the formation of personal wealth today makes the least bit of sense. One index rises, another falls, and no one knows what to make of either because there are no central tendencies.

Property and physical possessions were once the benchmark of personal wealth; ownership conveyed real value. Today, the vast majority of the cars driven by residents of Westport, Connecticut—one of the toniest of New York City's bedroom suburbs—are leased, not owned. Elsewhere, a car-leasing service was launched not long ago that will essentially give you time-shares in three different vehicles—a four-wheel-drive utility-sport vehicle for the winter, a convertible for the summer, and a station wagon or minivan for taking the kids to school.

Houses stagnate in value while bundles of stock rise along a curve no one can understand. Instead of planned obsolescence, we have moved into the era of inherent obsolescence. The computer is outdated the moment we open up the box it has come in; the food processor breaks, we chuck it; the television breaks, out it goes. In the epoch of inherent obsolescence, consumers have become conditioned to discarding things when they break. Real wealth is intangible, not tangible. The temporary is everywhere. And the temporary and intangible, lo and behold, are a perfect fit for the Age of Chaos.

•   •   •

Traditional employer-employee relationships have been turned on their ears: Because leverage in a chaos world goes to the critical variables, the person able to cut the best deal in a corporation today is not the most loyal one, but the one willing to leave himself or herself the most outs. (The corollary of that, by the way, is an unpleasant truth: Anyone whose first priority today is job security is absolutely screwed.)

Not only do patterns not distill in a chaos world, their roots are not even discernible. By the mid–1980s, unassailable reason told us that the American economy was doomed by its lack of internal harmonies, the absence of a government-business partnership, and, most of all, the blinding, grinding short-term orientation of corporations and their shareholders. Small libraries were written on the subject. Reputations were established, fortunes made. Exhortations filled the airwaves to take the long view. By the mid–1990s, it was apparent that the American economy was sailing along in ultra-high gear precisely because of its incredible short-term orientation. Short-term taught discipline, it turned out, and as the new General Agreement on Trade and Tariffs (GATT) and the North American Free Trade Agreement (NAFTA) beat down borders and opened up vast new opportunities, discipline and the ability to turn on a dime were just what was needed.

For its part, Wall Street pretends to science with its theories, systems, and indicators—the wave, random-walk, Dow, odd-lot, firm-foundation, and castle-in-the-air theories; relative strengths and price-volume systems; the hemline indicator and Super Bowl indicators, to cite only a few and not the most absurd—but it's all sham science. For every arbitrage firm betting high, another is betting low, and the average broker in the average brokerage doesn't have the least idea what's going to happen in the next fifty minutes, let alone the next fifty days.

In a brief five days in June 1996, a share of Gateway 2000 stock fell 25 percent in value. Why? Because a high-ranking Gateway executive announced that the company's European sales were expected to grow only 65 percent in 1996, not 100 percent. It would be pure insanity if there were any benchmark of sanity to measure it against. The fact is, there is not.

●　　　●　　　●

In fact, Gateway 2000 is a good example of both the seeming illogicality of chaos logic and its glorious potential.

What does Gateway have that allowed it to grow to more than a $5 billion business in 1996? The answer is: nothing. Gateway produces no original technology. It simply packages computer technology in a way that satisfies individual consumer needs. Gateway's manufacturing operation at its North Sioux City, South Dakota, plant consists of assembling components—made by other companies—at the specific request of a specific customer. The company maintains an inventory of prefinished goods and parts of no more than two days because it presupposes, given the acceleration of the rate of change, that within any five-day window a component could transform dramatically enough to cause a seed-change in the entire marketplace. What Gateway produces instead of original technology is flexible manufacturing, and what makes the whole operation work is Gateway's almost complete lack of attention to the traditional selling model.

In the traditional model, a vacuum cleaner was dragged door-to-door in the hope of finding a consumer who at the very moment you rang the doorbell was having a very bad day with his or her vacuum cleaner. You spread the dirt on the floor and vacuumed it up; you put the handkerchief over the nozzle and sucked astounding amounts of grime from furniture previously thought to be clean enough to eat off. In the process, you created a dilemma—to stick with an inferior vacuum cleaner or to own a brand-new Kirby—that you hoped would be resolved in your favor.

The selling model varied, of course. Sometimes you advertised a product broadly, put it in the stores, and hoped the customers would come to it. Other times you shipped out a catalog of finished goods and hoped the customer would come to you by phone. But always there was the baseline assumption that consumers would buy what manufacturers had available to sell.

Today, as Gateway and other companies are proving, that baseline assumption is vanishing. Consumers now have so many choices and so much power that they can command the producer to provide the goods they want simply by withholding their purchases in a particular category until the solution they seek is available.

On the surface, Gateway's competitive advantages would appear to be anti-advantages; beneath the surface, they are a simple recognition of the true nature of the marketplace. Instead of fixed products, the company creates a new product every time a customer calls. Gateway does this by communicating directly with its customers, satisfying its customers' needs in a one-to-one transaction, aggressively changing virtually everything it does on any given day in response to both customers' needs and accelerating technology, and repeating the process every day with such discipline that change becomes endemic.

For a reason-based world, Gateway 2000 would be an object lesson in unbridled chaos, an MBA seminar in how not to run a business. Is it a manufacturer masquerading as a service concern or a service concern masquerading as a manufacturer? Does it build computers or merely edit component choices for the consumer? Is it a factory or a fulfillment house? Whatever the actual case is—and it's all of the above—Gateway resists traditional typology. It draws outside the lines, and drawing outside the lines has always been death to traditionalists. But for a chaos world, Gateway is a lean, clean fighting machine. In effect, it has particalized its corporate structure to seek congruency with a particalized marketplace.

Put another way, Gateway 2000 has met the market on its own terms.

The Wings of a Butterfly

To understand how the marketplace works in a chaos world, ponder for a moment the classic chaos model of the wings of a butterfly. Because a butterfly in Costa Rica moves its wings, a little bit of air moves. Because the little bit of air moves, a frog changes its point of view. Because the frog changes its point of view, it spots a snake in its hole and flees. Because the snake goes unfed, it comes out of its hole and bites an anthropologist on the heel. Because the anthropologist has been bitten on the heel, she falls down and discovers the bones of a five-thousand-year-old man. Because the bones have been found, a geologist comes to study the rock formations. Because the geologist studies the rock formations, he finds a massive gold mine. Because the massive gold mine has been found, Costa Rica becomes a world player. Because Costa Rica has become a world player, its delegate to an emerging-nations conference feels free to insult a Shiite mullah also in attendance. Because the Shiite mullah has been insulted, he directs a terrorist attack on the Costa Rican capital of San José. And thus is launched the long-predicted holy war between Christians and Muslims that becomes known as World War III.

Absurd, of course, but the absurdity is the whole point. Causality still exists, clearly. In hindsight, the horror of war can be traced directly back to the seemingly inconsequential fluttering of a single butterfly's wings. But the chain of causality itself is so diffuse, so random, so unpredictable that no statistical model could have foreseen the outcome.

Now consider a real-life story:

Once upon a time between the wars in the city of Oakland, California, there was a man who distributed Pepsodent toothpaste to neighborhood drugstores—and to drugstores only. This was in the days when every neighborhood had its shops, and every shop—the butcher's, the grocery, the drugstore—had its individual purpose. One day, Pepsodent was acquired by Lever Brothers, which was then in the process of amassing a line of hygiene products, and in one of the earliest examples of efficiency downsizing, Lever Brothers fired a whole bunch of people around the country who had been working for the product lines it had bought, including the Oakland Pepsodent distributor.

What was he to do? Being without a job in those days was like death. Well, it turns out that in the course of his old job, visiting neighborhood after neighborhood, he had noticed that people were five times more likely on any given day to go to the grocery than to the drugstore. That being the case, he reasoned, if he could assemble little racks of very basic personal hygiene products from a variety of manufacturers and put the racks in grocery stores, he could create a higher volume of sales than he had when he was selling only Pepsodent exclusively to drugstores.

One of the first Oakland stores the former toothpaste distributor put his hygiene rack in was owned by a man named Sam Seelig. It didn't take Sam Seelig long to notice that people were perfectly willing to buy nongrocery items in a grocery environment, so he began offering other lines of nonfood products along with his basic grocer goods. Pretty soon his inventory space was so crowded that he had to move to a bigger store, and that one did so well that he opened a second one in Oakland, which the customers flocked to as well. If two, why not more? So he came up with the idea for a chain of stores, all within a fifty-mile radius, and a warehouse near the center that would allow him to consolidate purchasing and distribution. To do that, he needed capital. To raise capital, he formed a board and went to the public with a stock offering. And just about that time, he decided to change the name of his stores to something that would indicate to his customers that he was managing their risks, that this would be a safe way to shop—in short, to Safeway.

But the story doesn't end there. One of the original members of that Safeway board was an investor named Charles Merrill—one of the founders of Merrill, Lynch, Pierce, Fenner, and Smith, now simply Merrill Lynch. Merrill, in time, would purchase Seelig's chain, which by then had grown to 240 stores, and merge it with a 428-store chain that had grown up from a single local grocery in American Falls, Idaho, begun by a minister named S. M. Skaggs, who wanted to provide better food supplies for the local grain farmers. But it was at one of those original Safeway board meetings that Charlie Merrill got the idea that he could do what Sam Seelig had done: assemble and hold an inventory of stocks and sell them directly to ordinary people—everyday men and women who had no other ready vehicle for purchasing stocks—and in the process secure the best marginal commissions for himself and his salesmen. And thus from the flapping of a butterfly's wings—from Lever Brothers's decision to ax its Oakland Pepsodent distributor—was born the modern supermarket chain and what Charlie Merrill called "process marketing."

What is the moral of these two stories? That no one could have sat down at the turn of the century and described on paper a theory of marketing that would have arrived at a chain of Safeways, nor could someone have predicted that from the flapping of a butterfly's wings, the world would move to DEFCON 1. All you can know with certainty are the individual acts—the frog jumping, the ICBMs raining down on San José, the Pepsodent distributor losing his job, Charlie Merrill's serendipitously showing up on the original Safeway board—and you cannot know them until they actually happen.

This, in fact, is where chaos theory and particle physics meet. In order to understand any process in a chaos world—a world being steadily crunched by the acceleration of the rate of change, a world being bombarded by information in the Age of Access—you have to break it down into its smallest component parts and concentrate all your efforts there, because while other things will happen, while the flap of the butterfly's wings ultimately may cause World War III, all you have any hope of controlling is the individual relationship with the smallest component part. In the marketplace, that means the customer, but not the "customer" broadly writ.

As Werner Heisenberg discovered more than sixty years ago when he launched quantum mechanics, the more you concentrate on smaller and smaller units of analysis, the more you interfere with those units, and the more the units themselves subdivide into still smaller units. The more, that is, they become complex worlds of their own. That is the real "customer," the one writ small: one person, a little world all cunningly made, and the more cunningly made, the more you study him or her.

No statistical model, no assumptions from the average, no mountain of data about the mass market can predict how this one customer will act, because once you parse her at this individual level, you come to understand that she acts out of entirely individual motives. Nothing will lure this customer to move, because finally he moves from his own volition. That is why the balance of power in commercial transactions has shifted from the supply to the demand side, from manufacturer and retailer to consumer.

The world is awash in personal computers. As of the summer of 1996, roughly 35 percent of American homes had personal computers, an astounding absorption, and yet a new model is being introduced each week. Thanks to the rise of microbreweries, customers are drowning in beer-brand choices. Everyone from Eddie Bauer to L.L. Bean and Gloria Vanderbilt is turning out jeans by the trainload. Finally, any market supports only so much cash flow. For soft drinks, it might be in the range of $42 billion—$35 billion for Coca-Cola, $6 billion for Pepsi, another $1 billion for all other brands combined. Once the value of the competition for that $42 billion exceeds the amount of money that can be taken in, the customer takes over. Market surplus, not market share, begins to drive the economy. That, in essence, is where the economy has arrived.

・ ・ ・

Subconsciously, if not consciously, customers have come to understand that in a world supersaturated with goods—a world in which the once scarce is not only readily available but begging to be bought—they hold the upper hand.

This shift in the balance of power is also why corporations today have to go to where their customers are, one customer at a time. How do you do that? Through establishing one-to-one transactions as your medium of communication. Through penetrating the full dimensionality of not the marketplace, but the subatomic entities that compose the marketplace—each single person with cash in hand or credit in the wallet, waiting to buy.

You may be dying for a beer, but it is up to the Anheuser-Busch Corporation to convince you, individually, one thirst attack at a time, that what you are really dying for is a Bud. And to do that, they have to know not the abstract but the real you.

First Comes Love, Then Comes Marriage

How do you establish a market for a new product in a chaos world? As long as we're acting like economists here, let us resort to some boxes and matrices because, while there is no model that will predict who, from the total universe of potential customers, will purchase a new product, there is a model that shows with near iron-clad accuracy how it will be picked up by the market as a whole. Not surprisingly, the model is a graphic representation of the chaos process.

The boxes first. The one just below shows the initial stage of acceptance of any new product. (For argument's sake, we'll designate this one to be a state-of-the-art microwave oven.) These initial purchasers are people who are not only open to new kitchen technology, but predisposed to pursue it. We call them "early adopters," which is why we have marked them in this box as "EA." Since we are talking ovens here, let us think of these particular early adopters as kitchen geeks, the home-cooking equivalent of cybergeeks. The frame of the box represents the entire marketplace landscape. Note how the early adopters are irregularly spread across the landscape:

```
ooooooooooooooooooooooooooooooooo
ooooooooooEAooooooooooooooooooo
oo EAoooooooooooooooooooooooo EA
oooooooooooooEAoooooooooooooo
ooooooooooooooooooooooEAooooo
ooooooooooooooooooooooooooooo
```

Clearly, early adopters lack sufficient numbers to make a market themselves. Not only are they too few, they are also too demanding of newness, too hungry for fresh blood. To concentrate on nothing other than feeding them would exhaust resources with no hope of a concomitant return.

But if they can't make a market, early adopters are absolutely critical to setting one because early adopters are opinion leaders. It is their word of mouth, their interpersonal communication, their e-mail and faxes, their kitchen-geek example—the state-of-the-art microwave on *their* kitchen counter—that attract the second group of adopters, what we call "confirmers," and here mark with a "C." (Incidentally, most early adopters know that they are opinion leaders. Setting the market in their usually narrow spheres of interest is important to their sense of self-worth.)

Note that as the confirmers group themselves around early adopters, a market for the microwave oven has begun to form. Note, too, that as the confirmers group around the early adopters, they themselves begin to touch:

```
ooooooooo c o c oooooooooooooooooo
ooooooo coo EAo c ooooooo c o c ooooo
o c oEAo c oooo cc oooooo c ooooo coc EA
o c o c o c ooooo c o EAo c oo cc oo c ooooo
oooooooooooooooo c ooo cEAooooo
ooooooooooooooooooo c ooo c oooo
```

Now begins the final process of market-making—total adoption. Early adopters attract confirmers. Confirmers begin to overlap as the linkages move through subpopulations and media communes. As that happens, late adopters, or laggards (marked "L" below), join the parade—high-tech goes mid-cult—and with that, our box looks less like an orderly growth chart and more like a plot of some vast, new bacterial disease outbreak. (If this were a movie, Dustin Hoffman would now turn to Rene Russo and say something like, "The Ebola has broken out! There's no stopping it now!" And if this were a movie, we'd know with a concrete certainty that it would be stopped by the time the credits rolled at the end. But in fact, once this critical mass is reached, there *is* no stopping it.)

```
LLLLLLLLcLcLLLLLLLLLLLLLLLLLLLL
LLLLLLLcLLEALcLLLLLLLLcLcLLLLL
cLEALcLLLLccLLLLLLLcLLLLLLccLcEA
LcLcLcLLLLLcLEALcLLccLLcLLLLL
LLLLLLLLLLLLLLLLLLLcLLLcEALLLLL
LLLLLLLLLLLLLLLLLLLLLcLLLcLLLL
```

In the single dimension we can show here, this all appears to be an orderly process, both symmetrical and systematic. And indeed, in this single dimension, it is both. But the important thing to keep in mind is that the underlying basis of this seeming order is both extremely chaotic and thus completely unorderly and unpredictable.

You can predict that 60 percent of the populace will own microwave ovens within ten years, let's say, because social forces are compelling people to miniaturize their time in the kitchen, split-apart families need individual servings of food, and a microwave is a near-perfect vehicle for achieving both ends. You cannot, however, predict with any certainty which 60 percent of the population will own them. You'll know a person has bought a microwave only when he or she walks out of the store carrying the box, and you'll know it only one person at a time.

What does this mean in more specific terms for manufacturers and marketers? What does it mean for the allocation of resources and energy within a corporation? A great deal, but for that we have to go to the matrices.

Innovation Crunching and Product Confirmation

Tommy Hilfiger, the clothing manufacturer, had an interesting problem. Its clothing lines had become so popular with the group most likely to shoplift trendy clothing—young, black men from the ghetto—that the bottom line was beginning to suffer. No sooner would a new Tommy Hilfiger product hit the stores than a small but alarming percentage of it would be walking out again, stuffed under the last generation of Tommy Hilfiger shirts, stuffed into the now next-to-latest Tommy Hilfiger pants. What to do? Insist on tighter security at the stores that sell Hilfiger products? Come up with a new tagging system, a new system of alarm bells and whistles that would help alert store personnel to the shoplifting? Stop stocking the stores most likely to be stolen from?

In fact, the Tommy Hilfiger people decided to do just the right thing. They decided to do nothing. Why? Because young, black males from the ghetto establish the market in teenage clothing. What they choose to wear determines what rap groups wear on MTV. What rap groups wear on MTV influences what young, white suburban males with their own charge cards buy at the local mega-mall, and what young, white suburban males with charge cards buy at the local mega-mall influences what less affluent young males of all colors buy at their own malls with the money they have earned flipping Big Macs and delivering Domino's pizzas.

Young, black men from the ghetto are the early adopters. Young, white suburban males with credit cards are confirmers. Young males with French-fry grease on their hands, young males desperate to get home and shed their hideous orange, blue, and white Domino's shirts, fulfill the market. Yes, every Tommy Hilfiger shirt that is pilfered is a blow to the profit flow. It is perhaps even a small blow to public and private morality. But as soon as the pilfered shirt is put on and worn on the street, it becomes a walking billboard in absolutely prime sociological time—an advertisement that money couldn't buy. There truly is nothing rational about the "reason" of the marketplace today.

•　　　•　　　•

No mathematics, no equation can explain the etched curve shown below, but its shape characterizes the natural diffusion of every idea, every product, every service. The vertical axis (y-axis) shows the number of people who have adopted whatever it is that's being diffused. The horizontal axis (x-axis) shows the time it takes for adoption.

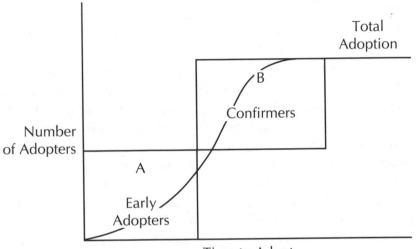

It's worth noting that the time it takes for all early adopters to get a new idea, to accept a new product, is about equal to the amount of time it takes for the general population to get it, but in a business you are not operating at all in the same domain during these two roughly equal time periods.

The first of these periods—Box "A," above—belongs to the engineering operation. Because early adopters know they are opinion leaders, because adopting early fulfills a critical ego need for them, they are actively seeking newness. The job here is not to create an appetite, it is to fulfill a preexisting and voracious one. The job, in short, is innovation.

The second of these periods, the confirmation process—Box "B," above—belongs to marketing. The challenge here is to alert confirmers through public relations, cultivating press contacts, stimulating word of mouth to the fact that early adopters have found something new.

Once the curve crosses out of Box "B," once it crosses from the confirmation process to total adoption and flattens out, the job again changes entirely. When you have full absorption of an idea or a product in the marketplace, conversation about it largely disappears. No one talks about Coca-Cola anymore as a great idea, a hot concept. Coca-Cola has no buzz. Coke just is. Coca-Cola now must direct all further investment into the daily readoption of the idea of Coca-Cola. Its challenge is not to sell to new consumers—there are virtually no new consumers for Coke in the Western world. Coca-Cola's challenge is to sell to consumers who have bought the product over and over again. And to do that, it has to constantly refresh the curve. How? By reinventing the existing product daily as if it were a new idea. By constantly redefining Coke's market position so that it remains innovative, so that it remains a clever idea. The only alternative is to invent an actual new product and try to diffuse it through the marketplace, using the goodwill built up by the old one. The New Coke debacle of the mid–1980s demonstrates why that is not always a good idea.

Technology inevitably hits a flatline, too, a similar discontinuity of growth. The small-block V–8 engine, to cite one example, grew rapidly from 40 to 1,000 horsepower along a curve nearly identical to the one shown above. But at 1,000 horsepower, there was almost nothing to be done to coax a single horsepower more out of the engine— the platform of a small-block V–8 had simply maxed out, given everything it had. Like Coca-Cola, automobile manufacturers—auto engines are now almost all they actually manufacture—had two choices: constantly reinvent the existing product as if it were a fresh idea ("the new Northstar system") or begin investing in fuel cells to create the engine of the future.

Discontinuity is the mother of innovation, both bad and good, but either way, corporations historically have had to function in all three domains: innovation, marketing for confirmation, and marketing for readoption. Increasingly, that is less and less the case. Only a handful of products globally have the luxury of reinventing themselves daily as Coke does. In the supersaturated marketplace that most businesses operate in today, the challenge is to return constantly to the early adopters, to the confirmers, and to start the process all over again. The acceleration of the rate of change has increased too sharply for most businesses to do otherwise. The social desirability of newness—new ideas, new products, new for new's sake—is too great. And except in soft drinks and a few other products, technology goes stale too quickly. To risk being seen as old is to be old, and to be old in business is to be out of the game.

How do you avoid growing old? By following the "vectrons"—new product ideas that push the company in what can seem like short-wave, relatively insignificant directions—because it's the vectrons that will keep you operating on the bleeding fringe. By resisting the creeping tendency of all products to move toward the central values of the culture, what we call "ecomagnetics." And sometimes, frankly, by investing heavily in "loss followers"—concessions granted to relocating businesses that you will never recoup, but that will make you credible as a place to invest in the future, and products that hopelessly chase a better idea, but will keep you viable as a brand to buy down the road. All three paths, it should be noted, are far easier to put down on paper than they are to practice in the real world, but doing both is absolutely essential to organizational survival.

Consider the matrix above once again, now with the time of adoption compressed:

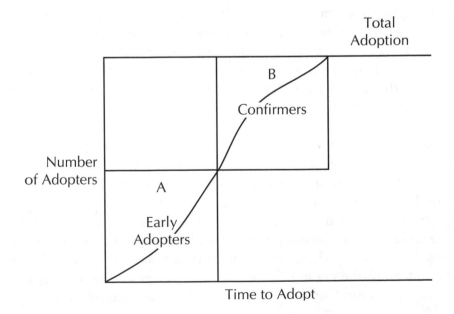

The same curve applies because there is no other mathematical shape to explain the diffusion of a new product or idea. The curve starts at the same place; it hits total adoption at the same number of adopters because the market is always finite. No matter how hard you scream, you will never convince a thoroughgoing Luddite to buy your state-of-the-art microwave or your solar-powered pencil sharpener. Just as early adopters get ego satisfaction from being at the cutting edge, Luddites get ego satisfaction from never jumping onboard. But under the force of compression, the curve rises more steeply; it accelerates faster to the same discontinuity. Sony, to mention just one of many examples that could be cited, has an invention cycle in electronics that now exceeds the inventory cycle in electronic stores. Because it relies on retailers, Sony can't get its products on the shelves fast enough to feed the early adopters. In effect, the present and future are merging. This is the world as it is.

Even Xerox—a company whose product is so much a part of the global vernacular that it has to maintain a roomful of lawyers to make sure the first x in its name gets capitalized in print—essentially stops marketing when its products reach the level of discontinuity. There is no point to further expenditure because the moment the product arrives there—the moment it enters into the social reality—it is obsolete. Within two years, the Pentium 100 chip went from being an essential, value-adding component of a personal computer to being a virtual giveaway. Why? Because the Pentium 200 chip makes the P100 look like stone and flint. And because there is no surer way to lose customers—and lose them for good—than to sell them stone and flint when you are just about to introduce safety matches into the marketplace. That is another corollary of the acceleration of technological change: Quality may still be job one, but mediating a consumer's risk of feeling like a fool is at least job two. More about this later.

What else comes from this crunch in time? Two things: First, as new products arrive on the marketplace with ever greater rapidity, the products themselves lose value and the ideas that drive them gain value. Second, as consumers increasingly drive the economic relationships of the marketplace, the need to massively accumulate data on individual consumers increases proportionally. As that happens, mass-market statistical models and other measures of uniform behavior lose value, and the knowledge that all consumers hold private about themselves gains value.

Back in late 1995 when AT&T announced that it was breaking itself into three free-standing, publicly traded enterprises, CEO Robert Allen told an Atlanta audience that "We're turning three companies free to compete in the principal markets of the Information Age." If that is what Allen really meant—if competing in the Information Age is to be the ethos of all three companies—AT&T stockholders might be well advised to head for the Montana compound vacated by the Freemen.

In fact, the Information Age had already come and gone by the time Allen spoke. The Information Age was about the building of databases. It was about the rise of computing. Today, the databases are already built; the ninth generation of personal computers is already passing through the marketplace; computing has merged with communications to create connectivity. Even as AT&T's CEO was lauding the Information Age, we had passed into the information economy. In the information economy, intellectual capital, not physical assets, drives everything.

Millennial Convergences

PART II

No span of years has held a greater power over the human imagination than that of the millennium—a thousand years. Herodotus wrote that the ancient Egyptians believed the soul of the dead had to pass through three millennia of incarnations so that it could be purified. Plato, in the *Republic*, calculated a dead soul's wandering at 1,000 years before it could be returned to life. Zoroastrianism teaches that the world is to last 12,000 years from its creation and that in the final millennium, the dead will be restored to life through a bath of molten metal that will wash innocently over the just while purifying the wicked. For its part, the Judeo-Christian tradition has spawned more than its share of millennial movements, all in expectation of the coming of the Messiah, that final kingdom when death shall have no dominion. The Judeo-Christian tradition has also given the world perhaps the most forceful and haunting description of its final days, in the apocalyptic revelations of St. John:

> *And there came out of the smoke locusts upon the earth: and unto them was given power, as the scorpions of the earth have power.*

And it was commanded them that they should not hurt the grass of the earth, neither any green thing, neither any tree; but only those men which have not the seal of God in their foreheads.

And to them it was given that they should not kill them, but that they should be tormented five months: and their torment was as the torment of a scorpion, when he striketh a man.

And in those days shall men seek death, and shall not find it; and shall desire to die, and death shall flee from them.

(*Revelation 9: 3–6*)

Apocalyptic visions seem to have found a special home in America. Back in the early 1840s, during the second Great Awakening of religion in the United States, as many as 100,000 people subscribed to the teachings of William Miller, a Long Island farmer and justice of the peace who had pored over the Bible and found finally in the Book of Daniel the numbers that allowed him to place the Second Coming of Christ between late March 1843 and late March 1844. (When the dates passed without the sort of slow-death neutron bomb envisioned by St. John or any other sign of a Second Coming, the period became known as the First Disappointment. When the recalculated date—October 22, 1844, known as the Great Disappointment—also passed, Millerism was finished, although the movement survives today in part in the Seventh-Day Adventist church.)

America's population totaled about 17 million when William Miller was traveling the land, preaching his version of the apocalypse. As a percentage of the U.S. population today, Miller's followers would equal about 15 million people. In fact, it is probably a fairly accurate estimate of the number of Americans who are at least willing to entertain the possibility of cataclysmic change as the twentieth century draws to an end.

We make no claim to the gift of prophecy, and this is not a religious book in any event, but a sense of millennial haunting—a disorienting sense of self and time—is upon the land and its people. Undoubtedly for many, the explicit root is religious: It is no coincidence that the third Great Awakening of America is cresting just as the millennium arrives. But implicitly, and perhaps explicitly for far more people, the roots lie in the convergence of change that we are describing.

What does it mean to have reason deposed? It means that we have to suspend our judgment about what is true. What does it mean to have organization—of the family, society, corporations, and government—overthrown? It means we have to restructure our relationships in every facet of our lives. What it does mean when the old rules of economics and the marketplace disappear? That we have to do business in an entirely different way. As the rate of change accelerates, the facts of life get altered daily, and as the facts of life get altered, so do the ideals that underlie those facts—of loyalty, nationalism, and democracy, to mention only a few. Those are the locusts upon the land as we near century's end, and their sting is as the sting of scorpions. Meanwhile, all this happens asynchronously. Everything accelerates at its own pace, according to its own internal rhythms. The only true constant is the acceleration of change itself—and the tonnage of change it accumulates.

Unlike Carl Sandburg's fog, meta-change of the sort we are experiencing never arrives on little cat's feet. It is dislocating, jarring, and the more so for its unpredictability. Just as important, meta-change never arrives alone.

Think once again of the shifts driving society in geological terms. Each of the fundamental changes described earlier is a river in its own right, and each is driving at flood tide toward convergence. But each cresting river is also the result of the sum total of innumerable phenomena along its tributaries. Stand on the banks of any one of these cresting rivers, watch the silty waters roil by, and you are seeing the work of drenching rains and melting snowfalls thousands of miles upstream.

It is the work of the tributaries that we take up here—the convergence of changes in values, motives, perspective, communications, information, lifestyle, and empathy that are both driving and being merged into the meta-changes in logic, organization, and economics. Like those changes, these already have occurred. It is not a matter of looking for them in the future, it is a matter only of recognizing their work in the present. The 500-year delta is here, waiting to be crossed.

Values: Authenticity, Connectivity, and a New Civility

Historically, the values that inform human behavior have been imprinted intra-generationally and stacked trans-generationally. As they got stacked, the values of previous generations were subtly transposed by new conditions. Tone changed—enough to distinguish one generation from the next. Morality was subtly altered. The impermissible slowly became the permissible, and the permissible the expected. The agenda that each generation built from its translation of values—the primacy of work, leisure, and consensus or disagreement, to cite only a few—bled from one generation to the next, but the bleeding was slow, the lines of demarcation blurry. Drop a person from 1940, say, into 1910, and he will share not only the collective memory of that time, passed on by parents and grandparents, he will also share the bulk of its beliefs. He may miss his comforts—safety razors, bottled beer, baseball on the radio—but he will still find himself in a comfort zone.

Meanwhile, as generations stack and translate their values, they also bubble forward through history, each generation according to its own rhythm. Like a mechanical Slinky going down a flight of steps, one generation will stretch out to move forward—exploring the edges of its experience—while the next pulls back to its center so the slinky can gather the momentum to move forward again. As with value translation, so with the Slinky: Historically, its expansions and contractions have been incremental and measurable. Our time traveler from 1940—a generation contracting under the multiple pressure of a war in Europe, unrest in the Far East, and the lingering effects of the Great Depression—might find himself shocked by the expansive spirit of an early-twentieth-century America just awakening to its global prowess, but he will still be in his comfort zone.

What holds this package together and binds generation to generation through the long time of history are core ethics. In the Western tradition, and increasingly in the Eastern one as well, there are five of these core ethics that drive all values.

With the fall of kingdoms and serfdom came the rise of the obligation to work—not because a higher power forced you to do so, but because work was an inherent part of citizenship, your own self-imposed duty. From the great experiment of America came republicanism; in return for the right to participate politically, you agreed to acquiesce to the decisions of the government that held you in its embrace. Mobility, the third of our core ethics, had its roots in America in the disruption of the Civil War and later of the Great Depression. In Europe, the roots of mobility were in the forced migrations of a succession of wars. But what began as a necessary diaspora—to find work or sanctuary—has since been transformed in the alchemy of ethics into a craving. Two generations ago, less than 20 percent of Americans lived more than fifty miles from where they had been born. Today, more than 80 percent do. Companies like Mobil—appropriately, given its name—have, in essence, organized around mobility, creating hub cities for their employees so that moving does not mean displacement.

Romantic love, our fourth core ethic, sounds like the oldest, but is, in fact, newer than mobility. The great love stories of the past—Shakespeare's tragedy of Romeo and Juliet, the equally tragic attraction of Peter Abelard for his tutee Héloïse—were stories of romantic love thwarted. It's only within this century that the concept of following one's heart wherever it might lead has truly taken root, and it's only within the last generation that people have been truly free to marry whom they want without regard to race, caste, social background, or even sex. The last of our core ethics, consumerism, is the most deeply ingrained of all, born with the rise of consumer markets at the end of the Middle Ages and sustained by the Industrial Revolution.

Like viruses, these core ethics may go dormant, they may mutate, but they never die out. Five hundred years from now, the core ethics that define our own time will still exist. Despite fevered predictions of a leisure society, people will still want to work, will still want to define themselves by productive output. Families may be dying out, social units are changing, but men and women—and men and men, and women and women—will continue to want to hold each other, will still thrill to the touch of flesh. The cry of our babies will rend our hearts whatever structure we might arrive at for the ownership and tending of children. On the horizon waits a much purer form of individualism than democracy as we now understand it allows, but the drive toward participation won't disappear. We will continue to treasure the freedom to get up and go, to redefine ourselves, to own. If not written in our genetic code, these things are etched in our collective conscience. What matters at the heart, time cannot erase.

What is already changing, and changing with breathtaking drama, is the speed of the value translations we make from that base of core ethics, the rapidity with which we build and discard generational agendas, the sheer mass of the value stacking each generation is required to do, the extremes each generation goes to in exploring its values, and the sheer quantity of the core ethics themselves.

Think of the core ethics as oranges lying in a bowl. Because each orange is a core ethic, it cannot disappear. But now we are going to add a new one, one that we call permanent flexibility, which is an essential survival ethic in the Chaos Age. To add this new orange, we drop it from ten feet into the bowl. Everything stays in the bowl, but the force of the collision rearranges the relationship between each orange that is already there. Now we'll add another one and another and another—connectivity, privacy, authenticity. And with each new core ethic, we'll tighten the time interval between adding them and thus accelerate the pace with which multiple ethics have to be absorbed into a single value set. And meanwhile, as we add these new core ethics, the generational agendas we form them into are changing, and the generations themselves are expanding outward and contracting back in at an ever more rapid pace. The Slinky buried within the orange bowl is on speed; the bowl itself has come alive and is pulsating at an ever more fevered pace. And as the acceleration of change keeps demanding more and more new core ethics, more and more new oranges themselves keep pounding down into the bowl.

This is the values world we exist in today. The simple fact is that anyone who has lived through the last forty years has experienced more value dislocation than had occurred collectively in the prior two centuries.

The Center Will Not Hold

In their book *Generations*, William Strauss and Neil Howe provide a solid base for the understanding of how generational values work. Working forward from the American Revolution, the authors create a generational typology of the American experience. We have tinkered slightly with their numbers and formulation here, but we are indebted to them for their work.

The generation commonly known as the Silent Generation extends from 1942, when the U.S. Navy victory at the Battle of Midway first turned the tide of World War II and gave promise of ultimate victory, through 1964, by which time John Kennedy's Camelot had washed up on the bloody shores of Dealey Plaza in Dallas. No generation perhaps has been better served by history, or by public munificence. America's economic hegemony was complete with the fall of Japan and the economic collapse of Europe. The GI Bill of Rights, the most profound piece of social legislation in American history, had turned a marginally educated general populace toward a maximally educated one. Before World War II, only 25 percent of Americans had high school diplomas and only 6 percent went on to college. The GI Bill democratized higher education. It created the middle class—2.2 million of the 15.4 million vets returning from the war used it to attend college. It built what Peter Drucker has called "the knowledge society." Thanks to its low-cost loans for new housing construction, it created the suburbs—most dramatically in the new "Levittowns"—and in the process began the destruction of the cities. And the commonality of those postwar suburbs, whether they were on Long Island or in Orange County, California, created in turn a commonality of wants and needs—separate kitchens and dining rooms, separate bathrooms, multiple bedrooms—that has since become the uniform ambition of people around the world.

As much as it was characterized by vast economic expansion, the Silent Generation was a time of value contraction, a drawing back toward its center. It was the generation that agreed: agreed on everything from cars (the Big Three) to entertainment (another Big Three—NBC, CBS, and ABC). When the Silent Generation began, it was still motivated by the work agenda that it had inherited from its predecessors; by the time it ended, the work agenda had yielded to the leisure agenda. Life had been organized around time away from the job, not time on the job. But at the Silent Generation's core lay a single ethic—upward mobility—that it had shared with at least the two generations before it and a single mechanism for achieving that goal, also shared with its two preceding generations: societal consensus. It was a center that would not hold.

Probing the Extremes

The rise of a new generation, best named by Tom Wolfe when he called it the "Me Generation," began in 1965. As the first Baby Boomers left home for college, the Me Generation reaped what the Silent one had sown and left the fields almost in ashes. Although there were inevitable blips in the economy, jobs were plentiful. So were graduate-school deferments for those who wanted to avoid service in Vietnam. So, too, was everything from marijuana to, finally, cocaine. And so, of course, was sex.

If the center could not hold for the Silent Generation, the center never formed for the Me one. Its goal became exploration, both inward and outward, and its mechanism was to drive toward the extremes. The generation was less than three years old when the first public "smoke-ins" began during the 1968 presidential campaign. It was four when Neil Armstrong left his lunar landing module *Friendship* and became the first human being to walk on the face of the moon. Before it was ten, the generation had burned draft cards and bras, protested against racism and for feminism, and found peyote and mescaline.

Romantic love endured, transmogrified, as sexual restraints vanished in a flood of IUDs, birth-control pills, and the Supreme Court's 7–2 decision in the 1973 Roe vs. Wade case, upholding Texan Norma McCorvey's unrestricted right to abort her fetus during the first trimester of pregnancy. The instinct toward participatory democracy endured, too, but consensus never arrived, in matters large or small. It was the generation that couldn't agree: on the Vietnam War, the scars of which never healed; on morality, the battle over which eventually would draw the Christian Right out of its churches and into the political arena; or even on consumer goods. America's core industries—cars and steel—tumbled as the Me Generation, in its love of extremes, turned to foreign automobiles from the eccentric (Volkswagen Beetles) to the exotic (BMWs instead of Corvettes) to the commonplace (Toyotas built in Kentucky, Hondas in Ohio).

Along with the collapse of core industries came the collapse of the core economic engine of the middle class—the labor unions, with their seeming promise of lifetime employment. If life had been organized around leisure at the birth of the Me Generation, life was organized around winning by its end. And then, on October 19, 1987, the economic engine that had funded this twenty-two-year drive to the extremes coughed .once, loudly and clearly, as the Dow-Jones Industrial Average tumbled 508 points on a single day of trading. Thus was born Generation X, and winning gave way to whining.

Victimhood

Forewarned by Wall Street's Black Friday on the day of its birth, pummeled by AIDS—the estimated number of AIDS cases worldwide stood at 1.1 million in 1987 and had grown more than tenfold by 1995—and born in the spirit of contraction, Generation X is the first in the history of America to be characterized more than anything else by its aversion to risk. It is the generation that returns home after college and has to be pushed screaming and yelling out the door; the generation that keeps its head down in the workplace because the corporate hatchet is swinging with wild abandon; the generation afraid that if it gets off the bus it won't be allowed back on; the generation that won't commit: to marriage, to belief, to political party.

Plagued by its insecurities, Generation X has a single overriding philosophy: to acquiesce on the surface and deeply reject authority underneath. And it has a single ethic of its own as well—the Victim Ethic: The devil, the television, impure water, song lyrics, *something* made me do it. The bizarre defense mounted by the Generation-X Menendez brothers—that years of abuse by their father made them kill, in premeditation, both their father and mother, against whom no abuse or even ill will was ever imputed—is only among the most extreme examples of a generational mind-set that shuns personal responsibility.

Absent any sense of itself, any clear sense of where it is going, Generation X increasingly harks back to earlier generations for its definitions. In the name of nostalgia—and thirty years after the surgeon general's office put to rest any lingering doubt about the ill effects of tobacco—cigars have become *de rigueur* for twenty- and thirtysomething bond traders, stock manipulators, and their wannabes. In the name of nostalgia—and sixty years after Myrna Loy and William Powell toasted one another over the cocktail shaker in *The Thin Man* movies—a bar devoted solely to martinis has opened on K Street in downtown Washington, D.C., there to be patronized by the most earnest young people in the most earnest city in the world. In the name of nostalgia, the generation clings to the belief that reason still prevails, that loyalty—despite all evidence to the contrary—still counts. Like the generation itself, its myths are lines of defense against the accelerated rate of change.

Generation X has powerful subsidiary values. Its very uncertainty about its economic future is helping to turn the fear of downward mobility into the virtue of downward nobility, and the rise of downward nobility—the desire not for many things but a few good things—will drive consumerism in the years immediately ahead. Numbed by advertising, Generation X is also helping to turn the mute button on for attack ads of all sorts. At the birth of the Silent Generation, the average American devoted an estimated 4.4 hours to media of all sorts and was exposed to 76 ads a day, according to a study by the Advertising Research Foundation. Slightly more than halfway through the life span of Generation X, the average American devotes nearly 9 hours daily to the media and encounters almost 150 ads a day, some 55,000 a year. No study, it should be noted, has yet to measure the increase in the raw shrillness of advertising over the last fifty years. The New Civility that we see as a powerful advertising force through the next decade is in part, though not wholly, a reaction to the acceleration and massive accumulation of advertising incivilities.

Perhaps more than anything else, Generation X is obsessed with personal energy, with its preservation and accumulation. For whatever bad things one might say about the generation—and we've said enough of them already—no generation in recorded history has had to internalize so much change so quickly, no generation has had its core ethics so pummeled, and no generation has seen its agenda so compacted, so densified. The work agenda endured for three decades; the leisure agenda for two; the winning agenda for one. Victimhood will have come and gone, we predict, in a mere thirteen years, roughly the span of time from the creation of Generation X in 1987 to the time the youngest members at its birth reach age thirty. It is the force of this miniaturization, the impact of stress upon time, that determines available energy. Stress grows exponentially with change—and even more exponentially the greater the inability to adjust to change.

In fact, this obsession with energy may be Generation X's most prescient value, because never before has a generation been less poised in its makeup and its whole value structure to meet the onrush of change that is already arriving. It is risk-averse when only those who embrace risk can survive and thrive. It is backward-looking when only those who embrace the future can prosper in it. Hardest of all, perhaps, it will, over the course of the next decade, enjoy the last fruits of the great accumulation of capital that began with the Silent Generation and will soon be largely passed on to Generation X through inheritance. Remember: Those who have the most difficult time adjusting to a new paradigm are always those who made out like bandits in the old one.

Perhaps the greatest myth of all that this last flower of the Baby Boom tells itself is that it will set the future. The reality is that it will become irrelevant as a generation at the very height of its supposed rise to power.

The Millennialists

Setting the values of the future will fall to the generation waiting directly in line behind the X'ers, the one we call the Millennialists. The Millennialists' credo will be built on a single overriding value: connectivity, access to everything. Their ethic will be a simple one—possibility—and we believe it will hold for generations and perhaps centuries. Where Generation X contracted to a whiny core, Millennialists will expand to explore the extremes because it is only by going to the edges and managing from there that you can control the center in a chaos world. Privacy will matter to Millennialists because in a world driving toward connectivity, privacy becomes scarce, and scarcity gains value. The cost of entry into this world will be precisely the opposite of the cost of entry into the world of Generation X: the assumption of personal responsibility. Millennialists will look out on the same landscape X'ers shrink from and see it for what it truly is: a world half full, not half empty.

Motives: Time Chits and Principles

Play a game with us. Choose any product you want to manufacture—a mattress, a car, a beer, it doesn't matter. The point is that unless you're in the business solely to get out of the house and have a steady negative cash stream, you will have to motivate a consumer to buy your product. To do that, you'll first need a focus for your sales strategy. In fact, there are only three of them. You can focus on the product ("Quality is job one"), on the marketing process itself ("We build excitement"), or on the consumer ("Built for the human race"). We've listed the three focuses in column A on the next page. Next, you'll need to appeal to a specific motive on the part of the consumer. Again, there are only three. Like values—and closely related to them—some motives are generationally imprinted. Others are life-stage oriented: You act as you do because of the point in your life you have arrived at. Still others are mass motives—they're in the air, the water. We've listed those in column B. Finally, since motives never operate in a vacuum, you'll need to pick a cause, an engine that drives the motive. These, too, are three in number: Motives are driven by a desire for status, a desire for a return, or by principles. We've listed these in column C.

A. Focus	B. Motive	C. Cause
Product	Generationally imprinted	Status oriented
Marketing	Life stage	Return oriented
Customer	Mass	Principled

Now, the item you are selling—mattresses, for argument's sake. Let's say you want to focus on the customer, target Generation X'ers, and appeal to their desire for a return on their investment. What's the ad campaign? How do you link all that in one salable sound-bite sentence? "Your back is too valuable to sleep on anything else"? It appeals to the generationally imprinted risk aversion of X'ers; it promises them a kink-free back for their money. It just might work. Twist the model slightly this time so you are now appealing to the status orientation of X'ers. How does the campaign go now? "Smart people don't take chances on a comfortable mattress"? Not bad. The act of purchasing the mattress conveys intelligence, and in the new information economy, raw intelligence is status. Now shift the motive parameter and the focus. You're still making mattresses, but this time you want to emphasize the product and you want appeal to the life-stage needs of people who are just starting to get chronic back problems—forty-five- to fifty-five-year-olds, let's say. What's the sound bite this time? "Serta—built for the back *you* have to live with"?

Now do it yourself. Pick a product and grab a focus from column A on the Chinese menu above, a motive from column B, and a motive engine from column C. A luxury car. A customer focus. An appeal to the generationally imprinted infidelity of the Me Generation. An orientation toward status. Create an advertisement: The room is elegantly furnished, the husband and wife elegantly dressed. The talk between them seems to be of enormous consequence. The implication is that he's having an affair. But, lo and behold, what she really wants is not a divorce but . . . a Cadillac!

Okay, that ad has already been made. The point is that it's easy, fun. The mystery is dispelled: Anyone can be a copywriter. But as you play, keep in mind Hans Reichenbach's analogy of the balls traveling through space. Unless the focus, the motive, and the engine driving the motive are the same color, they cannot merge, and if they do not merge, your mattress or car or beer brand cannot sell. And then remember that the balls themselves—now three in number—are changing color constantly as they travel. That is the real world of marketing today.

Proof, Not Guarantees

Two cartoons. In the first, a befuddled man stands in front of the return counter while the man behind the counter explains, "No, no, I think you'll see that it says that we guarantee you'll get pissed off if it doesn't work right." The second, a famous *New Yorker* cartoon of many years back, shows one side of a New York City block. A sign in the building on the corner closest to the viewer reads "Best Pizza in New York." The sign in the next building says "Best Pizza in the United States." Beyond it, in the next building, another sign reads "Best Pizza on Earth," and just beyond that still another sign proclaims "Best Pizza in the Universe." And then, finally, at the very end of the block farthest from the viewer, comes the sign that counts: "Best Pizza on the Block."

As dissimilar as the cartoons seem, they are both about motives— about what motivates a business to succeed and about what motivates a customer to choose one product from a universe of like choices. To be successful today, you have to be motivated to be the best pizza on your block. What does that mean? That companies have to segment themselves today to meet the segmented aspirations of their consumers. That it is far more important actually to be the best in a well-defined sphere than it is to claim to be the best in an ungainly one. One size doesn't fit all. The challenge is to find which segment of the population it does fit and to fashion a set of motives that will appeal to that segment alone. How do you do that? How does a company stay at the edge of its game? Four ways, and perhaps the four most important things any business can learn:

- The public has to believe you are the master of the basics in your category. Perhaps no one has ever done this more effectively than Sony did with its Trinitron, which both established the quality standard for the category and virtually renamed quality televisions.

- The public has to believe you are consistent.

- The public has to believe you fix your mistakes.
- You have to offer a value-added component that separates you from other choices in the marketplace and is meaningful for individual consumers.

Back to the Chinese menu for a second. You can position your car as the best automobile in the world (a product focus), as the most exciting automobile in the world (a marketing strategy), or as the automobile that—while neither the best or the most exciting—is the one most flexibly designed to meet the needs of individual consumers. Saturn owns the latter turf virtually free and clear. It has a category. It knows itself. It's the best pizza on the block, not the best one in the Universe. It offers a value-added component—haggle-free shopping and a promise that the car is made for you. Its recall programs have convinced consumers that it fixes its mistakes and is concerned about manufacturing a consistent product, and it has mastered the basics in its category, in large part because it defines its category so carefully. At a far lower level of U.S. sales, Saab knows itself, too. It's the ugliest sophisticated car in the world—a car for cantankerous futurists. As it happens, we know something about those, too.

Two last ways to plug into the motives of consumers: You have to know the difference between reliability and durability, and you have to offer proof, not guarantees. Reliability is easy: Every time you turn on the television, the screen fires up. Durability means that seven years after you first turn on the TV, the screen fires up just as quickly and the image is just as clear as it was on day one. That's Trinitron, not television—and consumers know the difference. Why proof instead of guarantees? Because one of the most powerful of all emerging values is the demand for authenticity and because every single one of us has stood at the same return counter that the man in the cartoon is standing at. To borrow from John Nance Garner's evaluation of the vice presidency, we all know guarantees aren't worth a bucket of warm spit.

This recognition of the devaluation of guarantees underlies MCI's business-oriented "Proof Positive" plan. Instead of empty—and fundamentally unbelievable—guarantees of savings, MCI now uses billing statements to help companies learn more about their own phone usage. Thus the savings generated become both an exercise in anticipatory economics for the company and an endemic part of its structure and practices.

Coca-Cola's brilliant series of ads that aired around the 1996 Olympics offered another sort of proof, but one every bit as effective as MCI's. The ads featured black-and-white footage of earlier Olympics dating back to 1924, when Coke first became associated with the games. In each scene was a Coca-Cola product—a vending machine, someone drinking from a bottle—with the single word "Coke" painted in red. The ads took a trivial product, nothing more than a soft drink, and tied it to the grandeur of the Olympic games. Most important, they tied Coke to the Olympics longitudinally, in deep time. The message: We were there then, we're here now, and we will always be. Coke has no new markets to win; in effect, its proof is its very history.

A last way you can offer proof, not guarantees, is to adopt the ancient methods of tribes to appeal to a rapidly tribalizing world. How do tribes do that? By initiation, by closing ceremony, and, most important, by the continuous reinforcement of ritual. Send out a letter once in a while to customers telling them how smart they were to buy your product. Or invite all your customers back to Tennessee annually for a barbecue. Few customers actually do go back to Saturn's picnic, but the proof of constant caring inherent in the offer is an absolute act of genius.

It is only when a business gets its own motives in line with a changing world that it can make its focus the same color as the changing motives of its customers, but even then it has to be wary. Nissan's "Built for the human race" created a wonderful customer focus; it hinted at a terrific value-added component. (Imagine, a car actually built for real hips, real elbows, real bad hair and myopia!) But when women went into the showroom and were told to come back with their husbands and their husbands' checkbooks, it became apparent that Nissan had been built for only 49 percent of the human race.

Starstruck

The motive that drives any individual person is the sum total of his or her experiences in life—what she wants, what she feels is most scarce, what will most validate her existence. In broad terms, though, motives can be broken down into the three categories we've previously mentioned:

Life stage.

Life stage motives drive you to join a health club because you just turned forty and "cardiovascular" now seems more than a long word in another language or a church because you've had those first grim flutters in the heart and intimations of mortality are beating in your ear. Life stage motives impel the recently divorced to scan personal ads and join singles clubs. They impel fathers of teenage girls to vote Republican for the first time because, suddenly, all the huff and puff about immoral lyrics and salacious movies has an objective correlative living under the same roof. These are the motives that lie closest to the bone, and they are the motives that cohort products both seek to exploit and are dependent upon.

Lite Beer by Miller, to cite one example, is a cohort product. It originally arose with thirty- to forty-five-year-olds and is now traveling with them through time. To do so, it has to change its message as the ambitions of its cohorts change while keeping the product constant. Rock 'n' roll is an even better example—a Baby Boomer cohort product that remains the same but continuously repackages memories as its cohorts move from life stage to life stage. Because golden oldies stations know their cohorts, because they don't try to force their cohorts to be something they aren't, they remain the most successful single category group in FM radio.

Other cohort products simply exist at a point in time that life stages pass through. Corona Beer is entered at about age twenty-one and exited mostly three to five years later. Still other businesses like Weight Watchers are virtually trapped by a cohort that had the will and energy to lose weight in its thirties and early forties, but has largely given in to gravity and cellulite in its fifties.

Trapped or not, though, products that live off of life-stage motives at least used to have fairly simple terrain to negotiate: Stay with your people or wait for your people to come to you. Today, that terrain more closely resembles the convoluted surface of the Moon than the flat plains of the Canadian Breadbasket. Like change itself, life-stage changes occur in ever more narrow bands. The old demarcations of youth, middle age, and old age long ago ceased to have meaning as life-stage discriminators. Now their more refined successors—early middle age, middle age, late middle age, to cite a few—are nearly as useless. The young act old; the old, young; life stages blur into one another. Meanwhile, products that attempt to lurch with life stages are cribbed in by the ascendant demand for authenticity—the imperative to be the cohort, not to pretend to be it. And products that attempt to break out of their cohort are equally cribbed in by the need to retain authenticity.

Mercedes is a life-stage product—a reward for faithful toil in the corporate or professional vineyards—which means that it, too, is a product effectively trapped in time. To break out of that box, Mercedes has begun marketing to younger audiences with its lower-priced C230 series in the hope that it will become a cohort product that will travel through time with its new, ultimately larger audience. Perhaps the effort will work, or perhaps Mercedes will find that fifty-year-olds no longer want to reward themselves with a car being driven by thirtysomething junior partners, and thirtysomething junior partners aren't interested in a car they associate largely with country-club parking lots. Destabilizing the motive core of a life-stage product can also destabilize its authenticity, and in the new age rising, that is a far harder hole to climb out of.

A final caution for products dependent upon life-stage motives: Flight impulse is building to critical mass. Undermined by the death of loyalty or liberated by the new freedoms to know, to go, to do, to be—it is all a matter of interpretation—forty-five- to fifty-year-olds soon will be seeking en masse completely different lifestyles and actively plotting their flights. Let your product stand in the way of that flight and it will be stampeded. Build a product that abets the flight, and you will ride it to riches.

Generational imprinting.

If each person is motivated by his own position in life, members of each generation share a collective body of motives. The risk aversion of Generation X'ers keeps them living under their parents' roof because they don't want to sign a year-long lease. Risk aversion has led to a whole new category of consultants—counselors who help X'er couples decide if they are compatible enough for marriage. It drives e-mail relationships because there is safety and protection in the long spaces of cyberspace. X'ers procrastinate. They are disinclined to climb on treadmills less because of their age than because their generation has rejected the health and fitness movement. The health and fitness movement, in turn, impels the Me Generation, even in its spreading years, to buy Gore-Tex running suits and rollerblade on ever more fragile joints and bones. For their part, the aging remnants of the Silent Generation seek products and solutions that won't require them to exercise control. Millennialists, on the other hand, will be obsessed with fixing the society they have inherited, which means that they will simultaneously be targets for guilt marketing and marketing to trigger guilt in others.

Generationally imprinted motives are subconscious ones; they come with our date of birth. And as change accelerates, as the sheer weight of change mounts up and buckles the infrastructure of lives and generations, generational motives come in ever faster cycles.

Mass motives.

For reasons that we'll show later, mass culture is dead, but mass motives live on. The least of the mass motives is annoyance. It is not just Generation X'ers who feel victimized, and it is not just X'ers who act out of a collective sense of victimhood. We make obscene gestures as we drive because there is a conspiracy to deny us our full rights of the road. We write letters to the editor because our microculture— senior citizens, white males, working mothers, mothers who choose to stay at home, slackers, gays—has not been paid adequate respect in an editorial or a news story. Peter Finch in *Network* and Michael Douglas in *Falling Down* were both playing to the mass motive of annoyance, of anger. "In your face" ads play to it, too: Get mad, get even, get happy, sort of.

Happily, we suspect annoyance is the most endangered of all mass motives. A New Civility, as we've written, is arising. The chaos of true freedom doesn't produce anarchy. Only anarchy can replicate itself. The chaos of true freedom impels very important rules about politeness, and does so very quickly, because it is only with important and binding rules about politeness that people can truly be free to pursue their rights to know, to go, to do, and to be. The "netiquette" that has emerged mostly of its own volition on the information super-highway—identify yourself; treat others with respect; no "spamming," or sending messages to totally irrelevant sites—is a forceful early example of what lies ahead broadly across the social spectrum. Like chaos, connectivity impels politeness; in the Age of Access there is no other way to get along.

The opposite of annoyance, and more profound than it, is the simple collective desire to have fun. Mass marketers such as McDonald's have worked long and hard to satisfy this desire, adding playlands, movie tie-ins, and even creating a specialized language in the pursuit of group enjoyment: "Melpu?" ("May I help you?"), almost always followed immediately by "Fries?" But no one understands the fun mass motive better than Walt Disney, Inc. In its theme parks, in its feature-length animated films, throughout its far-flung enterprises, Disney has learned to engineer fun and point it at the exact center of the populace—or more accurately, the exact center of the populace with enough discretionary income to partake of the fun at issue. At places like Epcot Center at Orlando's Walt Disney World, Disney has even learned to take a mildly educational experience and wrap it in a gift box.

Even more important as a mass motive than the desire to have fun, and closely aligned with it, is the desire for self-esteem. Everyone's a winner. All the kids on the soccer team get trophies. Every college student gets at least a "B," and in Lake Woebegone, as Garrison Keillor so charmingly puts it, "all the children are above average." In the world already forming, the achievement of self-esteem will be inextricably tied to the exercise of self-responsibility.

Of all the mass motives, the most profound—the one that straddles the motive world like a colossus—is the pursuit of celebrity. In the pursuit of celebrity, we make sure that the camera angle sweeping the football team as it charges into the stadium will include us in the background, or we hang around the fringes of accidents, hoping that we will be interviewed. The window that connects the *Today* show set to the street beyond is both an invitation to ambush celebrity and a form of ambush marketing: It allows people gathered on the street exposure on national television at the same time that it connects *Today* and its on-air personalities to the national craving for fame. Sometimes, we ambush celebrity literally as Mark David Chapman did on December 8, 1980, when he shot John Lennon outside the Dakota apartment building in Manhattan's Upper West Side—a crazed displacement of the same impulse to be known, seen, recognized. ITT's recent agreement with the Planet Hollywood bar-and-restaurant chain to build a series of hotels and casinos using the Planet Hollywood name and utilizing its Hollywood owners as drawing power even put an economic valuation on celebrity: ITT puts up 100 percent of the money and the star-owners of Planet Hollywood get 20 percent of the take, simply for being well-known.

It is by now both clichéd and incorrect to note that Andy Warhol's fifteen minutes of fame has been conferred on everyone. It clearly hasn't. But until now, no one has attempted to gauge just how near to prophetic Warhol was. We analyzed celebrity by counting the number of people from a given community who had appeared on local newscasts and in the local newspaper over a given period of time. Then we adjusted for size and for the median age of Americans and multiplied that out by the 39,000 localities in America today. Our estimate is that 64 million Americans—roughly a quarter of the population—have had a meaningful exposure in the media, long enough to validate their existence, long enough to be perceived by their peers as a star.

No motive today has more pulling power than celebrity. Ironically, it is a power that will grow both more compelling and less meaningful in the coming decades. Why? Because celebrity will be so easy to achieve. The drive toward access, the creation of the Age of Access, is ultimately about total connectivity, about the access of everyone to everyone and everything to everything. A personal home page on the Internet—self-created celebrity—is only the most primitive example of what lies ahead, but it is an instructive example all the same. Home pages are self-validation, and self-validation lies at the very center of the drive toward celebrity.

It is not public-relations consultants and managers who will prosper in the Age of Access. P.R. will be self-achievable, and publicity will come dirt cheap. It is, instead, privacy managers who will be in demand. Once again, we value most what is most scarce, and in the

Age of Access the drive to privacy will be among the most forceful of all motives.

The Declining Value of Status

As we said at the beginning of this chapter, the three motives that impel action are driven, in turn, by a desire for status, by a desire for return, or by the exercise of principles. To return briefly to our Chinese menu, the relationship between motive and cause breaks down as follows:

		Motive		
	Life Stage	Generational		Mass
C Status				
a				
u Return				
s				
e Principles				

For argument's sake, say you have just bought a Cadillac Seville with a Northstar engine system. The motive that impelled you may have been your life stage. The kids are through college, your economic future is secure. Perhaps you have bought a second home in Florida and want a spacious machine to carry you back and forth. Beyond that lies the reason that impelled the motive. A Cadillac Seville will make your neighbors and relatives sit up and take notice, in which event you are status-oriented. If the advertisements are correct, the engine system by Northstar—a wholly owned subsidiary of General Motors, though that is never mentioned in the ads—will go 100,000 miles before you need your first tune-up. If you buy for this reason, your action is return-oriented, you are looking for some savings out of your investment. Or perhaps you bought the Cadillac rather than a Mercedes 450 because it is American-made, in which event you have acted out of principle.

It is critical to marketing to understand that motive alone doesn't drive consumers, and it is equally critical to know what shifts are taking place not just in motives but in the forces that drive them. Those changes are, in fact, profound.

Status orientation.

Like precious metals, status draws its value from scarcity, but its value also is conferred by a shared assumption of what is, in fact, status. A Rolex on only a few wrists in a society that collectively agrees that a Rolex is worth having has status. A Rolex on many wrists loses its status, and even a scarce Rolex ceases to have status value if no one notices it. As the marketplace drives toward a supersaturation of products, scarcity disappears, and with it status orientation. As mass culture breaks up into, in effect, hundreds of millions of individual realities, there can be no shared assumptions of what is enviable to own. For that is yet another of the great ironies of total connectivity. As access draws people closer and closer together, it also drives them toward total individuation. Once there were three television networks to draw your view of reality, and with it your sense of what conferred status. Fiber optics will soon bring more than five hundred channels into every home that has a telephone. What will have status will be what is most unique, and what is most unique will be determined one consumer at a time.

The future lies not with conspicuous consumption, but with inconspicuous consumption, and by its very definition, *inconspicuous* consumption is the death knell of status.

Return orientation.

This, too, will be largely a casualty, for a simpler reason. To expect a return on a decision is to assume that cause and effect will prevail: I do, therefore I get. The chain of cause and effect has been broken, drowned in asynchronous bursts, swamped by chaos. The new mantra is far less demanding: I am, therefore I get. In the Chaos Age, the only way to appeal to an expectation of return will be to make the return implicit in the product: proof, as we've written, not guarantees; durability, not reliability; authenticity, not nostalgia. And the only way to do that will be to offer the proof, the durability, the authenticity time and time again.

Principles orientation.

This is far closer to where the future lies. In part, principles will assume an ever greater importance in motive formulation through simple default. Motives have to be driven by something, and if they are not driven by status or return, principles command the field. But the ascendancy of principles is more deeply rooted than that. When the capacity to plan your way from *a* to *b* to *c* dies, so does the old industrial model of doing things right. Doing things right implies a cause-and-effect relationship: You have to establish what is right and then plan your way to get there. In a world freed from reason, the biological model takes over. An ecosystem can't plan; it can't calculate what is proper and proceed to that point. Ecosystems simply have to do the right thing. The difference is more than semantic. Rightness has to be instinctual—there is no time for it to be anything else—and principles are instinctual rightness.

One other point needs to be made here. A marketing appeal to motives driven by status can survive chicanery—status is a floating target. An appeal to motives driven by the expectation of return is full of wiggle room—expectations are all over the lot. But a marketing appeal to motives driven by principles must be real, because principles are not only instinctually right, they have an instinctual crap detector. Some years back, when he was still serving as television spokesperson for the Chrysler Corporation, Lee Iacocca tried such a tactic. Buy the Plymouth Acclaim, he told viewers, because studies show that it is a better car than the Honda Accord. The appeal, in part, was to an expectation of return; buyers would save money and have a more reliable vehicle. But it was mostly to principle. Chrysler had gotten the message car buyers had been sending Detroit for years. It had fought back and now here, finally, was a chance to buy American and send a shot across the bow of Japan, Inc.

There were problems with the study Iacocca cited: Essentially, Chrysler had interviewed some two hundred people, none of whom had ever owned an imported car. In the business, it was what is known as a "strange sample." But the greatest problem was that Iacocca had appealed to potential buyers' instinctual principles, and potential buyers knew that what he was saying was instinctual baloney. Chrysler Corporation's Dodge and Plymouth minivans had been brilliant marketing concepts—a car that hit the Baby Boomer market exactly where it lived, between driving the kids' soccer team to practice and driving the family to the beach for vacation—but the Plymouth Acclaim would never be anything other than a discount Accord or Camry, with all the shortfalls "discount" implies. To suggest otherwise was standard advertising practice, but to tie the suggestion to an appeal to principles, as Iacocca did, violated authenticity.

Iacocca's own career trajectory offers compelling evidence that toying with principles digs a very deep hole. For those with a short memory, he had been widely credited with rescuing Chrysler, and his biography had been a huge best-seller. Like another industrialist, Ross Perot, Iacocca was frequently mentioned as presidential timber. Shortly after the Acclaim ads ran, he disappeared as the company's spokesperson. In April 1995, Iacocca resurfaced as part of an unsuccessful $20 billion bid by financier Kirk Kerkorian to take his old company over.

A final note on motives: What is true of motivating companies and motivating consumers is equally true of motivating employees.

At its test facility in New Jersey, Avis has been experimenting with time chits. When workers are particularly effective in the small details of their jobs, when they commit random acts of corporate kindness and perform in ways that are consistent with corporate strategy, Avis is rewarding them with time off from work. The exact value of the chit is still being fine-tuned—perhaps it will be worth five minutes, perhaps ten. The critical issue is that the combination of time length and frequency of bestowal must be meaningful. An effective employee should be able to accumulate enough chits to take two hours off each week during the summer to coach a daughter's softball team, or a week off of the work year to visit a distant parent. A time-reward system might mean that twenty employees would be needed to complete the work that nineteen are now doing, but if each employee is 10 percent more effective as a result of the chits, it's the same as getting a twenty-first worker free.

To motivate employees, in short, Avis is giving them the currency they most value, and the most valuable currency is always the most scarce. What is most scarce today for most employees is control over their own time. Even more important, to motivate employees Avis is giving them a reward that is both universally desired and open to individual interpretation. The beauty of a gift of time is that it can be used in any way an employee chooses to apply it. Best of all, time chits marry the self-interest of employees to the self-interest of the corporation. They are a proof, not a guarantee, that Avis will reward effective work.

Hats off to the experiment.

3

Perspective: No Walls, Without or Within

In the 1952 presidential contest between Dwight Eisenhower and Adlai Stevenson, 61.6 percent of the voting-age population cast ballots. By 1960—John Kennedy vs. Richard Nixon—participation had grown to nearly 63 percent. It stayed roughly there throughout the 1960s: 61.9 percent of voting-age Americans went to the polls in 1964 when Lyndon Johnson faced Barry Goldwater; 60.9 percent went four years later when Nixon defeated Hubert Humphrey. Then, in the 1970s, voter participation began to slide. About 55 percent of eligible voters cast ballots in 1972; in 1976, 1980, and 1984, participation hovered around 53 percent.

By 1988, with ever greater sums of money being spent by presidential candidates to bring their message to the electorate, participation appeared to bottom out. Slightly more than half of those eligible to vote—50.3 percent—bothered to go to the polls that year. Franchise exercise bounced back slightly in 1992—55.1 percent of voting-age voters cast ballots—and then it plummeted again in 1996, by far the most expensive presidential campaign in United States history, when less than half of eligible voters cast ballots. The bottom line: In the generation and a half between the Kennedy-Nixon and the Bill Clinton–Bob Dole races, participation in what is frequently cited as the most basic duty of a democratic nation declined by more than 22 percent.

Among Washington, D.C.'s, blue-suited army of political leaders and commentators, this decline in electoral participation is taken as an indelible ebbing of the civic spirit in America. Schools are blamed for failing to teach citizenship. Polling is blamed for making most political races foregone conclusions long before voting day arrives. New and looser interpretations of the right to vote are blamed for including in the body of eligible voters those—read eighteen- to twenty-year-olds—who are too preoccupied with themselves to exercise their franchise. Get-out-the-vote drives are blamed for bringing on to the voting rolls those—religious fundamentalists, the poor, blacks, depending on one's political leanings—who historically have ignored their franchise and will ignore it again after whatever single issue has brought them to the polls subsides. Even Washington's own brigade of political consultants is fingered, for reducing campaigning to the level of a schoolyard shouting match. (Indeed, a very serious argument has arisen in the advertising community over whether negative political ads have effectively destroyed the capacity of all advertising to deliver a message that isn't implicitly negative.)

But here's a radical theory as to why voter participation has declined: As we've already written, governments today—nations and those who control them—matter less and less. For most people in most industrialized nations, governments now exist as a mechanism for the transfer of payments and almost nothing more—save for their sheer entertainment value.

For a radical theory, that one, in fact, is about as plain as the nose on your face. Why has the Washington intellerati failed to grasp it? Because the centrality of the political process is intimately tied to the intellerati's own centrality—if government doesn't matter, it doesn't matter. Like other communes, the political commune talks mainly to itself, and thus has its worldview both set and confirmed within the confines of its commune.

It is all a matter of perspective. More accurately, it is all a matter of what we call truncated perspective.

The Parable of the Forest and the Trees

Some examples of truncated perspective in the corporate world:

Many have claimed to have heard it, but the president of General Motors actually once did tell us that as far as GM is concerned, Toyota can have the little-car market because it is never going to be profitable. He drove a GM luxury liner on wheels. His executive vice presidents drove lesser GM yachts. All around Detroit, loyal GM and Ford and Chrysler assembly-line workers were scurrying around town in the products they had helped to piece together. The General Motors president saw the world through the eyes of his own commune. He knew as much about the future of auto-buying motives as he chose to know. And because he did, GM and its stockholders saw untold billions of dollars that could have been theirs shipped across the Pacific instead.

When the Exxon *Valdez* ran aground off of Alaska on March 24, 1989, spilling 11 million barrels of Prudhoe Bay crude oil into Prince William Sound, Exxon's response was to concentrate on the oil—its containment and dispersal—because the company's ethos has been built around exploration, engineering, and refining. Oil is what Exxon understands. What the company couldn't predict, because it couldn't see it, was that someone whose perspective had been equally truncated by reading *Mother Jones* wouldn't give a hoot about the oil per se. Oil was the enemy. The *Mother Jones* commune's whole focus was on the tarred birds, the dying fish, and sea mammals. And because doomed animals make better footage than containment buoy lines, Exxon created a public-relations disaster that it is still crawling out from under. Technology, George Bernard Shaw once said, makes life meaningful for technologists. Similarly, oil makes life meaningful for oil men, and environmentalism does the same for environmentalists. Like Washington's political savants, it's easier not to look beyond.

United Parcel Service had a different case of truncated perspective. Its entire philosophy of managing a package business had been built around keeping the Teamsters in line and running an efficient trucking operation. Out of that perspective, UPS had created a wonderful system that could transfer a package nationwide at a modest cost if only customers were willing to accept deliveries on a given schedule. And then Federal Express came along and said, in effect, we'll up that modest cost, pick up the package whenever you want, and deliver it quicker. And, bingo, UPS's package-delivery hegemony was history. UPS could have done what FedEx did—it had the infrastructure—but it still thought the issue was money.

Truncated perspective is what drives companies to what we call "blue-chip ejaculation"—the tendency of very large corporations when confronted with massive amounts of change to ejaculate a single-point answer in a very large way. Why? Because like UPS they're still looking at the cost of the service when the issue has morphed into convenience and time.

Truncated perspective is also what drives them to competitive "uniphobia"—the absolute fixation on competitive situations, which, by their very nature, are transitory. Why? Because if you don't get out of the box of the present, the world will always look the same no matter how fast it is changing. And if that is the case, you will be steam-rolled by a future arriving at the speed of light.

How do you avoid a truncated perspective? By driving other manufacturer's demo cars, not your own. By meeting with others who share your business interests but not your corporate communalism or competitive set—Nike executives with Coca-Cola executives, for example; Boston Market execs with their Disney peers; Bank of America brass with the brass at Victoria's Secret. By realizing that what most interests you about your business is likely not to be your business's most critical variable. Oil executives, as we've said before, like to concentrate on oil—how much is in the ground, how to refine it. But the oil in the ground is fixed; refining engineering grows incrementally and predictably. Distance—the third part of the triangle of getting oil out of the ground and into a gas tank—is far less predictable, far more variable, far more evolving. How many oil men are looking there? Few, we would wager.

Our favorite box-breaker of all time was a scavenger hunt we witnessed for Bank of America branch managers. The managers were each given a camera and a list of service situations to look for and then set loose in a large mall with instructions to photograph each of the service situations on their list. The results were absolutely amazing. The managers' whole understanding of banking had been gleaned by running around and looking at each other's banks, and thus, quite naturally, they thought that a bank is a bank is a bank. But a bank has no more inherent claim on a customer's loyalty than does a car or beer brand. A bank is a service that happens to facilitate the exchange of money, just as McDonald's is a service that facilitates the provision of fast food and Victoria's Secret is a service that facilitates the acquisition of bras and teddies. To survive, to prosper, a bank has to be whatever each individual customer wants it to be. By the time the scavenger hunt was over, the Bank of America branch managers had come to understand that. They'd broken out of the box of their truncated perspective—seen the forest *and* the trees.

Take a look at the schematic below. The outside ring, the one we've labeled "Provocation," is people like us: provocateurs, people who are hired to force you to look at the world differently, to challenge your assumptions. (And, no, this isn't a job pitch—we've got all the work we can handle.) The next ring, the one we've labeled "Discovery," belongs to the imagineers, the scenario planners, mostly consultants who are brought in to take whatever ideas provocation has stimulated and try to engineer them for the business. Inside that is the ring we call "Momentum," where the scenarios of the imagineers are fine-tuned and made ready for implementation. "Momentum" belongs to the process people. And inside that is the bull's-eye of all this furious work, the "Mainstream," the heart and soul of whatever it is you are doing.

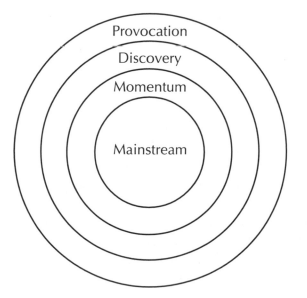

Most of the energy in any company goes to managing the uncertainty at the center, in the mainstream, but in a chaos world, a world in which change is not a luxury but an imperative, it is only by operating at the edge of the extremes—by courting provocation—that a manager can inject the information that challenges people to keep thinking about the business in a different way. There is the conundrum of managing in a chaos world.

What do you see when you finally do get the blinders off, when you finally do break through the barrier of a truncated perspective? That the world is both a far more complex and far more simple place than you thought it might be. Most clearly, you see that the American electorate in its broad wisdom really has been right. Borders don't matter. Nations are passé. Governments are old news.

Think Global, Act Global

By now, whole libraries have been written about the rise of the global marketplace, about transnational corporations, about how globetrotting CEOs have become the new princes of the economic and even social order. The evidence is more than abundant, and there is no need to regurgitate it here. Largely undiscussed, though, is the way in which the vacuum produced by the reduction in the power of governments globally has been filled by the expansion of the power of global corporations.

To attract businesses to Iowa, the legislature there recently passed a law that allows businesses relocating to the state to take a segregated tax deduction for salaries paid to their executives—this in addition to the preferential treatment on property taxes such companies already received. Italy provides similar income protections if you want to build an oil refinery or an air-conditioning factory there. In effect, governments are handing over their civic responsibilities to corporations, and corporations are thus beginning to function more like governments.

IBM, to cite one obvious example, is a virtual country unto itself. Like other transnationals, it has its own cadre of corporate diplomats—executives charged with the development and management of nation-state business relationships. IBM's loyalty to its subjects may be weak, but its loyalty to its true electorate, its shareholders, is very strong indeed. In effect, as globalism spreads, we are passing into—or perhaps *through*—an era of corporate feudalism.

Almost wholly missed in this rush to globalism has been the fact that as we arrive there, the traditional economic system begins to function far more like a traditional ecosystem. What is true of the shift in organization generally is true of the shifts in organization within this new world economic system: As with any ecosystem, all relationships are simultaneously symbiotic, competitive, predatory, and parasitic. And what is true of ecosystems is true of this new economy: There are no borders within it, only shifting communities of interest.

"Think global, act local"—the most recent collective wisdom of the sages that expound on the world economy—is what the internationally minded Mercedes Benz subsidiary of the Daimler Benz Corporation had in mind when it bought the Dutch-based Fokker aircraft manufacturer in 1995 for roughly $5 billion. Although its brand name has global recognition, Fokker essentially competed only in the mainland Europe airplane market. Not long afterward, the local Fokker slipped into bankruptcy, and the global Mercedes wrote off its $5 billion investment as a loss. By the summer of 1996, Fokker's court-appointed receivers were angling to sell the company to Russia's Aviatsionnaya Korporatsiya Yakovlev for about $216 million.

"Think global, act global" is what Volvo had in mind early in 1996 when the auto manufacturer targeted one million people around the world as its primary marketing audience. Volvo's 1 million potential customers weren't picked based on their addresses or their nations. They weren't selected by sex, race, religion, sexual orientation, ethnicity, or language. They were selected solely because they formed a specific community of interest—in this case, a community potentially interested in purchasing a slightly pricey, slightly dowdy, famously safe car manufactured in Sweden.

"Think global, act global" is also what MCI had in mind when it set out to create a new international "Friends and Family Social Monitor." The first thing a telecommunications giant like MCI is about is connectivity—connectivity is its entire ethos—and the last thing connectivity is about is borders of any sort. By measuring social attitudes internationally, MCI establishes itself as an icon of this new, borderless world at the same time that it develops a new metric for measuring the global marketplace.

Think global, act global is more than a slogan. Political battles over closing America's borders are in part about what government still does do best: the transfer of payments. Undocumented aliens and the black market in illegal workers rob the public till. Those who pay the bill must pony up more for those who don't. But the political battles also are about nostalgia, about a time when nationhood mattered, a time when to be an American—or a Brit or a Swede or a Saudi—distinguished. That time has gone. Think global, act global is a reflection of the world as it is.

One Corporate Culture, One Shopping List, One Life

Several years ago, we were involved in negotiations with Japanese counterparts. We were headquartered in New York and they in Tokyo, so San Francisco was chosen as the meeting place. Because stakes were high, we hired a consultant to teach our negotiating team the subtleties of dealing with Japanese businessmen. Because stakes were high, the Japanese hired a consultant to teach them the subtleties of dealing with American businessmen. At the appointed hour and the appointed place, the two sides met for the first time. And what happened? We bowed as we had been taught, and they thrust out their hands for a hearty shake. Had the Monty Python troupe caught the whole scene on film, it would have had grist for a feature-length movie. Finally, we sat down, rearranged our truncated perspectives, and with that all our differences disappeared because, finally, we had all come for the same purpose: to do a deal.

Just as books and books have been written about the new global economy, so books and books have been written about the subtle discriminators of national corporate cultures. And just as the global economy books so often miss the point, so do these: In the drive toward sameness, cultural discriminators are disappearing. It is in the interest of politicians to foster the impression of international business conflict, because conflict is drama, and politicians get to star in the playlets that ensue. But connectivity breaks down conflict. It turns bipolar

relationships into multipolar ones, because in the new ecosystic economy, nothing is as uncomplicated as me versus you.

At the same time, connectivity simplifies, because it sweeps away
artificial barriers—of nationality, gender, race. The plain truth of
international business is that a corporate CEO in Hong Kong wants
precisely the same thing as a corporate CEO in New Delhi, Milan,
Buenos Aires, Nairobi, or Chicago—to close the deal, pocket the
profit, and get his photo on the cover of *Forbes*, *Fortune*, or the *New
York Times Magazine*.

Intriguingly, workers and consumers want the same things, too. A
book-length collection of photographs titled *Material World* caught
this perfectly. It was a "stuff" book—the photographer, Peter Menzel,
had middle-class people from around the world lay out the prize possessions from their homes. If borders mattered, if nationality or race
discriminated in any meaningful way any longer, the objects would
have been different. In fact, the "stuff" was all the same, and adjusting for what a "middle-class" income means in different economies,
the houses were all the same, too.

Whether you measure it architecturally or by possessions, there is
now one and only one economic definition of middle-class life. It's
universal and it's as absolutely true in China and the Soviet Union as
it is in South Africa and Dallas and Westchester County, New York.

One of the reasons fraternities of strangers are so possible today is that
the drive toward sameness is equally a drive to familiarity. Half the
people don't come out of teepees and the other half out of mud huts.
There's a shared body of experience, a shared body of wants and
expectations, both up and down the economic food chain and laterally across it. New York City tenements are filled with the same base
core of consumer goods that Scarsdale mansions are. Indeed, one
study found that poor kids in Brooklyn's Bedford-Stuyvesant projects
had disposable incomes identical to those of kids living outside the
city in prosperous Westchester County: about $125 a month.

That may be an indictment on several fronts—of values, of the
welfare system—but most important, it's a basis that allows those two
sets of kids to know one another in ways that were hitherto impossible, because consumption is, at heart, a form of dialogue. What we

choose from the universe of available products and how much of it we choose speaks volumes about us and volumes to those around us. What we choose to give others speaks even more. (The corollary of that for companies, by the way, is that if you want to tell someone how much you care for them, how much you value their service, don't necessarily give them something new or expensive. Give them something they care about.)

Intuitively, people also know that barriers are disappearing in their own lives.

Canyon Ranch, the famed operator of upper-end health spas in Arizona and New England, had its own truncated perspective. It had been launched nearly two decades ago by Mel and Enid Zuckerman as a place meant to take you away from your everyday domain and all its psychic distractions. No drinking was allowed; more important, interaction with your office was strictly forbidden. Whether you came to the spas to shed pounds or addictions or just to reconnoiter with your spouse or yourself, you left home at the ranch gates. Over the years, the ranches had evolved into settings for corporate meetings as well, and as tax laws evolved, the meetings more and more had to produce a viable work product in order to be written off. But even then participants were expected to segregate themselves from the other communications of daily life. Canyon Ranch's ambiance was luxury, but its ethos was isolation, and the package had worked. For years, it has been rated among America's top spas.

Finally, though, there was a problem. Occupancy rates had held constant, but the average length of stay at the resorts had dropped from six to three days. Why? Because people no longer want isolation in the quantities Canyon Ranch had been accustomed to serving up. Inner perspective has shifted along with outer perspective. People don't define themselves any longer as working for one segment of their lives and recreating for another segment. Just as the barriers have fallen between peoples, barriers have fallen within people. The cartoon form of the work/leisure integrated person is the harried corporate vice president frantically cell-phoning from his golf cart as he rushes from hole to hole, practicing his own version of George Bush's famous speed-golf, but the cartoon hints at the reality.

Canyon Ranch has begun giving guests more of the tools they need to put business and leisure together—faxes in the rooms, ready e-mail access, a full range of secretarial services—and guests are now beginning to lengthen their stays once again. The challenge is always the same: to get ahead of where the customer has gone, not to stay where the customer has been.

The Drive to Free

A final point to be made about the shift in perspective: It is bone-chilling scary. The voice of Pat Buchanan's 1996 run for the Republican presidential nomination arches over the fears of thinking and acting globally. Think global, act global fears are NAFTA fears, GATT fears. It is the fear of competing for your job with a woman in Ireland, a man in India; the fear of your corporation disappearing overnight, merged out of existence in a boardroom somewhere across an ocean; the fear of losing the deal to two people dining over fettuccine Alfredo on the Piazza Navona in Rome while you are catching the morning red-eye from Seattle to Chicago. But at the other end of fear lies liberation. If nationalism no longer has meaning, if corporate identity can float away in an instant, if you are no longer identified by your race, your gender, your sexual orientation, by where you went to college or what clubs you belong to, you can choose to reinvent your life every single day.

Despite media efforts to paint a rising tide of intolerance, virtually every longitudinal study shows that we are steadily becoming a far more tolerant society. Barriers are falling, not rising. A high school student working on a fifth-generation personal computer in a cold-water flat in Newark or Cabrini-Green or Watts has as much access to information as a Harvard graduate student, and in any event, a Harvard degree is no longer a guarantee of a long and productive career—witness Ted Kaczynski, whether or not he proves to be the Unabomber. In the Age of Access, the opportunities to be whatever you want to be and to make your life better will be greater than they have ever been before in the history of mankind. Connectivity doesn't confine. Connectivity frees.

4 | Communications: One to One, Many to Many, All to All

In his classic work, *The Functions of the Executive,* Chester Barnard, who essentially invented the American Telephone & Telegraph Company, wrote that the most important role of any executive is communication. True enough, but communication where and to whom? Upward, to the CEO, the board, shareholders? Downward, to subordinates? Laterally, to peers? The answer: none of the above. The real problem for an executive is not the direction of communication, but its totality.

Think of every business executive as having a bucket. Inside the bucket are a collection of balls. Each ball is an hour of the workweek, and on each ball is the name of someone with whom he or she has an important business connection. The bucket is time and its capacity is finite. Perhaps it is sixty-five, maybe seventy-five, hours a week, whatever figure the executive has negotiated with his or her spouse as the maximum amount of time that will be spent on business each week—the amount of time, that is, beyond which there will be a major fight on the homefront.

It is the allotment of the names on the balls, the distribution of communication time within the time bucket of the week, that is any executive's most difficult role. Why? Because the bucket is always 100 percent full and an executive's communication time is always the most important political commodity of everyone below him or her—the more of it any one subordinate gets, the more powerful he is among his peers. And thus it is managing the competition for those balls that is an executive's most important function.

So far, so good. Bosses were coping with the time bucket long before Chester Barnard wrote his book. But now suppose that you want to change. And furthermore, suppose that an imperative of change is upon you. Suppose that you have to change how you are doing things to survive, and you have to change in ever more foreshortened cycles. Let's say you'll need to bring a new engineer into your life, a new project planner, someone to handle communications, and you need to do so in a hurry. In all, these three people will need eight hours of your communication each week, and none has been previously represented in your time bucket. Remember, the time bucket is of finite dimensions. To fit in the eight hours for the three new people, you will have to throw eight balls out. Your communication time upward—to your boss, to the CEO—cannot be altered, because changing it would entail grave political risks for yourself. That leaves lateral and downward communication. Your secretary had been getting four hours because she is terrific at defending your gates. Too bad, she'll have to make do with three.

You now have twelve hours a week set aside for clients, ten hours equally divided for your two key underlings. To get the extra seven hours you still need, you'll trim the clients back to ten hours a week, and cut out one of the key underlings entirely. Suddenly, you have displaced enough time balls to change, but in the process you have destabilized existing political relationships and will have a fight there, too. Therein lies the communication barrier to change: It entails more potential negatives than obvious positives. It trades the known world for the unknown one. It disrupts long-standing personal, interpersonal, and corporate communication schedules at the expense of political, social, and economic opportunities of unknown currency. And thus it is that change so often gets defeated in large organizations before it can ever really begin.

· · ·

Finally, let's suppose one more thing. Let's suppose that not only the totality of your communication schedule is under assault, but that the communications you receive are themselves massively accumulating. Where once corporate protocols and physical space protected you against unsought communication, e-mail has in theory freed anyone—literally, anyone—to reach out and touch you. Where once the phone in the outer office stood as a kind of drawbridge to protect you, it now stands as a permanent invitation to fax you. Pagers allow you to find previously incommunicado subordinates; cell phones allow them to find you. And the technology to do so makes the act of doing so almost irresistible. And all the while data services is cranking out more and more information on whatever decision is at hand and feeding it to you at the speed of light. Too bad that you incurred your secretary's ill will by cutting back her weekly communication time to three hours, because you are about to drown.

Welcome to the funhouse.

Human Synapses

Of all the rivers of change cresting as we race toward the millennium's end, none is more obvious, more disorienting to many, and more frequently misinterpreted than the shift in communications. Because computers are everywhere and are driving—though not controlling—the communications revolution, the evidence of the revolution is everywhere. As we noted earlier, the World Wide Web came into existence only in 1991; by the year 2000, some 33 million Americans—and 52 million people worldwide—are expected to be using it. Arguably, the communications revolution is even beginning to have a genetic effect. One study found that, given a choice of common household objects to grab hold of, babies were most inclined to grasp a remote-control box. Perhaps it's the first effort at adaptation to a totally wired world.

Just as in biology, where all growth is by definition exponential because cell division is exponential, so in connectivity, the heart of communications, growth is exponential. Communication expands faster than it can be cataloged. The richest man in America, one of the richest in the world barring sheiks and royalty, didn't make his fortune in steel or raw materials. Microsoft's Bill Gates made his fortune creating software, the tool of connectivity. For the first time in the long life of the planet, there are widely disseminated workers who are virtual human synapses: the worldwide delivery staff of Federal Express are such efficiently computerized links between shipper and addressee that you can instantly track the status of your package at FedEx's Internet site.

SHL System House is a near-perfect metaphor for the exponential growth of communications in the Age of Chaos. SHL produces 911 numbers. Call in an emergency, and an SHL system will receive the call, log it, record it, and forward it. For years, it was a straightforward business, but the growth of cell phones increased by a factor of at least ten the number of people who now witness accidents or crimes and can call them in immediately. SHL numbers, meanwhile, have built in redundancies, because there can be no margin of error in the reception of an accident or crime report and its forwarding. Multiple points of entry have to be provided for the receiving of a call, because emergency calls can't wait. Multiple systems have to be in place for logging, recording, and forwarding them, because response has to be as close to instantaneous as possible. What begins then as a tenfold growth in the raw number of 911 calls gets itself multiplied by another factor of ten in the necessary redundancies and backups, and becomes a hundredfold growth in the system that receives and processes the calls. And thus change compounds change.

The shift in communication and the connectivity that drives it also change the dynamic by which messages are made, received, and evaluated—in both interpersonal and commercial communications. We begin with the latter.

Commercial Communications: Get to Know Me

For centuries upon centuries, the model for commercial communications held constant: An advertisement was from one to many. A seller had a product, and he or she alerted either a broad sector of the populace to its existence (beer ads during Super Bowl time-outs), a more narrowly focused populace (Coppertone billboards on highways leading to shore resorts), or a finely honed slice (Rolls-Royce ads in *Town & Country*). Direct marketing changed that. Along with one to many came the model of one-to-one. Potential consumers were identified and approached by mail (because you belong to the Sierra Club, you are sent the catalog for Robert Redford's nature-oriented Sundance products) or by phone (the Dole campaign calls because you contributed to the 1992 Bush campaign).

Whichever way the commercial appeal was made—universally by broadcast or narrowly by direct marketing—the communication was of necessity close-ended. Word went out; it was either received or not received; it either influenced a sale or didn't. Connectivity is in the process of changing that dramatically. Advertise your used Toyota for sale in the classified section of the *Atlanta Constitution*, and your ad copy will read something like: "Toyota—'94 Corolla DX SW. auto. ac. cass. blue. 29K mi. Must sell. $10,500/obo," plus your phone number. Advertise it in *HotWired*, the on-line subsidiary of San Francisco–based *Wired* magazine, and your copy will say in essence the same thing, but the transaction will be open-ended. Anyone who wants to can come along and append your ad, to the help or detriment of the sale you hope will take place. Perhaps they had a wonderful experience with a similar '94 Corolla. Perhaps the automatic transmission failed at 35,000 miles, or the tape cassette kept jamming, or they have a friend who has a friend who thinks he once heard on NPR's *Car Talk* that the 1994 Toyota Corolla station wagon isn't half the car the 1976 Corolla wagon was. Maybe they just bought a '94 wagon with 29,000 miles on it for $9,300, or $11,400. In effect, each *HotWired* ad opens a chat room on the relative merits and demerits of whatever is being offered for sale.

The car ad in *HotWired* is simultaneously a communication one-to-one (seller and buyer), one-to-many (seller and the whole universe of potential auto buyers who click on to *HotWired*'s classifieds), many-to-many (the Greek chorus of kibitzers—pro- and anti-94 Corollas), and many-to-one (you ought to hold on to this little beauty; you've overpriced it; buy a Camry next time, it holds its value better). However much of a mess advertising now is on the Internet—and don't get us wrong, it remains a mess—the *HotWired* ad is the model of the future for one very simple reason: As the demands of consumers for maximized information merge with the technical capacity to supply them with maximized information, the possibility to advertise interactively impels the necessity to do so. Connectivity, too, has its imperatives.

Procter & Gamble, one of the biggest and savviest of consumer-goods manufacturers, recently cut its budget for traditional one-to-many advertising. If Procter & Gamble executives are as wise as their steadily ascending stock value says they are, they will redirect that money to advertising research and development—to developing new models of promotion based on the recognition that the commercial communications of the future must be simultaneously one-to-one, one-to-many, many-to-many, and many-to-one.

By itself, one-to-many advertising—a $2 million promotion for the movie *Babe*, say—can cause only arousal. Public communication—Siskel and Ebert give it two thumbs-up—validates the arousal, which is why finding the Siskel and Eberts in any commune or interest group is increasingly critical. But "sisbertizing" is only the second part of the new equation of commercial communication, because finally it is word of mouth that will put a product or idea over the top. "That's right, a movie with talking animals, and it's *great!*" If you are like us, you probably saw *Babe* precisely because someone you know well whose taste you have reason to trust told you to. In effect, you walked into a literal one-to-one chat room where the movie's validation was made real and personal.

Until consumers are involved directly in the communication transaction, one-to-many advertisers are shouting, very expensively, into the wind.

Interpersonal Communications: Masked Meanings

"How are you doing?"

"Oh, great."

It seems a simple enough exchange, but as Don Jackson, Janet Beavin, and Paul Watzlawick showed in their pioneering 1967 study *The Pragmatics of Human Communication*, interpersonal exchanges are never so simple as they look. Traditionally, all communication has taken place on three levels. There's first the denotative component—the dictionary interpretation of the words that have been exchanged.

At that level, "Oh, great" means precisely what it purports to mean: Stocks are up; the crop is in; I'm in the pink of health; my boss, my wife, my children or workplace underlings are happy with me and prospering. But stretch the "Oh" out another half-beat, give the "great" an ironic twist and some oomph at the end, and you arrive at the interpretive component of communication:

"How are you doing?"

"Ooohhh, *great!*"

What the response means now is up to you, the questioner, to decide from whatever clues have been given you—in intonation, in facial expression or body language—and whatever prior knowledge you bring to the communication. Does "Oh, great" mean "Oh, great"? Or does it mean "god-awful"? Or does it mean "Oh, great, you're asking me how I'm doing for the fifth time today. Can't we get beyond this?"

As Jackson and his colleagues showed, though, the denotative and interpretive levels of communication only frame the issue of understanding because there's a third, critical element to consider: the relational component between the speakers. "How are you doing?" has different values—and demands different responses—depending on the relation between the speaker and the spoken to and the balance that's being maintained in that relationship.

A doctor who asks "How are you doing?" on the golf course is spraying WD-40 on the social setting; he's greasing the moment. "Oh, great" is nothing more than a polite response between country club equals—unless, that is, the doctor is courting you as an investor in a chain of dialysis labs, or unless you are wooing the doctor for a slot on his very busy surgery schedule. A doctor who asks "How are you doing?" from behind his desk, wearing a lab coat, presumably wants an analytical response: "The palpitations seem to come less regularly." "The pain has gone to my right ankle." "I'm throwing up every morning." Or "Oh, great."

You the patient, in turn, answer differently depending on the relational balance that you are seeking to maintain. "Oh, great" might mean just that. Or it might mean "I'm good enough that there's no need to give me any tests that might uncover the fact that I'm terminally ill." And, as every parent knows too well, an "Oh, great" from a seven-year-old in response to "How are you doing?" has an entirely different meaning than an "Oh, great" response from a fifteen-year-old or a thirty-year-old: The assumption behind the first is "How nice of you to ask"; behind the second it's "Won't they ever stop prying?"; and behind the third it's likely to be "How much do I really want to share?"

Historically in the workplace, the relational element of interpersonal communications has been easy to decipher. Supervisors could be more brusque in their questions and responses, and subordinates were expected to be more polite in theirs, because it was assumed that the time spent communicating had more value for the boss than the worker. What's more, corporations were architectural and physical hierarchies as well as job-status ones. The chief financial officer might come down a floor or two to check on the accounting supervisor, but he rarely if ever rubbed elbows in the mail room. And these were hierarchies with durable casts. Personnel changes crept slowly across the landscape. Corporations weren't quite feudal—occasionally a serf found himself or herself elevated to the executive gym—but they were feudal enough that everyone knew his or her place. And the corporate ladder was so secure that every rung was readily identifiable to every player on it.

That this is no longer the case in the most successful corporations, and particularly the most successful American corporations, is by now so evident as to require little discussion. The true genius of Bill Gates's Microsoft Corporation hasn't been the software it has produced. That's been the economic engine. The genius has been to democratize communications: to give all employees a shot *and* to require them to bear the consequences of their ideas. Similarly, the genius of General Electric has been to move toward abandoning control of the parts in an effort to retain control of the whole—to recognize that in a chaos world you can control only by not being controlling.

That an essentially feudal structure no longer applies in interpersonal relationships should be just as obvious, too. What has been less noticed, and to our knowledge never properly limned, is the effect of this death of feudalism on communications.

• • •

A decipherable relational balance in communications requires, by definition, decipherable relations. When loyalty dies, when virtually every employee is working from deal to deal, from contract to contract—or from marriage to marriage—relationships become so fragmented and short-lived that deciphering communications can become the work of ages. Within the workplace, a decipherable relational balance also requires an identifiable chain of control—who's on top, who's not—but as the rate of change accelerates to the point where planning is impractical beyond, say, six months, power shifts toward the person in possession of the greatest variable: the serf who maintains the always iffy drawbridge chain, not the king swaddled in ermine.

Even where rank does exist, where it is decipherable, the democratized interactions of cyberspace have all but destroyed its usefulness for interpreting communications relationally. Electronic mail, voice mail, the fax, and their kith and kin allow people to break the norms of upward and downward communications, even lateral communication within organizations. On the Internet, we might be interacting with anyone from a pedophile to the president of the United States. There's no way of knowing, and because there is no way of knowing, the status barriers of normal discourse disappear as do interpretive signals. Voice mail leaves us no visible shrugs to help understand what is being said. Faxes and e-mail are death on irony.

Meanwhile, because all messages still flow to the hierarchical top of an organization, the person in titular control becomes an e-mail victim, and the quality of the information rising to the top diminishes toward zero.

Meanwhile, too, a new level has been added to interpersonal communications, a level that Jackson, Beavin, and Watzlawick never could have imagined: the fundamental issue of trust, what we call dimensionality. The question no longer is simply what is being said to me and what I will say back, but what is being said to me, to what extent am I prepared to believe it, and what kind of proof will I be required to produce to validate my response.

I'm from the Millennium: Show Me

When no industry sector in America save for telecommunications is trusted by more than half of the populace, when only 8 percent of

Americans say they trust advertising messages, when only 12 percent trust public-interest messages from large corporations, when only a quarter of Americans say they generally believe what they read in newspapers and even fewer say they generally believe what they hear on television news and talk shows, it should come as no surprise that a presumption of trust has disappeared from corporate, commercial, and interpersonal communications as well.

In the medical profession, distrust has been institutionalized by health-maintenance organizations. A doctor's expressed opinion about your illness may be accurate, or it may reflect pressures from an HMO to hold down group costs, and in any event a second and some-times third and fourth opinion will be required before procedures can be signed off on and payment approved.

In the teaching profession—another one-time bastion of unchallenged authority—distrust has been imposed by litigation and watered by the victim ethic. Johnny may have failed arithmetic because Johnny can't add, but he also may have failed it because the teacher is prejudiced against him—he is black or white, he is too short or too tall—or because he suffers from any one of dozens of maladies that the school system is too insensitive or hidebound to detect: dyslexia, attention-deficit disorder, aural-motor shortfalls, a tendency to speak out inappropriately or to speak not at all. (One teacher we know was recently berated by a parent for failing to understand that her son's disruptive classroom behavior was caused by "chronic heat aversion.") And in any event, our lawyers will be contacting yours if the grade isn't adjusted, if special training isn't provided, if Johnny isn't recognized for the victim he is, never mind precisely of what.

Within the family, too, distrust has been institutionalized by the simple realities of what "family" means today—a divorce rate now seemingly constant at greater than 50 percent, three in four children coming under new management during their childhood. Husbands and wives distrust one another, distrust the tenure of their relation-ship, distrust the veracity of what's told them over the dinner table or in the intimacy of the bedroom, all with statistical cause, because sta-tistics say that one of them has the name of a divorce lawyer scrawled somewhere in a wallet. Nearly every exchange between parents and children carries with it an element of risk or deceit, too, again with statistical cause. More and more, families are as deal-based as the new corporate world.

It is not just family relationships that this is true of. As the rate of change accelerates, relationships broadly tend to resemble starbursts. We meet someone on the Internet; we share a morning together in the United first-class cabin from Denver to Boston, or two hours over lunch between business meetings. We do the ritual courting exercises, the mutuality of disclosure: I tell you my name and you tell me yours, I tell you what my father did and you tell me what yours did. We can choose to terminate the relationship at any moment simply by refusing to answer, but if we choose to go on, we ingratiate ourselves through a reciprocity of intimacy—my fifteen-year-old daughter seems depressed, your twenty-year-old son has no direction in his life. We read the signs of human communication: denotatively from what's literally said; interpretively from anger to happiness. And along the way, we inferentially absorb and give away enormous amounts of information about ourselves: what's likely to be in our houses, our political persuasion, our racial tolerance, even what's likely to happen in our beds.

In effect, we are exchanging our "anthrolineages"—the résumé of cultural experiences that allows us to establish an immediate identity with a short-term other in a time-crunched world. If the exchange is successful enough, we will establish a situational intimacy that lets us move from strangers to friends. Situational love may develop, a spasm of affection driven by the intensity of our starburst relationship. If it does develop, we will leave the plane or the business meeting or sign off the Internet swamped by a kind of nanostalgia for the moment just passed, and the moment itself will become instant history for us. (It is this new hunger for nanostalgic moments that Krug champagne and other alcoholic products sell in their advertising—the promise that evenings spent imbibing them will become instant history for us.) But unless we can establish the dimensionality of our communication— unless we have time to, in effect, present our bona fides to each other and have them validated—we will never establish true friendship, true intimacy.

If our relationship has been solely a business one, we will never establish the one thing that truly matters in business: not friendship and intimacy—you don't want your accountant any closer to you than your money—but simply whether we can be trusted to do what we say we are going to do. And by the very nature of these relation-ships—starbursts of rising intimacy crunched into ever narrower slices of time—that dimensionality becomes harder and harder to achieve. By demanding more, the beast of communication is satisfied less.

How, then, is trust established in a particalized world? How is com-munication ultimately fulfilled? Here the paths of corporate commu-nication and interpersonal communication diverge. The issue in both cases is the same as it is in so many other matters as society rushes into the 500-year delta: authenticity. The divergence comes in how to achieve it.

The Two Faces of Honesty

In the purely corporate sense, the only way to add dimensionality to a message today is absolute rigor and honesty. At the denotative level, the message has to communicate a very clear and direct call to action. There's too much static in the world, too much ambient noise for it to be anything else. At the interpretive level, the message has to communicate how the company feels about the public the message is meant for. This doesn't necessarily mean that every message should let consumers know the company is consumer-driven. A utility com-pany, for example, can't be driven by the needs of individual con-sumers, because if it is, it might make a decision to keep one toaster working, one air conditioner running at the cost of the entire power grid. It simply means that the company has to create a context for the message it is delivering.

Relationally, the message has to do one very basic thing. It has to show respect. What does that mean? Two things. One, it can't embar-rass customers by, say, reducing prices on a product they have bought only a month earlier to such a level that it insults their intelligence. Price wars in the cellular phone industry have done just that time and again. Even more important in an age driving toward individualized realities, messages meant for individual members of the public have to convey that they understand who that individual is. They have to be segmented by communes, and they have to be in a format and language that speaks specifically to that commune.

Do all that and, in fact, wonderful things begin to happen. To the extent that your product is a trusted brand—to the extent that you have stood behind your deals and admitted your mistakes and not embarrassed your customers—the chances that your commercial messages, your calls to action, will be listened to rises, and the chance that your evidence will be challenged goes down. For more evidence, see Coca-Cola. Its brand equity is such that Pepsi will always be playing catch-up, and very expensively. For more evidence of that, catch the Super Bowl, where Pepsi in 1996 spent an estimated $8 million to debunk what for most global cola drinkers is simply the undebunkable.

But corporate trust goes beyond advertising and the reliability of advertising messages. To the extent that a corporation is seen as a good community player, to the extent that it is seen as an honorable employer, an innovator in the creation of goods and services, to the extent that it is believed by consumers to add value to its products through its manufacturing and distribution processes, to the extent that its leadership team is seen as outstanding—to all these extents the company itself also gains equity. It becomes more intrinsically valuable. Why? Because people are not only more willing to buy the products, they are more willing to buy the stock. They are more willing to deal with the company. They are more willing to tell the best young people they know to go work there. If all those things happen, the actual cost of capital diminishes, because a company is better able to negotiate interest rates. Just as central, the public at all levels is more ready to believe whatever messages the company broadcasts about its own political problems.

Who has dimensionality among America's leading corporations? Merck & Co., for one. It was able to communicate why it thought the Clinton health-care plan was wrong in its assumptions about the pharmaceutical industry and get immediate legislative relief precisely because it had established its trust over many years.

Who doesn't have dimensionality? Phillip Morris, which can write till hell freezes over about the perfidies of legislation affecting tobacco and never be believed, not because of the perceived inherent evils of tobacco, but simply because Phillip Morris has not earned trust. It has no reputation for sustained honor, and its management team is lightly regarded. Out of all that emerges a very real diminution in equity, in the value of the name "Phillip Morris," that has serious consequences for the bottom line of the company and for the well-being of its shareholders. Dimensionality matters. Trust counts. It drives to the heart of establishing empathy. And empathy counts every bit as much as trust.

In a personal context, dimensionality is established in three ways: through physical illustrations and objects (I show you a chart in *Fortune* to validate my thesis about capital-growth mutual funds); through statistics (you refer to the appendix to Table B); and most intriguingly and centrally, through myth, through storytelling. Strangely again—it is trust that is being established, after all—physical illustrations and statistics are the less effective. We have all seen Ross Perot's flip charts; we have seen statistics manipulated in political ads. Four out of five doctors have assured us that pain will be fought more effectively by products we know from our own experience to be less effective at that very thing. Even *National Geographic* has manipulated its cover image to fit all the pyramids into the frame. Like Mark Twain, we know that there are three kinds of lies: lies, damn lies, and statistics.

Which leaves us with myth, with storytelling. And which leads us to the media. For it is through the media that our shared stories are created and sustained in these times. It is by reference to the media that we most effectively establish dimensionality. And it is our capacity to manipulate the media—or our determination to steer clear of it—that tells the most critical information about us. In effect, the media has become a symbolic language of its own.

Think of how many conversations are, in effect, dances to find the media commune you both fit in: "Sometimes I feel just like that woman in *Friends*, you know, the one with the long hair." "Did you read Jane Smiley's *Moo*?" "God, wasn't Arnold great in *Terminator 2*!" And think of how many efforts at personal communication are terminated precisely because you couldn't find a commune that you both could occupy: In a world in which time is being progressively miniaturized, what is the point of spending any more of it on a person who has no interest in a satire about the Midwest and academic politics?

Myth is validation, and media is more than the message. Media is discourse. In a world in which time has become compressed, a world from which deep association is progressively vanishing, the media is how we talk with one another.

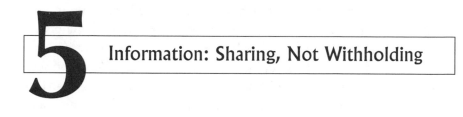

Information: Sharing, Not Withholding

It was Arno Penzias, the 1978 Nobel laureate in physics, who first theorized that computing had met communicating to form connectivity and that, in effect, everything eventually will be connected. Computing, in short, was never about data crunching. Data crunching was the means; connectivity was the end, which is why the data-pigs and cyber-pioneers will never inherit the Earth. Nor was the communications revolution about the machines and services that spawned it. Fax machines, modems, interactive TV, and Internet providers were all the means; connectivity was the end. Computing and communicating did more than intersect; they fused. And when they fused, connectivity was born. But connectivity finally is not the end, either. Connectivity is a state of existence, nothing more. The true end is what happens when things are in connection, what happens when connectivity itself fuses with information.

Man Bites Machine, Machine Bites Man

If reason had not died of its own weight, if linear progression had not proven inadequate to a chaos world, the sheer presence of connectivity would have spelled the end of sequential thought, because connectivity's true effect cannot be thought of in linear terms. The World Wide Web draws its name from the metaphor of the spiderweb that has long been in use in production theory, but the metaphor serves the Web well. A spiderweb is in turn many things at once: circular and linear, curved like space and arranged in flat planes, supple in its parts and powerful in its whole, an organized creation and an unfathomable maze. A straight line can be intersected. A spiderweb can only be met. To touch it anywhere is to come in contact with its whole creation. Lines link along a single spectrum. Webs connect across many spectrums. And connectivity connects across barriers that not long ago were thought unbreachable: the world of the made and the world of the born, for example.

Lost in all the hoopla over the introduction of Windows 95 was a single, highly pertinent fact: Almost 20 percent of the code that underlies the software package was written not by humans, but by Microsoft computers themselves. As an example of intelligent cogenerates, Windows 95 is actually rather tame. Every day, something like $2 trillion in Federal wire payments and U.S. interbank transfers flows electronically through downtown New York City. The computers that manage the daily task of balancing and clearing those accounts constantly rewrite their own codes. There is no time for humans to do it.

At the University of Southern California, something almost entirely different has happened. Researcher Len Adleman has built an operating system dubbed the TT100 computer that uses biomass as its core calculating device. By causing the DNA in the biomass to vary, Adleman has been able to convert the biomass into a binary computer that actually solved a linear equation. The process is slow, but watch for Adleman's name on the Nobel short list in the near future.

It is, in fact, no secret. The world of the made and the world of the born have been merging for some time. By the mid–1970s, Richard Dawkins was theorizing that all evolution is digital and that computers thus will evolve in their own right, and Dawkins's theory is now well in play. A new school of economic thought, bionomics, has arisen to explore the intersection and interplay of biological and economic theory. Vast shelves of science fiction have been written on the humanization of machines. But connectivity works both ways. Humans in a connected world imitate machines, just as machines imitate humans. And what has been less considered are the effects of the fusion of connectivity and information on humans themselves.

At its simplest level, this fusion leads to what labor psychologist Mike Moore calls the "activity trap." Because of technology, through connectivity information today arrives at such a rate and volume that you can be paralyzed if you don't manage it effectively. Simultaneously, each piece of information that does arrive is debased in value. A single electronic mail message demands attention. One of 200 e-mail messages—roughly the average volume of a senior-level executive in a technologically astute environment—has 1/200th the value of a sole daily message. Indeed, most such executives have a secretary who spends up to half of his or her time simply managing the e-mail flow.

No one but yourself can manage your exposure to commercial messages, but a similar debasing takes place as volume grows. A sole advertisement encountered on any given day also demands attention; it has context, contrast. One of 245 ads—the average potential exposure for an American adult to commercial messages on radio and TV and through the print media, according to the Advertising Research Foundation—has 1/245th the value of a single daily advertisement. All that has important implications for both corporate and commercial communications—they better be to the point, and they have to be smart—but it has even more important implications for the information revolution generally.

One of the reasons, perhaps the chief reason, the explosion in information has bred such widespread discontent is that too much information is chasing too few decisions—and too little interest. The tools of connectivity create capital on the Internet, sometimes spectacularly so. Shares in Yahoo! Inc., which provides an Internet search engine, more than tripled in value partway through their first day of trading, even though Yahoo! had never shown a penny of profit. But while the tools of connectivity grow astronomically in value, the information of connectivity floats profitless through cyberspace, random data randomly searching for users.

When another Nobel laureate, and the greatest of them all, Albert Einstein, was asked what was the most powerful force in the world, he replied without a moment's hesitation, "Compound interest." So it is, too, with compound information in the epoch of connectivity. Information feeds upon itself and expands to fill the space available to it, which in turn expands exponentially. To let yourself be drawn into the maelstrom of information is, in effect, to sacrifice control over time and ultimately energy. As man and machine meet, as connectivity and information fuse ever more tightly together, managing connectivity becomes a central job skill, and the greater the interface between man and machine, the greater the need.

Information is only germane in the presence of a decision to be made. To know that 200,000 people are likely to wear gabardine shirts on any given day or that 2 million people prefer their frozen broccoli topped with cheddar cheese is less than useless. It adds to the discordant noise of everyday life. Worse, because the data is universally available, it increases the information content of any decision without discriminating the decision. More and more data goes in. The same answers keep coming out. Unless, that is, you happen to be a retailer of gabardine shirts or a manufacturer of frozen broccoli products, and unless you happen to know exactly which 200,000 people are inclined to gabardine shirts and which 2 million diners like a dollop of cheddar on their broccoli. Then the information begins to gain real value for both the manufacturer and retailer, who can plan their production, distribution, and marketing schedules more effectively, and for individual consumers, who can be more certain that their passion for gabardine shirts or broccoli-and-cheddar will be more easily satisfied.

As this sea of ambient data groups itself into specific information transactions and as the transactions themselves become specifically refined, information gains direction. And as that happens, the information economy is born.

The Information Economy

Chicago-based Peapod was the first service to allow customers to buy groceries off their computer. Connect to Peapod via modem, and it will show you everything that's available at the supermarket that day and allow you to organize those goods in whatever ways you choose—by sale items, by nutritional value, by unit price, by whatever.

Click on ground beef, and Peapod will display the quantities ground beef can be purchased in and the lean-rating of each quantity. It will also give you the option of scrolling through ground beef–based menus from, say, Kraft. Find one you like, and you can order all the ingredients with a single click and have the recipe printed out. Sign on to Peapod multiple times, and it will begin to assemble a profile of your personal eating and food-shopping habits—whether you buy skim or whole milk; whether you prefer Folger's or Maxwell House; prosciutto or baloney. You then can use that profile both to increase your knowledge of your own nutritional habits and to enhance your options and shrink their universe.

Maybe you have a half-finished jar of forty-ounce Jif extra-crunchy peanut butter in the cupboard, but at the sale price being offered today, you'd like to purchase more anyway. Or maybe you normally buy peanut butter on a six-week cycle, and the sixth week is up. In effect, Peapod provides just-in-time inventory for the home (new peanut butter arrives just as you need it), for the store (it now can begin to predict more accurately its need for Jif extra-crunchy stock), and for the manufacturer, which can use the transaction to learn more about the consumption rates and patterns of its customers. Place your full order, and Peapod promises to deliver it within two hours, during any thirty-minute window of your choosing. Before starting the service, its owners worked at Domino's to study fulfillment techniques for pizza orders.

We mentioned in the previous chapter the classified automobile ads on the *HotWired* Internet site, but a Japanese car wholesaler has gone *HotWired* one better. It has created, in effect, its own Internet by putting up a satellite and giving potential buyers a server that allows them to use their computer monitors to view cars as they are going up for auction. Absent a car lot, absent any physical facility except a studio for displaying cars in, the company is selling a car every eight seconds it is in operation. Connectivity feeds information to a specific community of interest; the information creates transaction, in dazzling numbers.

Soon the automobiles themselves will be telling us when it's time to unload them. A 1996 Lincoln Continental already has built into it the equivalent computing power of a 1985 DEC mainframe. In fact, the value of its computing power exceeds the value of the sheet metal used in its construction by about 20 percent. Within ten years, in-car computers will be providing the same sort of survey of driving habits that Peapod is now providing of eating habits. Silicon chips will measure whether you ride the clutch, slam on the brakes, take curves easy or hard, find the bumps or avoid them. Based on those driving habits and its own knowledge of the car you are driving, a software program will be able to predict with near razor-sharp clarity the exact day you should sell your car for optimum worth based on how you drive.

Like Peapod's just-in-time inventory of the kitchen cupboard, this will be a just-in-time inventory of automobiles—for consumer, dealer, and manufacturer. If Ford or General Motors or Chrysler has the sense to get into the business—has the sense to turn itself from solely a manufacturing business to a service business that happens to manufacture a product—it will send you a letter thirty days in advance of the calculated day, offering you X amount of dollars for your car if you trade it in within the month. To do so would be to build a base of customer loyalty that would last for decades; it would be precisely the sort of value-added proposition that separates one manufacturer from another in a supersaturated marketplace.

If the auto manufacturers do not have the sense to alert you to your car's optimal sell date, it is almost a certainty that a company such as MCI would, because MCI is already in the connectivity business and what Peapod and the self-evaluating cars of the future are about is, finally, not computing, not technology. They are about the use of connectivity to create information transactions.

Connectivity, simply put, turns information to transaction, and the greater the connectivity, the greater the potential for transaction. Peapod isn't just about crunching time, even though the service claims to cut your food-shopping hours by approximately 80 percent. Peapod is an information transaction. It integrates manufacturer, supplier, and customer into a single unit.

Individual Inc., out of Burlington, Massachusetts, operates an online news service called NewsPage. Subscribers—and 50,000 people signed up for the service during its first two months, at rates of up to $6.95 a month—select their specific interests from a menu of more than eight hundred business topics. NewsPage then uses its software to scan some six hundred publications, from daily newsletters to weekly magazines, and provide, on demand, a news digest customized for each subscriber. That also is an information transaction. In return for this time-saving, highly individualized view of the reality of the total business world, subscribers give advertisers a highly individualized target audience.

The just-in-time auto computers of the future will be an information transaction as well. You surrender information about your driving habits; whoever is gathering information at the other end gets to know you better. In return, you can sell the car before its worth begins to plummet; in return, the information gatherer can build customer loyalty or pinpoint you for a targeted sales campaign on high-absorption shocks. Nobody loses. Everybody wins. Nobody loses, everybody wins in the transaction inherent in the *HotWired* classifieds. You surrender knowledge about the peculiarities of 1994 Toyota Corolla wagons, and you are paid in knowledge about 1992 Saabs when you go shopping for one of those. Suddenly, America has 264 million consumer critics—bad news, by the way, for the franchise now held by *Consumer Reports*—and everybody gets paid in kind for their expertise.

Or paid in real capital. AT&T has been developing drug-store kiosks that will allow AT&T card holders to swipe their cards through a machine and then choose from a variety of discount coupons. Why? Because the coupons any particular cardholder chooses will begin to form a profile of buying habits. AT&T understands that the sample statistics traditional advertising has been based on no longer apply, and it is willing to pay in discounts for the information each customer surrenders when he or she selects a coupon. That is the model for the future.

You, Inc.

As the world of the made and the world of the born flow together—as the two become more complex and complexify each other—every human life assumes some of the properties of the computer. Every human life becomes, in effect, a data bank. And as that happens, everything about you—your habits, your preferences, your buying whims, your opinions—assumes a transactional worth. They become more than the sum total of your wants and needs; they become your intellectual property, to be valuated and protected as strongly as any other property you possess. More strongly, we contend, because in an economy driven by information and dependent upon appealing to ever more particalized marketplaces, it is individual information that has the greatest worth. Connectivity burdens. It deluges. It dumps the universe of available data at your electronic door. It sends more and more messages to less and less interest because the very massiveness itself devalues the content. (For more on the latter, visit Japan, where seemingly trillions of consumer messages are chasing a very low level of consumer interest.) But connectivity also empowers.

Some years ago, researchers at General Electric identified what they called the "Hawthorne Effect." Simply put, the Hawthorne Effect holds that when people know they are being studied, they behave differently. A polling firm calls to ask if you would vote for Colin Powell were he to run for president, and because you want the pollster to like you, because you want to be thought of as someone who is prepared to vote for an African-American for president of the United States, and because you want to think of yourself that way, you answer yes. Perhaps you would have in any event, but the Hawthorne Effect impels a positive response. (Although it was rarely cited by name as such, the Hawthorne Effect was the major reason why the phenomenal polling data on General Powell that emerged in the summer and fall of 1995 were always considered so suspect by political professionals, and by Powell himself.)

We live today in a state of perpetual Hawthorne Effect, not because we want to but because the data-pigs and the information mongers won't let us live any other way. The capacity to study us through connectivity impels the necessity to do so. Three effects, we contend, will flow from this condition:

- As privacy becomes rarer and rarer, it will assume greater and greater worth, and privacy management will become one of the great growth industries of the twenty-first century. The freedoms to know, to go, to do, and to be imply as well the obligation to respect our freedoms, to respect our privacy. The Clinton administration's ham-handed handling of FBI files struck such a powerful chord precisely because privacy is at the bedrock of the new value system of the Age of Access.

- As consumers become more and more aware of the degree to which they are being studied and the worth of the information they surrender, they will become more and more apt simply to lie in response. Wanting to be liked is important, but in the Chaos Age, authenticity is more important, and authenticity is a two-way street. If pollsters don't provide honesty on the front end, they'll get dishonesty on the backside. Besides, lying on questionnaires can be fun, even rewarding. We have a friend who received a questionnaire from Dun & Bradstreet asking how much money he made and what his total worth was. A cool $110 million in the bank, our friend answered, without a blink, and $9 million annually. The answer bore no more relation to the truth than chicken croquettes bear to duck l'orange, but Dun & Bradstreet doubled our friend's credit rating.

- Finally, as people become more and more aware of the economic worth of their own privately held information, they will come more and more to realize what a fortune about themselves they have absolutely pissed away. Therein lies the beginning of anger. And revenge.

Subscribe to a new magazine under a slightly different name—Hank Smith instead of Henry Smith, Suzette Jones instead of Susan Jones—and you can see marked clearly as a city street the trail of commercial transactions that flow from the information you surrender about yourself with each choice of a magazine you make: the charity appeals from, say, the United Negro College Fund addressed to Hank or Suzette because you have designated yourself as left-leaning through a subscription to *Rolling Stone*; the telephone solicitations to Hank or Suzette for vacation packages to St. Lucia because you took a two-year renewal on *Travel & Leisure*.

For an extra $5 annually, Citibank will send holders of its Visa cards an annual summary of all credit-card expenditures, broken down by category. At tax time, it's a handy document to have, but as an economic transaction, it's as ludicrous as the free-information sur-render now inherent in magazine-based solicitations. The Visa data—which already has been collected and sorted—costs far less than $5 to print out and mail, and it's worth infinitely more to Citibank than $5. In a world of sane economic balances, Citibank will pay you for that information, for that profile of your financial and purchasing life and thus in a very real way of your actual life, and that sane world is nearly here.

Computer chips in automobiles and electronic shopping systems that create profiles of your eating habits are not the only ways that the data bank of your life is being augmented. Soon credit cards will be wallet-size software capable of holding as much information as is found in the twenty-seven volumes of the Encyclopedia Britannica. And AT&T is not alone in recognizing the new economic worth of your personal data bank. The Saga cable channel is available for $15 a month *if* you take it with advertisements, and for $25 a month if you want it ad-free. In effect, you are being paid $10 a month for your individual attention to advertising messages. In Seattle, pay-phone calls are now free *if* you will listen to a thirty-second ad before dialing. Again, you are being paid for your individual attention.

Time really is money; so is attention. The balance of power in information transactions is shifting to consumers as surely as it's shift-ing in all other marketplace transactions. Subjects—you, us, each person individually—will be paid to be subjects of studies, paid to sur-render information to pollsters and surveyors for exactly the same rea-son that the information revolution can seem so dissatisfying. Because we really are drowning in the stuff. Because too much infor-mation really is chasing too few decisions. Because information truly is germane only in the presence of a specific decision to be made.

The supply side of the information-transaction equation has been worn out. Marketers in a particalized marketplace have, in fact, no other choice than to get to know you. Each consumer really is a little world all cunningly made, and every factoid of information about that cunning world will have a specific economic worth. You will be paid to surrender information about yourself for one very simple reason: because you should be paid to do so. Consumers now own the dynamic of the marketplace.

Look for a moment at the graphic below. This is the theory of market surplus developed by David Court of the McKinsey consulting group. At each step of the process of moving a manufactured good through the marketplace, the entity that controls the step tries to create a value-added proposition—that is, it tries to create a surplus of return over investment. A boom box manufacturer, for example, tries to wholesale his boom box for more than the raw materials, capital investment, and production and distribution costs. A retailer tries to retail it for more than his wholesale, display, and advertising costs. And a consumer tries to buy it for less than the intrinsic value the product has accumulated along the way. The sum of all these added values, Court theorizes, constitutes the product's market surplus, and whichever entity controls the lion's share of the market surplus controls the market itself.

Market Surplus

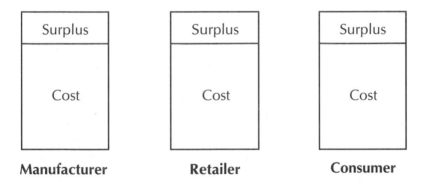

Who controls the market surplus in the information economy? The same entity that controls the surplus in the automobile market by exercising its individuality. The one that can demand the most of the other two entities while giving the least away, the one that manufacturers and retailers are desperate to know about: the consumer. You. The information economy empowers each of us by virtue of the information we hold and choose to share.

The Beehive Effect and The Law of Increasing Returns

We wrote at the beginning of this chapter about the decreasing returns of information in an age overrun with it, but a law of increasing returns equally applies. A single bee has a life span of six to eight weeks. A beehive, because it is the repository of all the transactions of information individual bees make, has a memory of four to six years. The sum of the information is greater than the individual parts. Information expands as communications expand, as the sum of information transactions mounts.

Communications, in turn, expand in raw numbers and in value as connectivity mounts. The first fax machine had no worth other than its curiosity and its scrap value. Who were you going to fax? Ghostbusters? It was the second fax machine that gave the first one economic worth, and the third fax machine that increased the worth of the first two. Returns increase with connectivity.

Returns increase, too, as information is shared in real time, in the present tense, and they increase in direct proportion to the degree to which the information is shared. To cite one obvious example, the high-gloss annual reports that publicly held companies send out to their stockholders are today virtually worthless—the news is dinosaur news, blips from the Mesozoic Era. Stockbrokers and accountants already have proven that companies that make their data available in real time are better able to attract new money for investment and simultaneously to raise their stock prices. Real-time information sharing creates authenticity. Sharing in the past tense feeds nostalgia.

Connectivity also drives information-transaction costs to zero. Fax a forty-page document from Los Angeles to Washington, and it will cost you about $9 for the phone time. Overnighting the document via Federal Express will cost $16 for delivery by 10 A.M. Sending the document by the U.S. Postal Service—snail mail—runs about $3. Delivering that same document via e-mail on the Internet costs approximately nine cents. Once again, returns increase. Individuals and small businesses are no longer encumbered by diseconomies of scale. They're no longer prohibited by cost from using the same resources. The Age of Access democratizes not just thinking, but business. It's worth saying again: Connectivity frees.

A new math is at work—a math based on access to information, not the withholding of it. And a new calculus of information is taking hold, too—a calculus based on the creation and valuation of the intellectual property that is shared. Technology—computers, modems, the Internet, the Web—will be the tool, connectivity will be the engine, but the information economy is the end.

6   Lifestyles: From Mass to Situational

Life used to be simpler for advertisers and marketers. Variables reflected actual variations. Consumers' "lifestyles" were discriminated by the demonstrable and measurable—whether they lived urban, suburban, or rural; their orientation to health and fitness; whether they thought their work was a job or a career—and the discriminators actually discriminated. Hobbies counted; socioeconomic status counted more. If you knew this data, you could begin to form a reliable profile of aspirations and wants, and if you could do that, you could predict consumption patterns.

Better still, you could predict at what points in their lives people were most susceptible to having their consumption patterns altered. An ingenious bit of research familiarly known as the "Welcome Wagon Study" found that 40 percent of consumers switched the brands of at least two products they commonly bought when they moved. Having to find a new dry cleaner, a new dentist, a new mechanic—all the small dislocations that go with the larger dislocation of changing jobs, homes, and marital status—creates stress. Stress makes those who move more susceptible to change.

128

Couple the move with a stress-provoking reason for moving, and the susceptibility to change is all the greater. A 1967 study by two University of Washington doctors, Thomas Holmes and Richard Rahe, created a do-it-yourself stress test. At the top of the Holmes-Rahe scale was the death of a spouse, valued at 100 points of stress. In second and third places were divorce (with a 73 score) and marital separation (65). Both came in ahead of being detained in jail and the death of a close family member.

Do such variables and discriminators still apply? In several senses, yes. Life changes continue to beget changes in product choices, and the more profound the life change, the more profound the change in choices. But like any other commodity, change depends for its value on scarcity. When change is frequent, it diminishes in significance as a discriminator. As change approaches constant—as the change in the rate of change accelerates, as change itself assumes mass—the value of change as a marketing tool plunges to zero. The old variables hold in another, stronger sense as well. For better or worse, study after study has shown that working women still can be broken into two groups: those who think that what they do is a career and those who think it is a job. Otherwise, the lives of women who work outside the house for money are virtually indistinguishable one from the other. Otherwise, too, the old lifestyle discriminators discriminate almost nothing.

Today, people live rural, work suburban, and have the mind-set of a city dweller. Neutralize skin tone and obliterate the backdrop, and it would be next to impossible to discriminate a group of country boys playing basketball on a dirt court next to the barnyard from a group of inner-city kids playing hoops on a blacktop court inside a chain-link enclosure. The Nikes, the Michael Jordan T-shirts, the Shaquille O'Neal signature ball, even the music coming from the boom box are all the same—culture has been universalized. Or people live urban or suburban and have a rural mind-set: Witness the explosion of trucks in bedroom-community driveways and on city streets. Or witness the near ubiquity of sports-utility vehicles along streets where the hardest thing drivers have to negotiate is a pothole. In 1965, full-size cars, led by the Chevrolet Impala, accounted for nearly 50 percent of all cars and light trucks sold in the United States; in 1995, the three top-selling vehicles in America were the Ford F-series of pickups, Chevy C/K pickups, and the sports-utility Ford Explorer. The Ford pickups alone nearly doubled the sales of the best-selling traditional car, the Ford Taurus. The moral is clear: The country mouse and the city mouse have become one.

Where someone actually lives or works—where her business or personal mail is delivered—continues to be of interest to the U.S. Census Bureau, but it determines nothing about lifestyle, because it is in no way definitive about life. Driven by connectivity, we have entered into location transparency. Thanks to telepresence, a doctor in New York City can virtually operate on a sick child in Bombay. The scalpel is not in his hand, but the intellectual property that drives the surgical procedure belongs entirely to him. Telecommuting gets much maligned. Absent a physical presence, so the argument goes, telecommuters lose political standing in an organization, they fall out of the loop. But many telecommuters are willing to trade marginalization for freedom. In the Age of Access, the freedoms to go and be sometimes mean never having to leave home.

Nor is lifestyle in any meaningful sense discriminated by earning power, possessions, or other measures of socioeconomic status. Middle-class residential aspirations are now absolutely uniform across the planet. The use of space in houses changes—formal dining rooms give way to kitchen/dining/den combinations as family meals diminish and simultaneous food-and-TV grazing rises; the three-bedroom, one-bath home becomes the two-bedroom, three-bath home as families splinter and daily baths replace weekly ones. Values stack and change, and as they stack and change, the use we make of our physical space changes with them—the garage, for example, is now the second-most-used space in American houses during waking hours—but the transforming values don't discriminate.

Nor do possessions discriminate. Connectivity connects more than people; it connects wants. Everyone has the same "stuff" list, everyone aspires to the same sets of possessions, and, increasingly, everyone has access to the same base possessions, whatever the brand name might be. The image might be clearer on a $2,000-plus thirty-five-inch Sony Trinitron than it is on a $100 black-and-white Emerson; the data will arrive faster and be more manipulable on a $6,000 computer equipped with a 33.6 modem than it will on an $800 PC hooked to a basic modem, but the information available on both—the exposure to possibility—is the same. Access spawns freedom of choice, in lifestyles as in everything else.

What, then, are the new discriminators of lifestyle? At least four are clearly emerging.

One is the personal orientation toward time, including the predisposition toward death. As Baby Boomers cross into their late middle years and old age, the lament that "life is too short" increasingly will become "life is too long." Jack Kervorkian and the assisted-suicide movement's continuing battles with the Michigan courts hint at the political and social issues inherent in the orientation toward time, but how one chooses to use time—whether one seeks to extend it, to sacrifice quantity time to quality time, to convert time to energy, or even to end time for themselves—has important implications for manufacturers and marketers as well. To know a person's time orientation today is to know something fundamental about that person's life and consumption patterns.

A second new discriminator, and a more important one, is personal orientation toward the media. Whether people choose to cruise broadly through the universe of available media choices or focus on the choices that reinforce their own worldviews, whether they merely use the Internet or whether they seek to help others learn to use the Net provides far more meaningful information about them than their job titles or their IRS 1040 forms. It also has a powerful effect on their perception of reality. Just as central as attitude and behavior toward the media is facility and proclivity—knowing how to manipulate the media and the degree of desire to do so. A smart turtle has it all over an eager hare.

More important still in an age being shaped by the acceleration in the rate of change is someone's personal orientation toward change. The simple fact is that all of us alive today have lived through so much change that it has become part of both our personal mythologies and our collective consciousness. To recognize the ubiquity of change to overwhelm, though, is not necessarily to embrace it. That finally is a personal choice, a lifestyle choice. Whether one slips into this stream of change and lets herself be carried by it or swims against change or simply stands on the banks and watches it all go by has enormous implications.

The final emerging discriminator is less abstract, but it is the most profound of them all. In an age being bombarded with new information, what most discriminates lifestyle is how someone handles the onslaught of fresh input.

Lemmings and Digerati

Two jokes about consultants: A consultant is someone who borrows your watch to tell you the time, and a consultant is someone who is convinced the whole world is explainable in a two-by-two matrix. We won't borrow your watch—*this* time—but in seeking to understand how input processing discriminates lifestyles, we did turn to a two-by-two matrix.

The end points of the vertical axis are defined by skill set. Are you proficient or not proficient at processing input? Since merely being able to do something well is no measure of whether you actually do it, we defined the end points of our horizontal axis by energy set: Do you aggressively or passively pursue processing input? The resulting matrix looked like this:

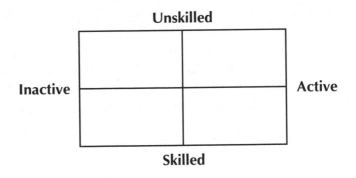

Next, we took a sample testing population and submitted it to a series of questions designed to determine both skill and energy levels at processing input. When we analyzed the data, our test sample fell neatly into four groups, none higher than 28 percent or less than 22 percent of the whole. Then we analyzed a second set of questions on attitudes toward new information, and that's when the real fun began. Before we begin the explanation, here's how we arranged the results:

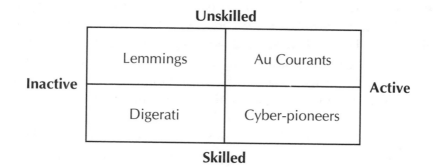

	Unskilled	
Inactive	Lemmings	Au Courants
	Digerati	Cyber-pioneers
	Skilled	**Active**

Like other microcultures in a steadily segmenting society, these input-processing microcultures were not fungible. They bled very little at the edges; concepts about input and the use of it, our surveying showed, were essentially nontransferable from group to group.

Not surprisingly, the upper-left-hand corner of the matrix produced what any diffusion of innovation curve always produces: a group of followers who lack both the skills to handle the innovation and the energy to gain the skills. We called them lemmings, for obvious reasons. The group in the upper-right-hand corner—active at processing new input but unskilled at it—proved on our survey questions to be the most interested in pop culture, which is why we named them the au courants. Au courants are heavy users of media, but they lack sophistication in doing so. To return for a moment to motive, they are the ones most likely to be driven by the desire to attain celebrity, however fleeting it might be.

The group in the lower-right-hand corner, both active and skilled at processing input, we affectionately dubbed cyber-pioneers. These are the ones who led us through the wilderness of the Information Age simply by being—less affectionately put—data-pigs. Along the way, they created a virtual language of their own and an ethos that we refer to as "nulture"—the blending of nerds and culture. The problem for the cyber-pioneers is that the wilderness no longer exists. The trails have been blazed, the bears driven to the high ground. Women and children are safe. The Information Age, as we have written earlier, is dead and gone, replaced by the information economy.

That brought us to the fourth group, the skilled and lazy. These, it turned out, were the most educated of all those we tested, the most affluent, the ones with the highest economic status. They know how to process input as well as the cyber-pioneers, but they don't do it simply for fun. Having left the hard work of pioneering the Information Age to their data-pig cousins, they are also the most prepared to take advantage of the information economy. Unlike the cyber-pioneers, they know what is important and what is not—they are primarily knowledge driven, not primarily information driven.

Lemmings make the lifestyle choices they make because they are told what is right. Slaves to fashion, au courants do what looks right; cyber-pioneers, what feels right. But the skilled and lazy do what is right. We named them the digerati, a word first coined so far as we know by Nicholas Negroponte in his book *Being Digital*. Digerati don't do, they are, which is why they will set the agenda for the future.

(An aside: Whichever Internet provider figures out the skilled-lazy connection to the World Wide Web wins, big.)

One more surprise awaited us. We were explaining one day to our friend Frank Wayne how neatly this matrix serves to discriminate lifestyles, when he asked us if we had ever heard how Erwin Rommel, the German field marshall who commanded Nazi forces in Africa during World War II, deployed his troops. By way of illustration, Frank Wayne drew us a matrix of his own. (We've added the parentheses to suggest the correlation with our matrix):

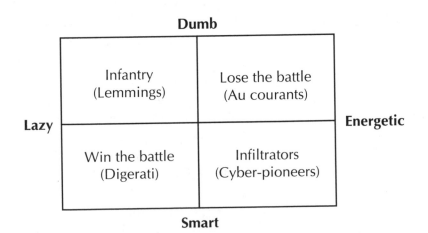

For Rommel, Wayne explained, the deployment of the dumb and lazy was easy to figure out: They're the infantry; they take spears well. The smart and energetic get behind enemy lines and make sure supplies reach them there. They push the envelope and bring you to the point where you can win the battle, but they don't put victory over the top. The two most critical groups, Rommel believed, were the lazy and smart, and the dumb and energetic. The dumb and energetic are the most dangerous of all the groups, because they look a great deal like the smart and energetic, but if you trust yourself to them—if you trust them to infiltrate and destroy from the rear—you are doomed. The smart and lazy win battles and wars because, in their aversion to doing rote work for rote work's sake, they are constantly trying to figure out a better way. They are the creators, warfare's equivalent of the digerati.

Field Marshall Rommel is rightly reviled for the cause he fought for, but he is rarely criticized for his strategies or his understanding of human behavior.

Ad Hoc Lives

The old lifestyle discriminators had the comfort of concrete. As circumstances changed, behavior changed, and as behavior changed, consumption patterns changed as predictably as the change of seasons. A move from the city to the suburbs brought a new list of demands; a move from $40,000 a year to $120,000 a year increased both the scale and the nature of consumption. Fifty-year-olds wanted what thirty-year-olds didn't. It was never that simple, but at least it seemed that way. There was loyalty—to spouse, to job, to age group, even to lifestyle, because lifestyle was, in effect, the accumulation of all loyalties. And it all worked so long as change remained slow and constant, because loyalty is a function of a low acceleration in the rate of change. Ratchet up the rate of change, compound the change itself, and loyalty falls apart.

The new lifestyle discriminators—the orientation to time, the media, change, and processing information—are nowhere near so set. Income is income, but someone who is knowledge-driven in one context may be information-driven in another, depending upon the outcome he or she is seeking. A mailing address is a mailing address; age is age, immutably. But how one looks at time, the choices one makes from the sprawling universe of information sources, the ways in which one embraces and rejects change are liquid. They run all over the place.

Like the lives they reflect, the new lifestyle discriminators are situational, deal-based. None of them relies on loyalty, because the future itself isn't about loyalty—it's about contracts. Nor does any define itself by a single data set or pay homage to a single relationship, because in a world of multiplying change, no data holds for long and no relationship is binding. Indeed, the two greatest predictors of future success in the workplace may be the capacity to live as "multiple you's," to re-create yourself constantly as the situation demands, and what we call "filocity"—the ability to adapt instantaneously to multiple relationships and move easily among multiple cultures.

(Filocity might also be thought of as the Ferris Bueller effect, after the slick teenage hero of *Ferris Bueller's Day Off*. As the white-out-sniffing high school secretary tells the assistant principal who has made it his futile life's work to catch Ferris cutting school, "The sportos, the motorheads, the geeks, sluts, bloods, wastoids, dweebies, dickheads—they all love him." And Ferris? Near the beginning of the movie, he sums up his own life philosophy by quoting John Lennon: "I just believe in me.")

All of the new lifestyle discriminators, it's also worth noting, are intrapersonal, not interpersonal, because the abiding irony of a world driving toward connectivity is that it leads to highly individualized interpretations, singular realities. The model of the new consumer is the same as the model of the new employee: Deion Sanders; free agency; me, me, me.

Situational lifestyles mean just that in the marketplace: Products have to fit the situational needs of consumers; transactions must be tailored to the particular situation at hand. Sony's new record store at 56th Street and Madison Avenue in Midtown Manhattan recognizes that today, in retailing as in every other facet of the marketplace, there has to be a value-added proposition that ties into not just people's shopping needs but the full dimensionality of their lives, a proposition that addresses lifestyle directly. Park yourself at the Sony store's interactive kiosk; enter "Woody Guthrie," "Bob Dylan," and

"Allman Brothers"; and the computer will tell you about the musical roots of all three, the music they had in common, and the mutual influences on all three careers. In effect, the Sony store merges education and utility. No one has to use the kiosk, but if consumers do, they leave the store smarter than when they came in. More to the point, to a remarkable degree, consumers leave with purchase in hand. The Sony store sells only at full retail; it's directly around the corner from a Sam Goody's store offering CDs 20 percent cheaper, and it is selling CDs to the tune of about $100,000 a day gross.

Range Rover has used different principles in renovating its dealerships, but they serve the same end. Instead of using Henry Ford's traditional model of the central dealership, Range Rover has been setting up smaller satellite dealer kiosks with a limited number of models for sale at each. The kiosks are patterned on Frank Lloyd Wright's Adirondack House, with fireplaces and comfortable sofas, and each kiosk offers for sale not only cars but the sort of peripherals and apparel that a Range Rover buyer also is likely to aspire to. In effect, Range Rover has created a highly individualized environment for a highly individualized transaction. The result: A company with one of the worst sales records in the auto industry is now in the process of turning its bottom line around completely. Why? Because the newly configured mini-dealerships take the latent personalization inherent in nearly any product and make it real. Buying a high-end new car is not the same as buying a high-end new washing machine, but even more important, buying a Range Rover cannot be the same as buying a Lexus. The dealerships give Range Rover its own thumbprint. They create a singular, not a mass, auto shopping experience, and thus they connect with the singular, not mass, realities of auto consumers.

Like Range Rover, Nike doesn't have to create a brand connection with someone who walks into its stores. The very act of entering implies that the connection has been made. What that person wants inside the store is a maximization of entertainment, fantasy, and utility, because just as work and leisure have merged, so have shopping and leisure. The miniaturization of time impels it. At its recently opened store in Chicago, Nike has devoted roughly a third of the space to pure utility—the selection and purchasing of shoes, sweats, socks, and T-shirts. Another third has been turned into a museum, a showcase of Nike products that have been worn by athletic champions. The final third is, in essence, a theater—a place where shoppers can watch great sports events and figures on film and videotape, always with the emphasis on Nike products to reinforce the final function of the store, which is to sell. And to assure shoppers that they are getting the best Nike has to offer, there is no discounting. If the latter seems counterintuitive in a world drowning in outlet malls, it is absolutely central to the value shift toward authenticity.

For multi-product environments—a Sears & Roebuck, for example—the rise of situational lifestyles teaches the same lesson. People don't want a store where everyone has the same shopping experience, because no two people go into a store under the same situation of need. People want a store where the experience is tailored to their specific needs, at the specific time at which they choose to exercise those needs. How, then, do you create a shopping experience that looks at the future of lifestyle discriminators instead of one that relies on the past? One way would be to create a kiosk at the front of the store where shoppers can pick individual employees to advise them, based on the employee's experience, or where shoppers can announce that they want virtually no employee interaction. That way, each time customers come into a store, they can change the terms of the shopping contract depending on their needs at the moment. The mass shopping experience is as fossilized as the mass market. To create customer loyalty in a multi-product environment, you have to be structured to be different each time a customer enters.

Situational lifestyles represent something else as well: yet another fundamental shift in the balance of power between seller and buyer, between manufacturer, retailer, and consumer. Until new metrics are developed to measure the new determinants of lifestyle, manufacturers and sellers will be more in the dark about their customers' wants and expectations than they have been at any time since the dawn of modern marketing. In the meantime, consumers know more about what they want—and are more determined to get what they want—than they have ever known before. Perhaps the greatest question about consumers today is how vengeful they will be in exercising their newfound power. The answer, we suspect, may be: very. They have much abuse to make up for. But that gets to the issue of empathy.

7

Empathy: Not Guilty

"And now abideth faith, hope, and charity," Paul the Apostle wrote at the end of the thirteenth chapter of his First Epistle to the Corinthians. "But the greatest of these *is* charity." The greatest and, in many ways, the most difficult.

Just as values are stacked generation by generation and transformed as generations reach out to explore their end points or contract back toward their center, so it is with the deeper impulses that inform the human experience. They, too, are transformed generation by generation, epoch by epoch, millennia by millennia. And they, too, will not only endure but prevail.

What does faith mean in a Chaos Age? In fact, it means a great deal. As reason wanes, disbelief becomes permanently suspended. And as that happens, faith grows, because the deeper one looks into the heart of chaos, the more one comes to find, as Albert Einstein did when he looked into the chaotic heart of space, that only a divine power can explain it. "God is subtle," Einstein once explained, "but He is not malicious." Think of it as a working mantra for the Age of Chaos.

What shape will this faith take once the apocalyptic, end-of-the-century scurrying of the neo-Millerites has passed by? Not necessarily the shape it takes today. Mass religion, we contend, is as doomed as mass culture, not because people will believe less, but because group reality is becoming particalized and because loyalty to a single over-riding interpretation of the divine is as dated as loyalty to family or to a corporation. The God of today—the God that we call Gosh because His job is to be everyone's best friend and to assure them that they, too, will be okay—will vanish as well, not because God will be any less kind, but because the greater kindness is to teach them that they will not be okay unless they actively pursue okay-ness. Gosh worshippers will be left standing on the banks of the river of change. People who don't need Gosh will be swimming in it.

To the extent that places of worship as we know them will continue to exist, we foresee a rise of loosely confederated, highly individualized denominations—situational churches, in effect, to fit situational lifestyles. Eastern religious thought and philosophy will continue to affect Western systems of belief because East and West are fusing as borders disappear and nationality fades into the background. But fusion works both ways: Eastern thought will be equally affected by the Judeo-Christian tradition. There will be a rise in pragmatic spirituality, as well: ad hoc beliefs to fit ad hoc lives. The New Age is many things odd, from male bonding rituals to Mozart accompanied by Amazonian chirping. At heart, though, the New Age is a transitional era between reason and chaos, between science and faith—an attempt to find in nature and in spirituality what the promise of science and reason has failed to deliver on. As far back as 1990, Americans were spending nearly $14 billion annually on alternative medicine, on everything from herbal cures to primal screaming, and paying for $10.3 billion of that out of their own pockets—compared to the $12.8 billion paid out of pocket that year for all hospitalizations. The public, in short, has already arrived at pragmatic spirituality, while the health-care analysts and HMOs were looking the other way.

We also foresee a rise—driven in part by New Age values—in the popularity of sacred spots, places invested by their natural features or ancient inhabitants with spiritual power. Unlike the New Age, though, these sacred spots will be as highly individuated as the people who are drawn to them.

• • •

What of hope? It will endure because it has to. Under extreme duress, humans have been known to live for more than an hour without air. The body shunts blood from the extremities to the vital organs—the heart, the brain; it closes down extraneous life so it can preserve final life. Without water, humans have lasted about a week; and without food, more than two months. In both cases, the body cannibalizes itself, feeding on the extraneous to preserve the central. The drive toward life within a living body is nothing short of astounding. But without hope, no one can live. The body has nothing to shunt to feed hope, nothing it can cannibalize in the interests of its own psychic self-preservation. Hope will endure because it has to. But hope will also prevail. We are entering into an epoch in which for the first time "possibility" has true meaning, has real resonance. It is the Age of the Fulfillment of Hope as much as it is the Age of Possibility.

And what of charity, the last of Paul the Apostle's triangle of abiding virtues and the greatest of them all? Paul undoubtedly meant charity not as in the giving of alms but as in what Protestant and Catholic theologians call "the Christian love of our fellow men." The word "charity" itself is drawn from the Latin "caritas," for "love," and translators subsequent to the King James Bible have generally used "love" instead of "charity." (Modern translators are careful in their commentaries to point out that they are talking about spiritual love, not sexual love.) But whatever word we use, this, too, will endure, this, too, will prevail. The instinct toward love, toward charity is too strong for it to do otherwise. What is already changing is the way we translate that instinct, the way we enter into the lives of our fellow humans: our empathy.

New Winners, New Losers

Our perspectives, our motives and values, the ways we communicate and the way we organize our lives—all these cannot undergo fundamental change without a concomitant fundamental shift in the way we feel for others. To project ourselves into the lives of others in order to understand their thoughts, to sense their wants, needs, and emotions—to be, in short, empathetic—implies inevitably a judgment based on our own experience of life. As we change, as the rate of change that shapes our lives accelerates, as change accumulates and assumes density, so our capacity to empathize also changes, and so change the judgments we bring to that effort. Revolutions have winners. And they have losers.

The empathy losers are already surfacing in the political marketplace. In statehouse after statehouse, workfare programs are being advanced that would alter or replace traditional welfare structures. Wisconsin, a state historically notable for its progressive political tendencies, moved in the spring of 1996 to abolish welfare altogether, replacing it with a system that would eliminate Aid to Families with Dependent Children, require every adult recipient of state aid to work, and cap all transfer payments at five years. In Washington, D.C., the 104th Congress sought systematically, if largely unsuccessfully, to erase three decades of social legislation meant, in theory at least, to enhance the lives of the downtrodden. Not to be outdone in the seeming rush to dis-empathy, President Clinton in April 1996 signed legislation tying transfer payments to unwed teenage mothers to their continuing enrollment in school programs. A month later, three days before Bob Dole was to deliver an address on welfare reform, Clinton endorsed the Wisconsin workfare plan in its entirety. By the time he delivered his second inaugural address, President Clinton could speak with confidence about the need for "each and every one of us [to] assume personal responsiblity not only for ourselves and our families, but for our neighbors and our nation."

Is an epidemic of unkindness loose upon the land? Certainly, in the short term, there is a danger of severe social dislocation if welfare reform is too draconian, if the screws are turned too tight on those who are now dependent on transfer programs and payments. The welfare legislation seemingly soon to be dismembered did not arise in a vacuum. It followed hard on the heels of the August 1964 race riots in Rochester, New York, and Patterson and Elizabeth, New Jersey; the July 1965 riots in the Watts section of Los Angeles that left 34 people dead, injured more than 1,000 people, and caused $175 million in property damage; and later racial outbreaks in Detroit, New York's Spanish Harlem, Oakland, and elsewhere. Wealth may accumulate more and more at the top of society, but history is still driven from the bottom up. And if history is forgotten, there can be hell to pay.

In the long term, though, we would argue that something like precisely the opposite of an epidemic of unkindness is happening. The new freedoms to know, to go, to do, and to be constitute collectively an opportunity economy never before seen in history, a chance for everyone literally to share in the pie. Connectivity, as we've said before, frees; access unburdens. Together, they level the playing field. But together they also change our understanding of success and failure. Although cruelty can and does surface in the debate over welfare reform—although unspeakable stupidities and facile misassumptions get cast about the political arena as received truth—what is going on now is not a rush to dis-empathy. It is rather the reflection of a vast reorganization of the very nature of empathy. The impulse to be kind, to love one's neighbor as one's self, holds, but kindness is and always was relative.

That Was Then, This Is Now

The entitlement programs that began to take shape with Lyndon Johnson's Great Society legislation of the mid–1960s are at heart historically based. Transfer payments, government preferences, and set-asides—the whole panoply of social engines that drives the modern welfare system—are meant to redress the wrongs of time. African-Americans are favored not just because as a group they have the greatest need, but because it is the obligation of Caucasian-Americans to atone for four hundred years of history stained by the slave trade and systematic exclusion from the mainstream of national social, economic, and political life. Women are favored out of a sense of debt to thousands of years of male social, economic, political, and sexual hegemony.

As a package, it works so long as a shared sense of history holds. When history falls apart, though, the underpinnings of empathy as we have understood it for the last three decades fall apart as well. And when reason is dethroned, when the organization of our personal and working lives is transformed, when macroeconomics and microeconomics are reconfigured into something wholly new, interpretations of history are swept away as well. Generational memory lasts 150 years because there are six generations alive on the planet at any given time, and thus the memory that informs empathy can last only as long as collective experience applies, as long as history is shared and continuous. The Holocaust is only about a third of the way through its generational transfer. Slavery, officially eradicated in the American South by the Emancipation Proclamation of 1862, is almost through with its transfer. That memory is about to be sealed. Empathy for the descendants of slaves won't be sealed with it, but it will be transformed.

The New Ethics Agenda

By definition, freedoms free, but they also sweep away excuses. The new ethics agenda already emerging in the American—and global—society works both ends of that formulation. To be free to know whatever it is you need to know to pursue your destiny means that there will be little sympathy for those who fail to arm themselves with the essential knowledge to succeed. To be free to go wherever it is you need to go to pursue your destiny means that there will be little sympathy if you elect to go nowhere and suffer as a result. To be free to do whatever it is within your intellectual and physical capacity to do means that if you fail to make an attempt to do it and suffer as a result, there will be little sympathy. To be free to be whatever it is within your intellectual and physical capacity to be means that if you don't pursue possibility and suffer as a result, there will be little sympathy.

Simply put, at the bottom line of the new ethics agenda lies one thing: the exercise of personal responsibility. True freedom, which is what the four new freedoms offer, entails true responsibility. It is impossible to have one without the other, impossible to demand true individual rights on the one hand and claim group victimization or demand group redress on the other.

The widespread refusal of whites to accept the verdict of O. J. Simpson's peers that he was innocent of the murders of Nicole Brown and Ronald Goldman had less to do with the implausibility of Simpson's defense, implausible though it was, than with the fact that Simpson had allowed his "dream team" of legal counselors to cast him as a member of an oppressed minority. Simpson, who had been living in a Brentwood mansion valued at $10 million and had rarely been seen in the Los Angeles ghettos, simply didn't fit the bill. The almost universal contempt for District of Columbia mayor Marion Barry that D.C.'s white minority was expressing by the summer of 1996 had far less to do with Barry's race—"West of the Park" white voters had given him strong pluralities in earlier elections—than it had to do with the fact that Barry was choosing to use his race to shield himself from the consequences of his erratic personal behavior.

Bio-schisms—interspecies divisiveness driven solely by biological and genetic distinctions—will remain a real, present, and fractious part of the social landscape. However much we may wish to deny it in our antiseptic age, biological and genetic distinctions between men and women, between the old and young, between races, are real and present and fractious. But to recognize such distinctions, to be honest about them, is not to endorse using them to subjugate or disadvantage a particular element of the population.

Racial tolerance, sexual tolerance, age tolerance—all have never been more alive and well in America and the world. It is collective guilt that has died, collective victimization, whether of blacks or women or white middle-aged men or white Christians of either sex who claim to have suffered for their age, their whiteness, their system of beliefs. The four freedoms empower individuals, not groups, and they mean that individuals, not groups, rise or fall. The fact of class, race, sex, and age will continue to exist, but the old barriers of class restraint, race restraint, sex restraint, and age restraint will no longer prevail, because in a world without barriers, a world of universal access to information, a world where individuals and careers can and must be made over constantly, there are no collective restraints to hold accountable for failure. Like success, failure is a solo act; individuals alone are responsible for both.

Who wins under the new ethics agenda?

Corporations who exercise their full measure of corporate responsibility. Corporations who are good citizens, who offer authenticity, who treat the individuals they employ with respect and individual customers with even more respect. Corporations who align themselves with causes that themselves evoke empathy.

Back in 1982, when he was head of the United States Olympic

Committee and planning for the 1984 Summer Games in Los Angeles, Peter Ueberroth, with the help of Jerry Welsh, discovered that the identification of products with the Olympics was not only a sign of corporate beneficence, it also attached to corporate products a sense of international excellence, global expertise, and competitive perfection. Good ideas often get out of hand, and this one is no exception. Scattered among the more than 171 hours of Olympics television coverage in the summer of 1996 were 26 hours of commercials, and somewhere among them—who could keep track?—must have been ones for the Official Olympic Breath Mint and the Official Olympic Hemorrhoid Relief Preparation. Who could keep track, too, of the endless eighty-four-day, 15,000-mile Coca-Cola–sponsored Olympic Torch Relay—a rite that, as Roger Angell reminded *New Yorker* readers, was invented by Adolf Hitler for the 1936 Berlin Games. But the excesses shouldn't hide Peter Ueberroth's accomplishments. Ueberroth, who had become Major League Baseball commissioner by the time the 1984 Summer Games took place, had promised the City of Los Angeles that he would use the program to raise enough funds to finance the Games, and he kept his promise and raised enough additional money to finance the American Olympic movement for many years to come. In the process, he set a model for corporate endorsements that other good causes have followed.

The American Red Cross, for one, has gone to school on the Olympic Sponsorship Program, and in some ways improved on it. Unlike the Olympic program, the Red Cross has kept the number of sponsors low, and it has made a particular appeal to companies whose business depends upon their ability to deliver services quickly and effectively, because the Red Cross is today associated not with service in wartime but with response to disasters. The Red Cross gets the money, which it sorely needs, and the sponsors get the reflected halo of the Red Cross. No one loses. Everyone wins.

Who else wins under the new ethics agenda?

At least part of the not-for-profit sector. As governments abrogate their traditional civic responsibilities and as corporations in effect become nations and take on more and more of the roles of traditional government, the not-for-profit sector will emerge as a fusion point between the two. It is through the not-for-profit sector that services to the needy will be delivered, through it that the needs and wants of the powerless will be brokered and discriminated. Meanwhile, the parallel fusion of downward nobility and the Millennialists' generationally imprinted drive to fix the world will create a new class of not-for-profit elites, a ruling class that will set the empathy agenda for decades to come.

Who wins most importantly?

Those who by reason of genetic defect or simple bad luck can't keep up. Those who are victimized not by their group identification but by their individual powerlessness. The victims of child abuse or spousal abuse, children born with Down's syndrome or spina bifida or neuro-motor disorders or AIDS, the family maimed because a drunk driver plowed into their Dodge Caravan at eighty miles an hour, the psychotic, the insane. Kindness is relative, but for the those who can't help themselves, those who couldn't avoid a bad fate, kindness will be bottomless. And there will be no race test, no sex test, and no age test on who receives it.

Who loses?

Corporations who won't exercise their full measure of civic responsibility, corporations with a reputation for less than honest actions, corporations who abuse their employees and customers. These are the ones that consumers will wreak their revenge on. Who else loses? Movements that continue to insist on group guilt, group redress, group victimization, along with their leaders. (It is not by accident that the ever supple Jesse Jackson has been lately seen talking about individual responsibility in the black community.) The group-guilt industry that forms so significant a part of the nonfederal economy of Washington, D.C. That portion of the charity industry that has aligned itself with the group-guilt industry, and it, too, is huge. The whine industry, and it is huge as well, in the nation's capital and throughout the land. Any group that seeks to subsume individual responsibility into collective explanations. Any group that claims for itself excessive privileges, excessive rights. As empathy shifts, the understanding of social fairness shifts as well, and as that happens, rights are earned, not given.

Who loses in particular?

The drunk driver who plows into the Dodge Caravan at eighty

miles an hour and is rendered a quadriplegic as a result. Slackers. Drifters. Addicts. The lazy. The indolent. The idle. School dropouts, for whom the quality of mercy will be severely strained because they have not put themselves in a position to take advantage of their freedoms. Not those who can't help themselves, but those who won't help themselves or won't accept efforts to help them. To the extent that it depends on historic victimization or group victimization, the victim ethic is dead.

The new ethics agenda can be glimpsed at work in the $162-billion-a-year charity marketplace, as well as in the political one. Alzheimer's disease is an easy cause to raise money for, because no one actively seeks to expose himself to the danger of suffering from it. Alzheimer's simply happens. Diseases of old age are generally widely supported, because even those of us gifted with the best of genes eventually grow old and die. AIDS is another matter. The disease gets a share of federal monies out of all proportion to the number of deaths it causes because gays, the group that most suffers from AIDS, are seen as a bloc vote. But rightly or wrongly—and it is certainly wrong for the ravaged hemophiliac population and for babies born with the disease—AIDS will be judged in the emerging new ethics agenda as an elective ailment. A similar dis-empathy, we suspect, awaits the victims of smoking-related diseases. And it certainly awaits both women who don't assure that adequate precaution has been taken to avoid pregnancy and the men who impregnate them. The four freedoms mean that everyone falls or rises on individual choice. "Dying for a smoke" is a choice made one cigarette at a time. And whatever teenage boys might claim to their dates, no one *has* to have sex.

The intersection of the new ethics agenda and the charitable sector is perhaps most neatly tied up by the example of a charity we just mentioned, the American Red Cross. Almost 90 percent of the Red Cross's annual budget of nearly $1 billion goes to its institutional responsibilities—in effect, helping the downtrodden—and for this, the group has a terrible time raising money. Less than 10 percent goes to disaster relief, but for this—hurricanes in Florida, flood damage in the Midwest, earthquakes in California, acts of God wherever—the money comes pouring in. It was this dichotomy that the Red Cross had in mind when it changed its slogan to "Help Can't Wait," and "Help Can't Wait" has worked.

Charity will abide in both senses, as the specific act of giving and as the broader exercise of love. But it only makes sense that people who live situationally—who redefine the terms of their personal realities from moment to moment—would give and love situationally as well. That is empathy in a chaos world.

Unreal Realities

PART **III**

We've focused thus far on the broad changes that are converging as the century and millennium drive toward their end. Let us stop here for just a minute and catalog the specific changes that all of us have lived through in whole or in part. In fact, their numbers, their breadth, their scope, the speed with which they have arrived are nothing short of breathtaking.

Consider, first, the speed of change:

In 1960, 925,000 Americans were age eighty-five or older. Today, that number has more than quadrupled, to 3.8 million. By the year 2010, nearly 6 million Americans will be at least eighty-five years old.

In 1960, 45.7 million American households had televisions, and the average television household had one set each. Today, 95 million American homes hold 213 million TV sets.

In 1960, the average computer could handle less than 1.5 MIPS—or millions of instructions per second—and serviced 550 people. Today, the average computer can handle 150 MIPS and services one person.

In 1960, the average CEO traveled 12,000 miles a year. Today, the average CEO travels 112,000 miles a year.

In 1960, 23 million American women worked for pay. Today, more than 61 million do.

In 1960, the average person had one job and one career over a working life. Today, the average person at the outset of his or her working life can expect to have seven jobs and two careers.

In 1960, the average person needed to learn one new skill a year to prosper in the workplace. Today, the average person needs to learn one new skill a day.

In 1960, the richest 5 percent of Americans controlled 17 percent of the nation's wealth. Today, the richest 5 percent control 21.5 percent—an increase of more than 26 percent in less than four decades.

In 1960, the average American was middle class. Today, the average American is either rich or poor.

In 1960, the average child had one set of parents and two sets of grandparents. Today, the average child has two-and-a-half sets of parents and six sets of grandparents.

In 1960, 224,000 American infants were born to single mothers, and the *Statistical Abstract of the United States* referred to such events as "illegitimate live births." Today, more than 1.3 million infants are born to single mothers, and the *Statistical Abstract* calls them "births to unmarried women."

In 1960, the average American father spoke with his children forty-five minutes a day. Today, the average father speaks with his child six minutes a day.

Since 1960, the annual per capita consumption of meat in the United States has declined by 32 percent, the average per capita consumption of eggs by 31 percent, and the average per capita consumption of fresh citrus by 23 percent. Meanwhile, the average per capita consumption of potato products has grown by 35 percent, and the average per capita consumption of sweeteners has grown by 78 percent.

In 1960, the average person saw 107 commercial messages a day. Today, the average person is faced with 145 commercial messages daily, an increase of 36 percent over less than two generations.

In 1960, the average American spent about sixteen hours a year attending movies. Today, the average American spends about eleven hours a year in movie theaters and about fifty-seven hours a year watching movie videos.

In 1960, nearly 1,800 daily American newspapers had a total circulation of 59 million, and 60 percent of those papers were evening dailies. Today, some 1,500 dailies have roughly the same total circulation they had almost four decades ago, and 72 percent of them are morning dailies.

In 1960, the average American household owned one car. Today, the average American household owns no car, but controls two.

In 1960, the number-one car in America sold nearly 1.5 million units. Today, the number-one car sells 366,000 units annually and is outsold by two lines of trucks and a sports-utility vehicle.

In 1960, the number-one selling song in America, the theme from *A Summer Place* performed by Percy Faith and his orchestra, stayed at the top of the hit parade for nine weeks. In 1996, the number-one selling group, Hootie and the Blowfish, was spending its second year on top of the charts.

In 1960, the most important American industry was manufacturing. Today, the most important American industry is ideas.

And all this in less than two generations.

In the long reach of time, the span between 1960 and today hardly registers. Dinosaurs roamed the face of the Earth for nearly 100 million years; compared to that, four decades is less than an atom. Humanoids have been in existence for some nine hundred generations, and intelligent humans for five hundred generations. Eighty generations have passed since the birth of Christ. The slightly less than two generations we are talking about encompasses just 2 percent of the time since the dawn of the Christian era. In just forty years, culture has been universally diffused. That is why Hootie and the Blowfish managed to stay on top of the pop charts for twenty-four months: MTV has created a global marketplace. In just forty years, the family as we once knew it has been completely remade. In just forty years, the great American middle class—that bulwark of national values—has been dethroned, dissolved, virtually destroyed. In just forty years, corporations have been particalized and borders have turned porous. In 1960, Europe was still recovering from the last of its bitter, bloody wars over national boundaries. Today, you can travel from the tip of Scotland to the Turkish border without once showing a passport. In a mere four decades, chaos has shifted from describing extreme disorder to describing a viable theory of organization.

Someone born in 1960 is likely—in the modern calculus of family making—to just be entering parenthood; actuarial tables will tell you that he or she has lived barely half a life. Think of the speed of change, the acceleration, that person has had to live through. And then remember that that person is at least in some part you.

Here's another way to look at the speed of change and its acceleration. From 1963 through 1975, the U.S. Patent and Trademark Office issued 48,571 U.S. patents annually. From 1990 through 1995 it issued 59,942 such patents annually—an increase of 23 percent over the earlier period. In 1990, the office issued 52,972 U.S. patents; in 1995 it issued 64,509 such patents—an increase of 22 percent in six years alone. Is it any wonder that we all feel such an enormous compression of innovation?

Speed is only one part of the whole story of change, and in many ways the lesser part. The speed—and particularly its acceleration—dazzles us. It gives us psychic whiplash. But it is the raw tonnage of change, its massive accumulation, that we finally feel most in our bones. Back during the Cold War, when debate raged in Congress over whether there was a megaton gap between Soviet and American nuclear weapons, the late Senator Henry "Scoop" Jackson of Washington state explained that the missile inventories of the United States and the Soviet Union had both reached such massive proportions that a few more megatons wouldn't be decisive in the outcome of a nuclear war. As Jackson said, "It's how high we want to bounce the rubble." That is where change has brought us today. The social upheaval of the sum of all the changes that are upon us is a given; it is only a matter of how high the rubble bounces.

We've cataloged the speed of change. Now consider all the *things* that existed in 1960—the cultural artifacts of the times, the totems, the ceremonies, the global concerns—that have either ceased to exist or ceased to matter in any deep way over the last four decades. Like the previous list, this one is only partially complete:

Fizzies   Oxydol
The cha-cha   Ipana

Railroad Express
Civil defense
Communists
The Soviet Union
Nike missiles
H-bombs
Veterans' Day
Patriotism
Strategic Air Command
The Domino Theory
The Berlin Wall
Bomb shelters
Family doctors
House calls
Plaster lathe
Family meals
Whole milk
Spam
Canned vegetables
TV dinners
Gimbel's
Studebaker
Pan Am
Propeller-driven planes

Whole-life insurance
Mimeographs
Adding machines
Univacs
Typewriters
Latin mass
Cash payrolls
Single-entry bookkeeping
Comptrollers
Silver coins
Postal money orders
Relief
Lifelong employment
Mill towns
The numbers racket
Ten-cent hamburgers
Taverns
Trading stamps
Hi-fi
The three R's
Inner tubes
Silk stockings and girdles
Old maids

And then think of all the things that are fundamental parts of our daily existence today, yet didn't exist at all or were barely creeping off the planning boards less than two generations ago. If anything, this list is even more incomplete:

Cable TV
Halogen lamps
Cellular phones
Software
Databases
VCRs
CDs
Color TV

Fax
FedEx
Microwaves
Call forwarding
E-mail
Answering machines
Post-Its
Personal computers

Baby monitors	ATVs
Home burglar alarms	Visa cards
The Club	Transplants
Calculators	HMOs
747's	NASDAQ
Area codes	Biotechnology
Zip codes	Food stamps
Birth-control pills	Space shuttles
Space shuttles	Feminists
Compulsory seat belts	Political correctness
Catalytic converters	Miranda rights
Radials	Diet Coke
Cruise control	Starbucks
Condos	Wal-Mart
AIDS	Martin Luther King Jr., Day
ATMs	

Next, for good measure, add these elements:

- In 1990, the World Wide Web didn't exist. In 1996, 11.5 million Americans used the Web and more than 28 million had access to it. The best predictions are that, by the year 2000, 52 million people worldwide will be Webheads.

- In mid-December 1995, the Alta Vista server was launched in Palo Alto, California, to scan the Web's roughly 225,000 sites for information. By late June 1996, Alta Vista was processing 8.5 million requests a day.

- In 1996, the Web was expected to generate about $500 million in on-line shopping revenues. By the year 2000, that figure may grow to $100 billion in U.S. transactions alone.

Then add this: Thanks to genetic engineering and biotechnology, the world today is creating new life-forms at the same rate that it is losing old ones. Indeed, the next new step is to define precisely what life is. Is human sperm in a sperm bank "stuff" or is it "life"? Are brain cells being harvested from aborted fetuses and farmed to repair the damaged brain tissue of Parkinson's disease victims "stuff" or "life"? Is the biomass computer that uses stimulated DNA to solve mathematical problems "stuff" or is it "life"? We have not even begun to ask the questions that bioengineering soon will be requiring us to answer.

Last, just for fun, consider this: So slow was the rate of change in business two generations ago that your grandfather may have had to memorize only 25 names in a working life. So fast is the rate of change today that many executives have to memorize the names of 25 people every month—300 names a year, 3,000 a decade. That's why memory courses have replaced computer courses as the hottest item being sold on late-night TV. As much as we have yet to truly consider the definition of life, we have yet to truly consider the genetic limits of human consciousness. At what point do we stretch the limits of a person's hard drive and memory? At what point does the human computer, like the man-made one, become so overloaded with operating systems and databases that it simply goes slower and slower?

It is out of this mountain of change—and most particularly in defense against it—that we create the sustaining myths of our times. We've mentioned a number of them already:

- The myth of reason when, in fact, the only thing you truly can count on in your personal or professional life is that people and organizations will act irrationally.

- The myth of family that so drives the political debate over family values. The reality is that "families" are largely a status symbol today, a luxury for those who can afford to keep them intact. Something similar, it should be mentioned, is going on in the political arena in the debate over drugs. The myth is that we can return to something like an addiction-free society—an American society, incidentally, that never existed. The reality is that there are 247 twelve-step programs in America today. James Danowski's entropic theory of the adult personality deserves mention here. Danowski contends that increasingly over time human behavior becomes dictated by body chemistry. We, for example, take risks to produce the adrenaline that our bodies crave, and as our bodies come to crave it more and more, the more risky our behavior becomes. In effect, as a species we are becoming addicted to addiction itself.

• The myths of business organization. In fact, there are many. Perhaps the most persistent is that power necessarily belongs to the person who sits at the top of a decision pyramid. The reality in a chaos world is that the greatest power belongs to the person who controls the most unstable variable. A second, related myth is that it is only by assuring certainty in each part of an organization that you can create certainty in the whole of the organization. The reality is that the uncertainty of the parts assures the certainty of the whole. A third is the myth of the career. The reality is that there are only two kinds of workers in any business organization: owners and employees. And the further reality is that there are only two kinds of employees: the 5 percent who would stay where they are if they were offered twice their salary to leave and the 95 percent who would be gone in a flash. The myth is loyalty; the reality is that it's a deal-based world. As employer and employee, you are never not at risk.

• The myth of relations of economic worth. The myth is that all relations are either symbiotic, predatory, competitive, or parasitic. The reality is that all relations of economic worth today are all four at once.

• The myth of governments. The myth is that they matter. The reality is that they matter mostly to those who have an economic stake in their day-to-day operation—that is, to government employees and those who receive federal transfer payments.

• The myth of nations. The myth is that they, too, matter. The reality is that connectivity penetrates borders and access destroys them.

• The myth of action. The myth, made famous by the Nike sportswear slogan, is just do it. The reality is that in a chaos world, you cannot "do" your way to anything. You can achieve an end only by focusing on outcome and letting each individual decision be dictated by your final goal. Don't do it. Be it.

To this list, let us now add two more myths.

• The myth of singularity—the myth that each individual change that collectively makes up this mountain of change can be analyzed and dealt with separately. The reality is that the effect of change is both interactive and cumulative. As we write, the front page of the *New York Times* informs us that there is to be a change in the federal minimum wage, that terrorism prospects in Saudi Arabia are changing for the worse, that a new prime minister has brought a change in U.S.-Israeli relations, that relaxation of U.S. human-rights policies has brought a change in the trade prospects with China, that there has been a change in the presidency of the New York City Board of Education, and that the Russians have changed for the better in their willingness to confront corruption in their government. Each of these changes may be singularly interesting for any one of us. Perhaps we are a member of the Russian military or the New York City parent of a school-aged child. But in a world driving toward total connection, all the individual changes announced on this single front page of the *Times* have a collective consequence, a cumulative effect. Terrorism in Saudi Arabia could affect oil supplies, which could mean long gas lines. Improved trade prospects with China could send Pacific Rim stocks plummeting, which would affect mutual funds that are heavy holders of Pacific Rim stocks, which could spell trouble for your plans to move from New York City to Pelham Manor because you are afraid that a combination of a new school board president and the joblessness brought on by a higher minimum wage will turn Manhattan into a towering inferno. Remember how the wings of the butterfly left Costa Rica in ashes in the classic chaos-theory example we cited earlier. To touch a spiderweb anywhere is really to affect its whole creation. To paraphrase John Donne, no change is an island, entire of itself; every change is a piece of the continent, a part of the main. As we've said before, a myth without validation is a fairy tale.

• Finally, the myth that reality is real. The reality is that each individual edits reality for himself. The reality is that the combinations and permutations of media choices allow each person to have an entirely idiosyncratic view of reality. The reality is that today reality is constructed.

Is it any wonder that most people today have an expectation at variance with the way the world actually operates? Any wonder that most people sense a disconnection between their experience and their beliefs, their attitudes and their behavior? Indeed, wouldn't the true wonder be if most people felt at all otherwise? This sense of variance, of disconnection, of dis-ease, is the defining condition of our times. We call it cultural schizophrenia, and we take up cultural schizophrenia in the next section of this book.

The Search for Meaning

PART IV

The first novel of the Age of Chaos, the first fiction of the twenty-first century, was written more than thirty-five years ago by an author born in Brooklyn, New York, on May 1, 1923. His name is Joseph Heller; the novel, *Catch-22*. As millions of college students have learned in American literature courses—and millions more of movie fans have seen through Mike Nichols's brilliant screen adaptation—it's a dark comic scream.

Heller was writing about the chaos of war, particularly the chaos of the European theater during World War II, but the madness he describes will be familiar to anyone trying to run a business today, anyone caught in a corporation's maw, or for that matter any fan of the *Dilbert* comic strip: Milo Minderbinder's commodities trading schemes ("A strong Egyptian-cotton speculating industry means a much stronger America"); the casual manner in which nurses Duckett and Cramer rotate the feeding and urine-collection jars for the "soldier in white," wrapped entirely in plaster casts and surgical bandages ("Why can't they hook the two jars up to each other and eliminate the middleman?" a baffled artillery captain asks); the IBM machine that promotes a private named Major Major Major to major; and the comically magnified idiocies of war that lead to the neurotic Major Major becoming the air squadron commander.

Indeed, in the annals of chaos culture there may be no single scene more perfectly descriptive of the world as it is today than the one in which Major Major explains the new rules for the air-squadron commander's office to his orderly:

> "From now on . . . I don't want you to come here while I'm here to ask me if there's anything you can do for me. Is that clear?"
>
> "Yes, sir," said the orderly. "When should I come here to find out if there's anything you want me to do for you?"
>
> "When I'm not here."
>
> "Yes, sir. And what should I do?"
>
> "Whatever I tell you to."
>
> "But you won't be here to tell me. Will you?"
>
> "No."
>
> "Then what should I do?"
>
> "Whatever has to be done."

Sound familiar?

It's in his central character, the bombardier Yossarian, that Heller most fully captures the conflicted world that the convergence of change has created. Yossarian is paradox personified, moving through a world from which reason has been routed. Instead of being at war with Nazi Germany and Fascist Italy, he is at war with the institutions of war itself.

In effect, Yossarian is trapped in a classic double bind: All demands on him are contradictory, and thus any action he chooses is wrong. He flies mission after mission with a single thought in mind—to achieve his quota of missions and be rotated back to the States—and every time he reaches the quota, his hated nemeses, Colonels Cathcart and Korn, blithely raise the standard. Insanity is the only grounds for being sent home, Yossarian is told, but if you are sane enough to declare yourself insane, you are by definition perfectly sane. Finally, Yossarian simply refuses to fly again, and to solve the problem, Cathcart and Korn offer to promote him, give him a medal, and send him home a hero. But there's a catch, a catch-22. Yossarian's side of the deal is simple, Colonel Korn explains: All you have to do is, "Like us. Join us. Be our pal." And there's a last catch. Seconds after Yossarian accepts the offer, he is set upon and nearly killed by a prostitute he had tried to befriend.

In the last scene of the Mike Nichols movie version of *Catch-22*, Yossarian, by now nearly recovered from his stabbing wound, decides to forego the deal Cathcart and Korn had offered him and row himself to freedom. "That's insane," protests a fellow captain who has come to visit him in his hospital room. "Of course it's insane," Yossarian shouts as he grabs a dinghy and leaps from the hospital window. "That's why it's the only sane thing to do."

Perhaps that will sound familiar, too. In a chaos world, as we wrote earlier, the only way to manage a life is from the edge, and the only thing you can depend on is you. Each reality is created on its own terms, one person at a time.

How do you find meaning in such a world? By abandoning the search for unifying theories. By particalizing attention—focusing it at the subatomic level. By concentrating on the confusion in the parts to find coherency in the whole. By being the ball, not playing at ball. In a reason-based world, it makes sense to proceed reasonably. In a world that treasures loyalty, to be loyal is to be wise. But in a double-bound world, there is no way to reason your way to rightness. In a world without loyalties, there is only loyalty to yourself. In the midst of chaos, the only way to survive is to get in touch with chaos, because it is only by doing so that you can make chaos work to your advantage.

"Of course it's insane," Yossarian says of his plan to row his way out of the war. "That's why it's the only sane thing to do." With that, bombardier Yossarian became the ball—and finally found meaning. Which is why, just as Heller's novel is the first fiction of the Age of Chaos, Yossarian is its first citizen.

(In the spirit of chaos, too, we should point out that Joseph Heller's memorable title, now so much a part of the language that it has become a dictionary entry, was going to be *Catch-18*. Unfortunately, "18" was also in the title of novelist Leon Uris's *Mila 18*, which appeared at roughly the same time. Heller went with "22" instead, and the rest is history. In the same spirit, and in the spirit of the war we've just been writing about, we also could mention that just as Heller is the first novelist of the Chaos Age and Yossarian its first citizen, Adolf Hitler is arguably the last politician of the Age of Reason. Elected to office by a reasonable political system, he applied reasonable methods—systematic plans and perk charts—to an unreasonable outcome. That, too, is history.)

In this section, we take up the search for meaning—the connections that these converging rivers of change are forging, the broad outcomes they are driving to, and, finally, what to do about it, including specific skills and strategies needed to thrive in the Chaos Age. But we begin where any quest for meaning has to begin—not with the search, but with the searcher.

1

Cultural Schizophrenia and the Noble Truth of Pain

At the outset of this book, we asked you to find yourself in the story of the uneasy sleeper lying in bed in the middle of the night, toting up the balance sheet of his or her professional and personal life. An employee, you may recall, had come in the afternoon before, bearing a $1 million contract. To deliver it, she was demanding a 10-percent commission. There was worry about the house or condo, the career ladder or lack of same, a son or daughter, a younger brother or sister. Love pure and simple existed between our uneasy sleeper and his or her significant other, and tension pure and simple crusted the relationship. A five-year plan needed doing; a $15 million proposal sat on the desk, waiting approval. The salary pool was too shallow to water all the best people. Worse, the business itself seemed too perilous. Change was washing at its base, threatening to topple the whole structure.

Now we ask you to find yourself in that same person's next day: *Noon.*

The worst ones stay, you are telling yourself. The best ones go. By sliding your chair over to the far right of your desk, you can just see the security guard hovering as your brilliant thirty-three-year-old systems analyst clears out her desk. Except she is not "yours" anymore. She came to you an hour ago to announce that she was leaving. You asked where she was going. She answered: your biggest competitor. Company policy is very clear on this issue. She waits in your office; you call security; security gives her two hours to pack up her personal possessions, sign the appropriate exit forms, and drive out of the parking lot, never to return again. While you were waiting for the guard to arrive, you made small talk: Why was she leaving? The answer both surprised and didn't surprise you: Because. Because movement seems built into her. Because she never really saw herself as part of the company. Because, you now understand, she was always a kind of insular pod within the larger pod of the business, was always really working for herself, not for you. Now you ask yourself: Is that why she was so good?

She turns—a last look in your direction, a last nod. Instead of responding, you slide your chair back to the middle of your desk and stare at the stacks of paper there. The whimsical clock on the edge of your desk—fire-engine red, with oversized hands—reads 12:12.

12:12.

Paper stack A: the departments' input for the five-year plan. All the bulls in all the world, you tell yourself, could not defecate enough to fill up this five-year plan. The variables embedded in one department's input flatly contradict the variables embedded in another department's input. Where they don't contradict them, they subvert them. And where they don't contradict or subvert them, they are simply inane. Perhaps this is how people come to religion, because no chain of predictable causality, nothing short of a leap of faith, can get your division where you know it has to go.

Paper stack B: the $15 million proposal. It now seems to you to have been printed on ancient papyrus. You are afraid that if you pick it up, it will crumble in your hands, turn to dust. You are afraid that in your assiduous attention to the parts of the proposal, you have missed the whole, that you have let yourself drown once again in detail.

A comforting thought: Now that your systems analyst is leaving, you will have enough money in the salary pool to keep your management information director.

A discomforting thought: Does the fact that your management

information director is willing to stay for more money mean that he is not as valuable as you thought he was?

A further discomforting thought: Accounting is not on your side any longer. Accounting yelled at you this morning when you ordered it to cut a $100,000 commission check on the $1 million contract you now have locked in your top drawer. We do not pay commissions to employees, accounting had screamed. We do now, you informed them. And then to appease accounting, you had mentioned that as of the close of business tomorrow, the employee for whom they were to cut the $100,000 check would no longer be working for your company. You have struck at best an uneasy peace.

12:42.

The phone. Your secretary informs you that your son or daughter's school is on the line. The school, in turn, informs you that your son or daughter has been caught smoking marijuana in the woods behind the gym. Somebody will have to come and get your child immediately and take him or her home. The assistant headmaster will be meeting with the parents of all the sons and daughters involved in the incident at 8:30 tomorrow morning.

Is it your turn to deal with this? Or is it your significant other's turn? Whose time is more valuable? Who will demand less in retribution for having dealt with it? How is it that a child so smart, so handsome, so lovely can make such terrible choices?

Someone will be there, you inform the school. Someone will be there soon. How would it look to send a cab to pick up your son or daughter after such an event? Would it be an indication of your displeasure? Or of your lack of engagement? You instruct your secretary to dial your significant other.

12:50.

Finally, you. More and more, it comes to you that the business you labor so mightily for, the product you have worked so hard to put on the bubble, the bleeding-fringe service your company exists to provide, will soon be dead meat, road kill on the autobahn of change. Your grandfather worked a lifetime in the service of his own entity— his farm, his store, his garage. You father spent a lifetime in the service of a single corporate entity. Was he happy? You have your doubts. Was he secure? That and more. He worked. He rose. His career flattened off and he coasted. Then he retired, and when he did, there was a steady enough stream of income arriving from his former employer and the federal government that both he and your mother could golf happily into their golden years.

And you? If this is income security, if this is job security, if this is career security, you would hate to meet their opposites. If this is happiness, too, you wonder how awful sadness might be, but that is not to say that you have given up on the latter, because somewhere you sense a great deal of happiness awaiting you if only you can find your way there.

Congratulations. In the midst of your pain, you have arrived at the beginning of wisdom. Now go pick up the kid.

The Noble Truth of the Cause of Pain

The above, we acknowledge, is not *Catch-22*, certainly not in its prose and not in its drama, but today, every working life, every personal life, assumes some of the chaos of warfare. Like Yossarian, we all exist today in a double-bound world. The rules we were taught to live by no longer apply. We are entrusted to manage assets in a world in which direction is impossible to figure out. Lines of demarcation have disappeared. Discriminators don't discriminate. Variables are everywhere, and the balls are changing colors constantly.

We could cite one hundred reasons why this is the best of times. As we write, the stock market is in the stratosphere compared to a decade ago; there's no more mutually assured destruction, at least for the moment; everyone is living longer. Leave aside the promises of genetic engineering; what has happened in standard medicine in recent years is astounding enough in its own right. Many Parkinson's disease victims can have their flailing and rigidity allayed by a pallidotomy—a procedure in which holes are drilled in the skull and, while the patient is awake, minute areas of the brain are killed by laser beam. Two decades ago, prostate surgeons had to operate almost by touch in a sea of blood. Today, many prostate cancer victims can have their malignant gland removed and return to virtually normal sexual lives. Only three decades have passed since the first artificial and human hearts were transplanted—by Michael DeBakey in Houston and Christiaan Barnard in South Africa. Today, organ transplants of all sorts, from livers to eyes, are approaching the commonplace, and thanks to pharmaceutical advancements, the chances of rejection have been dramatically reduced.

Microbreweries have restored taste to the humble beer; fruits and vegetables once available only seasonally are now available at the supermarket year-round; driving is safer; cars are better; cable TV and satellite dishes have made every den a true home entertainment center. Jupiter's moons have been mapped. We've toured the neighborhoods of Uranus and Neptune with the incredibly durable Voyager space probe.

We could cite all that and more, and if you are like most people, you could cite one powerful reason in return why our optimism is pure hooey: You don't feel optimistic. Instead, you feel anxious, tense, scared of what the future holds. Therein lies the greatest double bind of all.

Not long ago, we heard a guest minister preach at a Unitarian church in the Northeast.

"It's interesting to come here today," he began his sermon, "because I'm always struck by the fact that we live in the most affluent times in history. In fact, we live in the most affluent country in the most affluent times in history, and right now I'm in the most affluent state in the most affluent country in the most affluent times in history. And not only that, I'm in the most affluent county and the most affluent community in the most affluent state in the most affluent country in the most affluent times in history." (There was a slight exaggeration there, but the point was nearly accurate.)

He paused briefly to let his premise sink in, and then got to the kicker: "How come," he said, "you feel so bad. Why don't you feel good? You have got everything they said was going to be good."

Being a Unitarian, he couldn't follow his text to too religious a conclusion. (Joke: What do you get when you cross a Unitarian and a Jehovah's Witness? Someone who knocks on your door on Saturday morning for no particular reason.) And since his full-time job was to run a church-supported homeless shelter, he had his own prejudices about why the affluent are rich in everything but contentment. But without meaning to impugn his message, we believe something far larger is at stake. We believe that we are living in an era characterized by dis-ease, discontentment, and anxiety precisely because we have arrived historically where we have: at the 500-year delta, at the end of five-century-long experiment with reason as the controlling force of logic, at the breakup of consumer markets and economic relationships as we have known them, at the breakup of a pattern of social organization far older than consumer markets or the regency of reason. As we mentioned earlier, we call this condition "cultural schizophrenia." Before we get to it, though, a word about definitions.

No word describing a specific psychobiological condition may be more abused than "schizophrenia." It does not mean "split personality," although it is commonly used that way. Nor, despite what romantics of the mentally ill might contend, is there any deeper insight into the true nature of the world inherent in the condition. The movie *King of Hearts* may have painted the schizophrenic inmates of the asylum as the only sane people, but real schizophrenics hear voices, not insights. They suffer crippling delusions, not blinding illuminations.

We once asked a man who had been diagnosed with clinical schizophrenia for almost twenty years what his strongest sensation was. "Anxiety," he answered. "Constant anxiety." Why, we asked. "Well," he said, "for example, when I go outside at night and see the stars, I think they're all spaceships, part of an intergalactic fleet, and that they are looking at me for direction. If I turn left, they go left with me. If I go right, they go right. If I make a mistake and go the wrong way, they'll make a mistake and go the wrong way, too. And who knows what would happen to the Universe then?" His medication happened to be right on the money at the time—he could talk about his condition coherently. A few weeks later, we asked a woman on a park bench—a woman who had been "deinstitutionalized" years earlier and was far removed from her medication—to tell us about her condition. "I'm really a man," she explained. "My penis was cut off when I was three by some boys who were jealous of how big it was."

That is the real voice of schizophrenia, and we mean no disrespect to it, either. But something similar and far broader, if far less individually horrible, is going on in society at large. Caught between reason and chaos, we do hear voices, and they carry contradictory messages. Trapped between past and future, we suffer delusions—the myths of family, government, nations, business, and even reality. With one foot, we cling to the comfort world of what has been—loyalty, nationalism, career. With the other, we step hesitantly into what is to be—individualism, globalism, a working life spent deal to deal. And straddling both worlds, the lure of each is equally strong.

We grasp at so-called "paradigms" to explain the new world, and as each new paradigm proves inadequate, we feel more and more pinned. Meanwhile, as society unconsciously reinvents itself, as it unwittingly redefines how it is going to conduct its affairs in the future, our attitudes and behaviors move in disparate directions, and in the disconnection between the two lies the fountainhead of our ambient anxiety.

Why do most people have it so good and feel so bad? Because most people today have an expectation of the world at variance with the way the world actually operates. Why do most people today feel such anxiety? Because most people today know in their bones that this disconnection exists.

The bad news we bring is this: There is no way to avoid this anxiety, no way to avoid feeling this pain, because everything that is causing you to feel the anxiety is real. The good news we bring is that this anxiety is your own best friend.

The Noble Truth of the Cessation of Pain

Whole businesses, large tomes, enough psychotherapy groups to populate a large island have been built around the premise that anxiety needs to be eliminated from our lives. We don't argue that anxiety is good for you—it is, in fact, the silent killer of our times, and when it compounds upon itself, it can become as debilitating as schizophrenia, if not so absolutely bizarre in its most profound symptoms. We argue instead that when you can't depend on institutions as you have known them, when you can't depend on relationships, when converging rivers of change are rushing forward into a new world, and when uneasiness, chaos, and disharmonious conjunctions have become the organizing principles driving those rivers of change, anxiety is simply unavoidable. And we further argue that the larger part of our cultural schizophrenia—of this disconnection between attitudes and behaviors—comes not from the onrush of change, but from the fact that we are being programmed to avoid anxiety at the same time we are coming to intuitively understand that we must embrace anxiety to survive.

There's a lesson in the longest times of history. "Lucy," the theoretical "first hominid mother" that Don Johanson discovered at Hadar in Ethiopia in November 1974, has survived through some 15,000 generations of offspring not through sheer luck—although luck is always part of evolution—but because each of those 15,000 generations in their own way learned to use its anxiety to survive. Anxiety is transformed from generation to generation—from fear of saber-toothed tigers to fear of ax-wielding Huns to fear of ax-wielding CEOs—but whatever shape it takes, anxiety is a useful emotional predisposition. Judged reasonably, the ambient anxiety of our time may seem a failing; judged evolutionarily, it is just right.

What do you find when you embrace anxiety? That it turns to enlightenment. And what does enlightened anxiety bring you? The $15 million contract your proposal seeks, maybe. A good night's sleep, in any event, because in the midst of all the ambient gloom and doom you find that there really is a better world out there.

To fight anxiety is the same as fighting a war on crime. You can't get rid of crime—crime exists. To complain about crime is like complaining that rocks are too hard. All you can do is to recognize the most critical variables with relation to crime and you. You can arm your children with sensible strategies about crime—don't get in cars with strangers, beware of people who want to talk about sex on the Internet—and arm yourself with sensible strategies, too: *no* ATMs after dark. You can decide whether to buy a weapon, and if you do, you can take all the precautions to learn to use it properly. But crime itself is immutable. You can only affect it as it is most likely to affect you.

So it is with anxiety: The millions of inconsistencies that confront you in any workweek are immutable, too. You can't stop them from happening—inconsistencies are in the nature of chaos—all you can do is stop them from controlling you. Enlightened anxiety doesn't mean that you ignore problems or that you worry over them at random. It means that you allow problems to take their course and do the best that you can within them. It means that you recognize that there are enormous numbers of things in your personal and professional life over which you have no control, no ability to effect an outcome, and that you recognize further that there is great liberation in having no control over them. It means that you stay permanently flexible, because it is only by being so that you can achieve synchronicity with a world that has itself entered into a state of permanent flexibility, a world that is being subtly and meaningfully altered every single day. Here's the real secret of successful people and businesses: They are different every day of their existence.

Think of yourself on a Los Angeles freeway at rush hour. To exercise control over your own car is a lifetime's work; to try to exercise control over every other car on the freeway will leave you as hamstrung as the clinical schizophrenic we mentioned earlier who thought he was directing the intergalactic space fleet. As millions of Los Angeles commuters have learned over the years, the only way to survive in the chaos of the freeway system is to learn to swim with it. So it is, too, with life in the chaos world.

To return to our uneasy office worker, what does enlightened anxiety teach him or her? That perhaps he can exercise influence on his daughter's or son's behavior, but not on the behavior of his or her friends. That perhaps she can uncrust the tension in her damaged marriage, but only by uncrusting the tension in herself because, finally, she is the only critical variable in the equation over which she has control. That the departure of the brilliant thirty-three-year-old systems analyst may be a loss, but that the loss is inherent in the nature of the modern corporation, where no loyalty is to be expected or given. That the only way to get the $15 million proposal right is to have focused on the outcome and let the parts arrange themselves in that service. That if he or she has done all that, happiness is not such a far-fetched concept. Pretend you are in the movie *Groundhog Day*. Reset the clock to the day before. Like Bill Murray, do it again and again and again until you get it right. Humans, after all, are meant to learn.

The bottom line: Accept chaos for what it is. Slip into it. Drift with it. Have some fun. Remember: The only person in charge of you anymore is you. If you've made the choices you've made based on your own internalized set of values, they'll be the right choices, whether they are right or wrong.

The Noble Truth of the Path That Leads to the Cessation of Pain

Throughout this section, we've used subheads drawn from the Four Noble Truths of Buddhism. The last of the Noble Truths leads to the Eightfold Path, which leads, in turn, to overcoming pain. These, the Buddha taught in his first sermon—known as "Turning the Wheel of Doctrine"—are the elements of that Eightfold Path:

> Right View
> Right Thought
> Right Action
> Right Speech
> Right Effort
> Right Livelihood
> Right Mindfulness
> Right Concentration

And these are what we take up in the next chapters of this section. The path that leads to the cessation of pain is the path that leads you to see the world as it truly is.

2

Right View: Fusion

Fusion food means many things, from Vietnamese cuisine—a fusion of Southeast Asian ingredients and French cooking techniques—to, in its more primitive form, the cross-border Tex-Mex style taco, tamale, and fajita. It is fusion food that drives the popularity of lemongrass as a seasoning in Western dishes; fusion food that has created all the chic Asian-American food boutiques that hug the Southern California coastline; fusion food in its broadest sense that lies behind a new line of drinks being developed by the Pepsi-Lipton partnership—bottled iced-teas flavored with exotic Eastern flavors—because culinary borders have fallen along with national ones.

Fusion food reached one of its most tortured expressions in the concoction of a trendy little restaurant called Bilbo Baggins in the Old Town section of Alexandria, Virginia, across the Potomac River from the nation's capital: Veal Viennois New Orleans Style with Japanese Bread Crumbs, a dish that leaps two oceans, joins three continents, and, by using veal as its base, even manages to offend animal-rights activists in the bargain.

But the ultimate fusion food is something far more humble:

Nabisco's lowly Ritz-Bits, those bite-size cracker snacks filled with peanut butter or cheese. Why? Because Ritz-Bits fuse things that matter. Nabisco took a product of the comfort world, a food item steeped in the lore of leisurely kitchen snacks, and turned it into a product for the anxiety world—hand, bag, mouth; hand, bag, mouth—without sacrificing any of the texture, taste, or even name. In effect, Ritz miniaturized itself literally to merge with a world in which time has become figuratively compressed and miniaturized as well. And thus Ritz Bits fused nostalgia with utility to create authenticity. Not surprisingly, it is now the engine that drives the entire Nabisco food business.

Hostess, we should point out, wasn't quite so successful when it rolled out its new Twinkies Lite. Twinkies Lite was meant to merge nostalgia with the health-and-fitness movement by substituting a low-calorie cream-and-sugar filling for the heavy-as-lead filling of the traditional Twinkie. But there was a problem, and it wasn't just that the health-and-fitness movement was already on its last legs, although that didn't help. The real problem was that nobody ever picked up a Twinkies for anything other than that heavy-as-lead filling. The name itself promised the filling. And thus Twinkies Lite was an oxymoron without authenticity—the balls weren't the same color when they met—and an expensive one at that.

Think of Twinkies Lite as fission, and Ritz-Bits as fusion.

A-bombs and H-bombs

It was the fission capacity of change that led Alvin Toffler in *The Third Wave*, published in 1980, to despair. Change was coming too quickly, on too many fronts. It could be neither contained nor absorbed. In effect, what Toffler saw happening was the same thing that produced the first controlled release of atomic energy on December 2, 1942, in a uranium-and-graphite pile thrown together in an underground squash court at the University of Chicago: nuclear fission—the fruit of Enrico Fermi and General Leslie Grove's supersecret Manhattan Project and the forerunner of the atomic bomb that two-and-a-half years later would be used to devastate Hiroshima, Japan. As happens in nuclear fission, where energy is created by splitting apart the large nuclei of atoms (*fission* and *fissure* share the same Latin root), so society under the pressure of accelerating change would explode into fragments.

We look out on the same landscape with eyes strongly influenced by Alvin Toffler's works, we study economic and social organizations, we see them being particalized, and we are convinced that something entirely different is being created from this process. Our model is fusion, not fission. Our metaphor is not a rending apart, but a convergence toward the center. As in nuclear fusion—the principle of the hydrogen bomb, not the atomic bomb—we see the small nuclei of all these swirling atoms of change being merged into a single mass, a mass that will be converted into enormous energy.

When these convergences of change take place within individuals—when the nuclei of these atoms of change fuse internally—enormous energy is available for consumption there, too. We look out on this acceleration of change, this staggering accumulation of change, and we see people massively empowered, not massively enfeebled, by their connectivity.

In fact, the evidence of fusion is nearly everywhere. Let us provide a checklist here of the most important examples:

- **The fusion of East and West.**
  Too much, we grant, has been made of this in some ways. The Easternized Western world that seemed such a sure thing two-and-a-half decades ago—a world in which Nehru jackets were *de rigueur* at Carnegie Hall, sitar music blared out of elevator speakers, and a quoting familiarity with Herman Hesse's *Siddhartha* was the baseline for being taken seriously—never arrived. Turned out, the vision had more to do with good dope than good fusion, which is why every kid today is not a "Karate Kid."

  The East may have the people, grouped primarily in two highly unstable political entities. Driven by population, the East may even soon have the bulk of the global purchasing power. The World Bank projects that by the year 2020, seven of the ten largest national economies—China, Japan, India, Indonesia, South Korea, Thailand, and Taiwan—will lie on the far side of the Pacific, with only the United States, Germany, and France representing the Old World economic order, and that China will be by far the largest economy globally. But the West has the vast bulk of economic firepower and business know-how, and will till the cows come home.

If fusion hasn't turned into absorption, as was once predicted, fusion between East and West has happened all the same. The most commonly spoken language in Vancouver today? It's Cantonese. Ride down the Kennedy Freeway in Chicago and you can see a billboard advertisement in Japanese. Go to the dining room of any major business hotel on the East Coast, from Miami to Boston, and you'll find a Japanese breakfast on the menu. Karaoke bars are fusion entertainment, and thanks to the globalization of Western rock, the same songs are performed in them globally.

The fusion foods we mentioned earlier are evidence of both the fact of fusion and of the way in which it occurs. Like values, elements from different cuisines are transformed in the process of creating fusion foods, but one doesn't replace or absorb the other. They fit tongue-and-groove together.

What is true of foods, by the way, is equally true of cultural products. The DreamWorks studio has been developing ideas for made-for-TV movies that would fuse the traditional Eastern journey inward with the traditional Western quest for manifest destiny. Why? Because if University of Nebraska undergraduates and twenty- and thirtysomethings across the Rust and Bible belts aren't walking around reading Lao-tzu, the Tibetan Book of the Dead, and the Upanishads, they have at least been infected by the language of Eastern mysticism. The New Age has made it part of their daily vocabulary. Alternative medical practices borrowed from the East—and transformed by Western values— have become part of their private regimens. For many people, too, the abiding theism of the Western world seems simply inadequate to the modern condition. Eastern mysticism gives us at least a language equal to chaos, a language that largely rationalized Western religions lack.

It's the incomplete fusion of East and West that created the Ayatollah Ruholla Khomeini, led to the 444-day captivity in Teheran of fifty-two American hostages, and toppled the administration of Jimmy Carter. It's incomplete fusion that has led to European tourists being slaughtered in Cairo; incomplete fusion between rapidly Westernizing South Korea and feudally Eastern North Korea that gives us the periodic saber rattling from Pyongyang. Indeed, no force in the world has remained more resistant to fusion than the 38th parallel, which is why Pentagon planners have North Korea largely in mind when they insist that the U.S. military not be cut below a troop level that would allow it to fight simultaneously on two fronts. We suspect that parachuting a million laptops with extra battery packs and preinstalled Internet connections somewhere above the 38th parallel might do the trick, but this is not a treatise on international affairs, either.

To the extent that they are insensitive to the consequences of fusion within their own borders, Western democracies have the potential for incomplete fusion, too. Witness the 1993 bombing of New York's World Trade Center or the bombing of Pan Am's Flight 103 over Lockerbie, Scotland, in 1988. Indeed, terrorism may be the ultimate expression of chaos in the international political theater—the particalization of anger, revenge, and violent death.

The headlines go to collision, not fusion, but it is in many ways the true fusion points between East and West that have the most to teach and the greatest potential. Not long ago, the World Bank came forth with an innovative measure of future national wealth based not just on raw materials, production capacity, capital resources, and the like, but also including a new metric that we call "mental flexibility"—the capacity to move comfortably among different mind-sets, to absorb different cultural practices. The United States finished fifth in the world by this measure. Number one was a nation that has been for many years a Western gateway to the East and thus a fusion point between cultures: Australia.

In some ways, an even more interesting study was one that attempted to rank nations by the strength of connection between couples—their personal bond, their attitudes toward childbearing and toward sharing the responsibilities of family and marriage. At the absolute bottom of the list was Japan, an historically isolationist nation steeped in sexually feudalistic practices. Very near the bottom was China, only now being touched by outside influences. At the absolute top was another of those countries where East and West touch, a nation that has managed to fuse Western political values with those of the Islamic world: Turkey.

Where else is global fusion occurring? South Africa, where black Africa and the white West are finally conjoining. Argentina and Chile, where South America is fusing with Europe and North America. Thailand, another site where West and East are becoming one. In alpha cities like New York, Bombay, Sydney, Berlin (but not Paris), Seattle (but not Atlanta), Toronto—places where cultures swim into one another. Most dramatically, maybe, from one end of the Old

World to the other in the European Community, an almost unimaginable pulling together after centuries of warfare and potentially an astounding economic engine. Fusion creates energy. Energy feeds values. Energy plus values creates wealth.

- **The fusion of men and women.**

  Too much can be made of this as well. Gender still counts. There still is a glass ceiling, although it thins out day by day. The Indians and the Chinese, 40 percent of the world's population, will not soon stop aborting many, many more female fetuses than male ones. Cultural practices don't crumble overnight, or necessarily over centuries. To the extent that it ever achieves anything close to a parity of sexes, the U.S. Army will continue to favor males for trenching and ditch digging. Genetically determined musculature counts, too. But if the genders remain separate, the roles of men and women in relationships have fused dramatically, and where economic initiative is concerned, they have even swung over to the woman's side.

  In less than a generation, women in middle- and upper-class households have assumed responsibility for managing the children's education; managing household purchasing, and doing it far more effectively than men, on a just-in-time inventory basis; managing a stream of household help that includes not just cleaning people, but a nearly continuous stream of baby-sitters, plumbers, electricians, yard workers, and more; managing the maintenance schedules of the family cars; and—a fact learned too slowly by many auto manufacturers—deciding which cars come home from the showroom.

  Three in four of all cars bought today are either purchased by women or purchased with their permission. That's why Ford introduced a "tall" sports utility vehicle called the Expedition—an SUV that sits high on the road, has the option of four-wheel drive, but has "majesty" as well. Men may want a sort of everyman's Humvee they can ride to war or up the Himalayas, but women want a car, not a glorified combination of Jeep, tank, and truck.

- **The fusion of time.**

  Some once upon a times: Once upon a time, there were luxury liners, trains had nice sleepers and clean windows for taking in the vista, planes celebrated the comforts—food, drink, little packages of cigarettes—they provided you with to make your trip as enjoyable as possible. Now luxury liners have largely disappeared except for those that cater to retirees, passenger trains are mostly on the dole, and airlines, instead of celebrating their comforts, celebrate their capacity to minimize the anxiety caused by the length of time it takes you to get where you are going. The moral: No matter how fast a plane goes today, it isn't fast enough.

Once upon a time, there was room in the day for long walks, speed golf had not yet been invented, good health was accrued by taking the steps instead of the elevator. Today, eating and health maintenance have been fused into health-food snacks. Bag, hand, mouth; faster, faster, faster.

Once upon a time in the very near past, stock traders would use satellite communications to process your order. Today, the time to uplink and download is too great. One second out, one second back, and two seconds collectively lose their edge.

A last once upon a time: Once upon a time, you could live in three tenses—the past, the present, and future. There was time to consult history; there was time to plan for what lay ahead. The present tense was spent managing the transfer of the past into the future and imagining what that future might be. Today, under the pressure of accelerating change, the past and future have been fused into a single tense: the present. The present is real time and real time is the only time.

• **The fusion of economic models.**
We've mentioned a number of these already: the fusion of economics and biology into a new model that treats the economy like an ecosystem because it is only through the metaphor of an ecosystem that one can begin to understand an economy in which billions of variables interact continuously; the fusion of the four economic relationships—competitive, symbiotic, predatory, and parasitic—into a single economic relationship that is all four at once. For more on the latter, see the joint venture between Fuji and Kodak to manufacture film, the joint venture between Toyota and General Motors to manufacture cars, the joint venture between Sony and Philips to produce digital compact-disc storage. The list could go on and on. We repeat it here only because it is so important: Nothing is as simple today as you versus me, you and me, you or me.

But a final economic fusion needs to be mentioned as well: the fusion of wealth and ideas. The socialized capitalism that grew up in the Western world was never pure capitalism, but its name was at least largely accurate: It depended on the preexistence of capital for the formulation of wealth. Labor demanded it, production costs demanded it; there was job security to be provided because, to a greater or lesser degree, loyalty was demanded and rewarded. Because capital was the starting point, capital begat capital, and capital created wealth. You couldn't get into the game without oodles of the stuff. Today, those relationships simply don't exist. Start-up costs for most new businesses are relatively small. The vision, the imagination, the intellectual property of the entrepreneur who stands behind the start-up is far more important today to the formation of wealth than the simple presence or absence of capital.

On the day it was first offered for sale in November 1993, the stock of Boston Chicken jumped 143 percent in value. Why? Not because the company had an alluring track record—it had yet to earn its first annual profit. And not because Boston Chicken controlled the production, processing, and distribution of poultry products. But simply because the market believed company CEO Scott Beck had a better idea about how to sell cooked chickens. Netscape got $2.2 billion on the first day of its initial public stock offering. Why? Not because it controlled the World Wide Web or the hardware required to access it, but simply because the market believed Netscape had a better idea about how to browse the Web's white noise of data.

It is this fusion of ideas and wealth that will continue to keep the United States on top of the world economic ladder. About one in twenty people in the world are U.S. citizens, but according to the National Science Foundation, better than one in three articles published in scientific journals globally—the raw material of innovation—are written by American scientists. Today, money goes to ideas, to intellectual property, to imagination. Fusion creates the energy. The energy frees.

The Fusion Game

Play another game with us. Take any two words and try to join them. If the words create fusion, the shared meaning created by the connection will be immediately grasped, and the new phrase itself will have greater energy than either word can have individually. If the words create fission, the new shared meaning will be splintered, and the energy dissipated.

Twinkies Lite? Fission, as we said. Miller Lite? Fusion. Why? Part of the reason is subject to explanation: Twinkies was lightening the best part of its food package; Miller lightened the calories, but kept the alcoholic punch constant. No one misses the calories; everyone would have missed the punch. Part, though, is non-sense—not nonsense, but non-sense. It's not subject to rational explanation, it just works.

Cyberpunk? Cybernaut? Fission or fusion? We would maintain fusion in the former and fission in the latter. Why? The combination of a computer and a rebel—a cyberpunk—resonates just as Web "wrebel" resonates; it conjures up a picture that is immediately grasped. Cybernaut? Space suits and microchips? What's a cybernaut look like, feel like, talk like? There's no there there, and when there's no there there, no energy can be created.

Safe sex, surrogate mothers, smart bombs (and that explosive ice-cream treat Smart Bombe), hot wax, minivan—they all fuse. California roll is a great fusion term, too, as well as a great fusion food. It doesn't mention sushi; it isn't even sold in Japan; but in the United States it *is* sushi because, both as word and food item, it fuses East and West. And thus, by blending culture and ideas into a single entity, it achieves convergence.

Products fuse or fiss as well. In the late 1980s, Volvo took a hard look at its position in the auto industry and found that it had been branded the "safe car." What to do? In Volvo's case, the wrong thing. The company launched its new luxury-oriented 850 series with a marketing campaign that emphasized the performance characteristics of the car over the safety characteristics, and the car sat in Volvo showrooms, gathering ever thicker layers of dust. Why? Not because Volvo looked at the wrong set of data—it *was* the safety car—but because it created a car model that exceeded what loyal customers would allow. A sexy Volvo, a fast Volvo, defused what Volvo stood for. It decoupled the name from safety and thus created fission. A safe Volvo fuses. It's tied to the long history of the brand, and brands are destiny as well as identification.

Disney learned about another face of fission when it located its European theme park outside of Paris. Disney is what it is—fun, fun, fun—and Parisians and the French generally are what they are, and never the twain shall meet. Fission. Disney in Japan? Fusion, straight and simple. Ditto for Lexus, for different reasons. The marketplace never would have accepted a luxury Toyota—the phrase itself is as fissionable as Twinkies Lite—but a luxury car built with Japanese know-how that never mentions its parentage is a different matter. It's a lesson that Mazda, which named its luxury 929-series entrant after itself, was painfully slow to learn.

Vacations and learning, funerals and occasions, adventure and business all have tremendous fusion power as the century draws to a close, because all of them conjoin activities in a time-crunched world. The refusion of hospitals and service would have great energy, too, if anyone could figure out how to do it. PC's and TV's, a long-predicted merger, may prove to be fusion or fission. Will the PC-TV combine the energies of both media? Or will they offend the enthusiast marketplace for both? We confess to not having a clue how it will work out.

Where else does fusion occur? In crimes, for one place, because in an instantaneously connected world, it is possible for a single crime to become an alpha crime, a crime that so fuses with social reality that it defines the category for years and years to come. Examples? Charles Manson, the alpha criminal of mass murderers, even though as mass murders go, the eight deaths he was responsible for are pretty tame fare. The bombing of Pan Am Flight 103 over Lockerbie, Scotland, the alpha crime of international terrorism. The beating of Rodney King by Los Angeles police officers, which so connected to the perceived social reality of black Americans that it became the alpha racial crime of our times. Michael Milken, the alpha criminal of financiers, who has been sent to global pillory and will neither be pardoned for the fact that he has prostate cancer nor allowed to atone no matter how much money he raises to fight the disease.

Maybe most notably, fusion occurs (or fails to occur) in advertising. We could cite hundreds of examples of advertisements where slogan and product fused to create vast energy, and hundreds more where the two split to create fragmentation of both message and image. Instead, let us cite just one of each and encourage you to page through your favorite magazine and judge the ads there for yourself.

Fission: Chrysler and "What's New in Your World?" The answer is self-evident—everything—and because it is, the ad does nothing to discriminate Chrysler and its products from the universe of auto choices.

Fusion: Breitling watches and "Instruments for Professionals," always against a background of a jet-plane cockpit. In a world in which everyone is going faster per unit of time than they ever went before, it only makes sense to track the passage of minutes with the watch of the people who go the fastest of all.

Managing Fusion

Fusion does more than create businesses. The job of any business today is fusion itself. It is to incorporate particalized identities, particalized positions, particalized points of view into a coherent whole so that it can compete in a particalized marketplace.

We've sat in corporate meetings, and you probably have as well, where the Christian Coalition caucus proposed opening with a prayer, where the women's caucus wanted to shift the whole thrust of the gathering to fair-employment issues, where the middle-aged-men's caucus wanted to shift the whole thrust to protecting themselves under those fair-employment practices. We've sat in other corporate meetings, you have, too, where there was not a single shred of interest in the business at hand because, today, it is not in anyone's inherent interest to be in a corporation. Corporations frustrate the four freedoms by their very nature. No matter how deftly they are handled, they limit the right to know, to go, to do, and to be.

How, then, do you create fusion in businesses that by their very nature have to be governed by the consent of the governed? How do you harness the energy created by fusion and bind it to an outcome? Three ways: by having a commitment, by making the commitment the entire core of your business, and by binding your employees to that core commitment.

Great businesses are businesses that have at their heart an entrepreneur whose long-term objective is everyone's objective. He could be dead—

Thomas Edison is, in the case of General Electric, and so is Walt Disney—but the founding entrepreneur's objective lives on in the business through thick and thin. Great businesses also make that objective the entire core of their existence. They fuse their businesses to the core, which is why diffusion—read, decentralization—is the wrong model for the Age of Chaos. To decentralize is to succumb to "macronomia"—the feelings of disgust and normlessness that large organizations often experience with their own size. The feelings are wholly understandable, but to give in to them is to admit you have no core, and without a core there can be no fusion. Eliminate instead the number of things you do. Downsize by activities that are not relevant to the center of the business so you can focus on that center. Instead of constructing a confederacy, practice value-based management. Take whatever values are inherent in the history of the company, declare them to be incontrovertible truths, and let those truths direct and manage the daily activities of the enterprise. That way, everybody sings from the same hymnal, no matter how diverse their voices might be.

And finally, great businesses find a way to fuse their core commitment with their employees' core commitment. How did Levi Strauss do that? Ingeniously. It told its employees that if the company achieves its cash-flow objectives for the year 2001, every worker will get a bonus check equal to his or her yearly salary—in Levi Strauss's case, an average of $25,000 a worker.

Do all that, and you liberate energy to focus on what the business has to do right. Do that, and the fusion produced by the convergence of change creates what it should create: enormous energy, energy that can be harvested. Do that and you win.

Homophyly

One more fusion element needs mentioning. We've noted before that one of the abiding ironies of the Age of Access is that as society drives toward total connection, it drives equally toward total individuation. Here's another abiding irony: As people drive toward individualized realities, they also grow more and more like one another. As borders become infinitely permeable, as national identities fuse into a single global identity, the ability to differentiate cultures becomes increasingly difficult.

What are we constantly told is one of the great cultural distinctions between the United States and Japan these days? The size of houses—ours are bigger than theirs. And how big a cultural differentiation is that? Teeny. As cultural differences disappear, language differences disappear, too. In the last twenty years alone, something like half the world's languages—3,000 of what two decades ago were 6,000 distinct tongues—have simply vanished, dropped off the face of the Earth. Meanwhile, English becomes more and more the global language of commerce, not just because the United States remains the world's economic superpower, but because, as the most hybrid of all major languages, English has the greatest capacity to absorb and fuse the useful remnants of dying tongues. And as connectivity spreads, as borders disappear, as language merges into a single tongue, aspirations—to own, to believe, to participate—fuse into a single aspiration as well, and consensus materialism is born. People globally want the same things; they define middle-class status by the same possessions. Instead of xenophobics, we are more and more "Xerophilics," in love with copying, and happily for us, more and more everything is able to be copied. The media may segment us into communes, a desire to belong may impel us toward the comforts of a tribe, but people line up for Big Macs and Cokes as eagerly in Moscow, Russia, as they do in Moscow, Idaho.

Biologically, there's a name for all this: homophyly, the tendency of life-forms when touching to assume the properties of each other. Figuratively, homophyly has much to teach business. It says that single global branding is the key to the future for both offensive and defensive reasons: offensively, because consensus materialism has turned the globe into a single marketplace and you have to treat it as such, and defensively, because as customers themselves slide easily over and through borders, they will become more and more aware of different messages sent by your product to different cultures and the discrepancy will inevitably appear to be pandering.

Coke is globalized—it sends a single message with a single set of design parameters to every corner of the world. So do Mercedes and Marlboro and Colgate. Lever Brothers is not globalized, because the company still believes that cleanliness and hygiene standards are highly regionalized. Our advice: Change or die. Homophyly also teaches that the Arthur Andersen global compensation model is the key to the future as well: one pay scale, no matter what office around the world you run or work in; one set of global work standards; one global commitment; one motto. In Arthur Andersen's case, that motto happens to be "One firm, one voice"—a nearly perfect expression for a homophylous world.

What else does homophyly mean for brands? That they need shelf-determinism: They have to remain the same from culture to culture, yet allow themselves to be defined differently by whatever microculture's shelf they happen to be sitting on. They have to sit under a message that communicates globally-distributed values—quality, aggressiveness, fun, adventure, whatever the values might be—yet is supple enough to not get in the way of individual microcultural interpretations.

When Hewlett-Packard sells a printer to the office environment, it's selling a printer that's fast. When it sells a printer to the household, it's selling one that's fail-safe. And the proof that an HP printer is fail-safe? It works in offices. Same machine, same message differently interpreted by differing market segments with differing needs, circular reinforcement. Brilliant, in short.

And then there's the case of the Chevrolet Suburban—the official car of very large, very rosy-cheeked American families and the official car of the hajj, the pilgrimage to Mecca that every Muslim is expected to take at least once in a lifetime. Why the latter? Because the Imam of Mecca looked around at the terrible traffic jams that plague Mecca during the pilgrimages and declared that no car that is not as large or larger than a Chevy Suburban could come within ten miles of the city during the hajj. And there is only one car in the world that fits that definition: the Chevy Suburban. The result: Some 75,000 Suburbans a year are sold in Saudi Arabia. Same vehicle, different appeal to different cultural discriminators, and in the Islamic world, at least, a locked-up market.

Taken literally in its biological sense, homophyly may have a far more interesting lesson to teach. One of the most interesting theories of why the dinosaurs died out in such a geologically brief time frame has nothing to do with meteorites or environmental calamities, but rather with genetic calamity. Dinosaurs stopped differentiating themselves as species, so this theory goes, and instead kept defining themselves within species—that is, they stopped creating new species and became genetically more and more alike. Like the Romanoffs, they inbred, and with each successive generation, the species became weaker and weaker until finally it reached a critical point of massive collapse.

Could the same thing happen to the human species as the drive toward sameness leaches variation from the gene pool? It's a stretch, we admit, but perhaps only because such matters are so very hard to think about. It would certainly be the final and greatest irony of the Chaos Age: to have been empowered at its birth by fusion, not destroyed by fission, only to have the ultimate expression of fusion lead to its end. But the simple fact is that every great epoch contains from the very first the seed of its own destruction. That's how history cleans the boards.

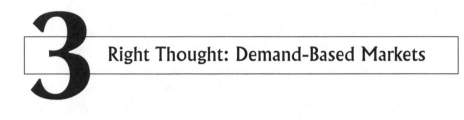

3 Right Thought: Demand-Based Markets

Take a look at the schematic below. It's one of several versions of a game known as Prisoner's Dilemma. (The game was patterned after a famous application of game theory by the same name, devised in 1950 by Stanford University professor Albert William Tucker to teach his students how individually rational choices can produce unwanted collective outcomes.)

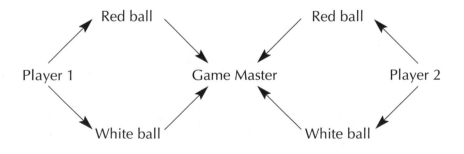

The game is played as follows: The game master in the middle passes his hat, and each player puts one of his balls into it without being able to see the color of the ball the other player has put in. The game master then checks his hat. If both of the balls are white, he gives each player a dollar. If both of the balls are red, each player has to give the game master a dollar. Easy enough to figure out. Both players keep putting white balls in, and very slowly they both get rich. Now here's the tricky part (and keep in mind that the red and white balls aren't identical—you can tell which ball belongs to whom): If the balls dropped into the hat on any round aren't the same color, the person who put the white ball in has to give the game master two dollars, and the person who put the red ball in gets two dollars from the game master. Let the game begin.

The fact is that it doesn't matter what culture you play Prisoner's Dilemma in. It doesn't matter whether the players are black, brown, yellow, red, or white. It doesn't matter whether the players are young, old, middle-aged, actual prisoners, Parisian boulevardiers, or boilermakers from Peoria, the results are always exactly the same. For the first eight or nine rounds, both players put nothing but white balls into the hat and collect their dollars from the game master. Before the tenth round, the first red ball shows up—one of the players wins two dollars and the other loses two dollars—and after that? Nothing but red balls. Boom, boom, boom. Dollar, dollar, dollar. And very slowly the game master gets rich instead. Why? Because greed eventually impels one of the players to drop in a red ball. And after the first red ball has been dropped, the players stop playing the game master and start playing each other. Prison guards—the game masters—use the game to break down camaraderie among prisoners, to set them against each other so the guards can control the prison population.

Guess what? The same thing has happened in the marketplace. So long as manufacturers and retailers played against the customer—so long as they dropped white ball after white ball into the hat and collected their dollars each round—the market surplus belonged collectively to them. But when they stopped playing against the customer and started playing against each other—through, for example, manufacturers turning to direct outlet stores to cut retailers out of the profit stream, or by retailers pressuring manufacturers for more and more concessions in order to secure shelf space—the customer suddenly began getting all the money.

What started this shift rolling? The intransigent greed of the Me Generation. Their ironclad determination to wring every penny out of the market equation for themselves put the first red ball in the hat. And it is the uncompromisingly greedy Me Generation that will pay the heaviest price. Just as guards consciously use Prisoner's Dilemma to control and discipline the prison population, so customers today unconsciously use the game to control and discipline the marketing equation—and the more they have been disciplined themselves, the more they will discipline in return.

The great illusion of the marketplace is a simple one: that it is supply-based; that those who produce and those who facilitate the transfer of product to the consumers' hands create and sustain the market; that if you build it, they will come. The great reality of the marketplace is simpler still: Nobody who produces is in control. Nobody who sells is in control. If you build it, they will come only if they want to, and if they decide to leave, there is nothing—not cutting your prices, not increasing your supply, not getting on your knees and begging for sales—that can stop them. When the world gets tired of cappuccino machines, they are *gone*.

The great reality of the marketplace is that it is demand-based. Customers own it lock, stock, and barrel.

Brand Latency, Customer Loyalty

When the market has become supersaturated with products, when customers have taken control of the marketing equation, how do you create and sustain a business? How do you put a product in the store and have it succeed? Two ways (and they are deeply intertwined): by fostering brand latency and by earning customer loyalty.

A question: If you were to be given the choice of being presented with (1) all the assets of the Coca-Cola Company, including the formulas for the drinks but not including the name, or (2) only the name, which would you take? Think hard about it, and if you picked (1), think seriously about a career in the arts. Why is the name Coca-Cola so valuable, more valuable than the entire assets of the company itself? Because Coca-Cola has brand latency. It has the implicit power to continue to sustain a market well into the future simply because it is what it is.

More questions: Would you take all the assets of Exxon minus the name, or the name Exxon itself? All the assets of Phillip Morris, or the name Phillip Morris itself? If you took the latter in either case, even a career in the arts might not be enough protection.

Great brands are more than just names. They are mission statements, they are value, they are language, they are even non-sense, because no rational explanation can wholly account for them. And they are all of this even when they are, or are supposed to be, inherently evil. A final question: Would you choose the Iraqi army without Saddam Hussein or the brand "Saddam Hussein" himself? History, in fact, has already answered that question.

Brands, in short, count. But in a world in which the cycle of innovation is being progressively crunched—a world of butterfly markets that grow, unfold, and die in what are comparatively nanoseconds; a world in which what is "in" is in for only a blink and what is "out" is out forever—brands alone cannot create customer loyalty. The only the thing that can create customer loyalty is loyalty itself. It is only by giving loyalty to your customers that you can get loyalty back in return, and it is only by recognizing that customers are under no obligation to give their loyalty that you can hold on to it day by day.

How do you prove your loyalty to customers? Not by pursuing customer loyalty, but by being loyal to your customers. In a customer-loyal world, your first concern is someone who purchased your product, not someone who might do so, because that customer with the product is now your best and cheapest billboard. In a customer-loyal world, you thank your customers, not in expectation of what they might do in the future, but for what they have done in the past. And in a customer-loyal world, you make your own value structure isomorphic with the value structure of your customer base. Build that, and loyal customers will come.

Prudential, to cite one example, will need decades to repair the damage done by its securities division, because Prudential has always portrayed itself as the Rock, and rocks don't lie. When Prudential brokers knowingly portrayed high-risk investments as financial instruments for widows and orphans—when they pocketed their commissions and, in effect, told their customers to like it or lump it—they were putting the first red ball in the hat. It is not the kind of insult customers forget, ever. TWA put its own red ball in the hat when it seemingly dragged its heels on releasing the passenger list from its Flight 800 that went down off the coast of Long Island on July 17, 1996. Whether it was listening to its own or its insurers' lawyers or simply involved in a colossal act of disaster mismanagement, TWA was acting in the past and future when its customers' families cared only about the present. Acting in real time is the only way to begin to repair the damage done by real tragedy.

To structure a business so that it meets its customers' real lives, make the ownership of a customer relationship a fundamental part of the creation of the business itself. The product matters, of course, but it matters less than customer loyalty. The brand matters, but it, too, matters less than customer loyalty. Products disappear, brands fall out of favor, and both happen in ever tighter cycles. All you can transfer from product to product, from brand to brand, is your customer's loyalty. And because your customer is under absolutely no obligation to be loyal to you, his or her loyalty is the most valuable commodity you can own. Scarcity creates value.

We limp along on many horrible economic metrics these days, because the science of measuring the economy has lagged years, perhaps decades, behind the reality of the economy. The Consumer Price Index, maybe the most ludicrous of all widely watched metrics, uses a market basket of goods and services that is changed every ten years. How many new services were developed in the past ten years? As the cycle of innovation closes, how many entire generations of products come and go in a decade? (Nine generations of personal computers during the ten years 1985–95, to be exact where one product is concerned.)

But no metric blinds us more to the true nature of the business world than the Standard Industrial Code's distinction between the manufacturing sector and the service sector. Making customer loyalty a central part of the creation of a business requires exactly the opposite. It requires recognizing from the first moment that no matter what you are making, no matter how brilliantly conceived your product is, no matter how fabulous a brand you create or how maximally efficient your delivery system is, you cannot possibly succeed unless you become, from the first moment, simultaneously a manufacturing and a service enterprise. Like every other form of loyalty in a particalized world, customer loyalty is as thin as the horizon. Abuse it once, and you have lost it for good.

One-on-One Marketing

The prejudice of macroeconomics is that the study of large changes—in employment, in income, and the like—will account for individual changes and behaviors. Consumers can have guns or they can have butter, as every Economics 101 student learned, but they can't have both. The reality of market particalization is that the prejudice of macroeconomics couldn't be more wrong. When consumers control the market equation, they can have whatever it is they want.

How then do you predict behavior in a marketplace that has become segmented into millions of individual realities? How do you market to that behavior? By microsizing your examination. By studying millions of individuals to track their millions of highly individualized behaviors and marketing to each of those behaviors. In short, by one-on-one research to create one-on-one marketing. (Don Peppers and Martha Rogers deserve mention here for their book *The One to One Future*.)

The drugstore kiosks AT&T is creating will let customers swipe a card through the kiosk to receive free coupons that then can be used over the counter for discounts. In order to get the card that is used in the kiosk, customers will enroll through their health maintenance organizations, and they'll receive a free benefit there as well. So far, so good—it's a trade that benefits both clubs. Customers have received an economic benefit in return for surrendering their name and coupon preferences. Because AT&T has worked through HMOs and is using drugstores that work with the HMOs for its delivery system, the company has customers in an environment in which they are likely to spend time.

What AT&T will also have eventually is a self-renewing study of millions of highly individualized shopping behaviors and preferences that then can be used to market individually to each behavior. That's why the information you own about yourself has such value—because it's only by your surrendering that information that you can be marketed to on an individual basis. And it's why people will demand payment for that information—because, they *should* be paid for it. But the self-renewing study can be used for something else as well: to predict larger trends in the marketplace, because, in fact, exactly the reverse of the macroeconomics model is what's needed today. It is only by accounting for individual behaviors that larger changes can be explained.

Scarcity Cravings

Why did two pairs of Kenneth Jay Lane earclips once owned by Jacqueline Onassis sell for $12,650 at the famous Sotheby's auction held in New York in April 1996? Why did a cigar humidor that was once a gift from Milton Berle to John F. Kennedy sell for $574,500 at the same event? Obviously, there was a certain ghoul factor to it all. Thanks to Lee Harvey Oswald, Jack Ruby, and Oliver Stone, the Kennedys will live forever on the margins of the macabre American fascination with conspiracies. Obviously, too, part of it was nostalgia. "In short, there's simply not a more congenial spot / For happ'ly ever-aftering than here in Camelot!" as Alan Jay Lerner's lyrics went in Lerner and Loewe's *Camelot*. But the larger reason, we suspect, is the same one that explains the quilts we recently saw for sale. The quilts had been machine-made in identical batches of five hundred, and on each one was a little piece of material appliquéd by hand that announced it was part of a "limited edition." By any reasonable standards, the assertion was absurd. What can be "limited" about a machine-made quilt produced in such numbers? What can possibly make it a collectible? Then again, who said the world is reasonable?

One of the abiding ironies of a world becoming steadily more tolerant of diversity is that, as we do so, diversity itself disappears. As it does, uniqueness inevitably gains in value. Jackie Onassis undoubtedly owned many dozens of earclips in her life, but she owned only many dozens. Milton Berle gave Jack Kennedy only one cigar humidor. The quilts may come in batches of five hundred, but there are only five hundred of them. As we connect societally, we come to crave scarcity, and as the Sotheby's auction proved beyond any doubt, we'll pay a near fortune for it.

How do you build scarcity into products for a marketplace controlled by consumer demand? By finding the scarce and marketing it. (All credit to Sotheby's and the Kennedy children for that.) By limiting production. (All credit to the "limited edition" quilt makers for that, too. They saw the world for what it is and took advantage of it. So far as we could tell, the quilts were moving like hotcakes.) By parsing customer preferences to the nth degree and marketing to the most discrete possible audience.

Best of all, maybe, you build scarcity into products by individualizing them for the individual realities that collectively compose today's marketplace. By becoming, in effect, a component editor for your customers, you allow them to create their own individual realities instead of imposing a collective reality on them. Nothing, finally, could be more scarce than that. And it is the future of marketing.

Hit 'Em Where They Are

Among the many wonderful explanations of baseball offered by the late New York Yankees manager Casey Stengel was this explanation of how to bat for a high average: "Hit 'em where they ain't." We've advised the board of the National Baseball Hall of Fame Association and have been consultants to the Baseball Hall of Fame Museum in Cooperstown, New York. We dearly wish that baseball were, in fact, life. But it's not. In a marketplace controlled by customers, not manufacturers or retailers, the only way to survive is to do exactly the opposite of what old Casey suggested: Hit 'em where they are. To do that you have to understand tribalism, membership, and the fraternity of strangers. We take those up next.

4 Right Action: Membership

Why will consumers purchase a twenty-pound bag of Iams puppy chow when they can buy a twenty-pound bag of Purina puppy chow for half the price?

Why is a U.S. Army veteran just an ex-GI, while an ex-Leatherneck is a Marine forever?

Why do pseudo-intellectuals rush to get their names and bios included in *Marquis Who's Who in America*, while real intellectuals avoid the book like the plague?

Why are two Los Angeles gangs, the Bloods and the Crips, among the most successful social organizations in America today?

Why are Harley-Davidson motorcycles one of the greatest marketing stories in contemporary business history?

How did American Express shoot itself in the foot?

The answer in every case is: membership.

We've talked earlier about the particalization of social organization. The family is dead and gone. Traditional families, to the extent that they exist today, are either a luxury item for those who can afford them or an economic necessity for those who can't afford to get out of them. Loyalty has died, too, and with it all the organizational pull that was based on a shared sense of ideals, of mutual obligations.

National political parties only rarely nominate consensus presidential candidates. Since the restructuring of the Democratic selection process prior to the disastrous 1972 nomination of George McGovern—and with the exception of incumbents—both parties have tended to endorse whatever fragmented political stance garnered enough support in the primaries to prevail at convention time. The electorate today votes less from ideals than from self-interest, enlightened or otherwise. Particalization prevails at the local political level, too, where ward bosses once held the neighborhood electorate in their benign—if often iron and greedy—grip. One of the many beauties of the movie *City Hall* was the sheer quaintness of the alderman's role played by Danny Aiello, with its assumption that all politics was local and all local politics revolved around mutual obligations based on the trading of favors. In a single generation, collegiality—venial or otherwise—has vanished from the political process, and as the Republican-dominated 104th Congress found, even a national mandate is a short-term loan.

Attend a meeting of the Elks, the Moose, the Odd Fellows, the Rotary Club, and you will see a species nearing extinction, as surely as the passenger pigeons that not much more than a century ago could still blacken the skies with their numbers. Why? Because while their rituals—the Pledge of Allegiance, for instance, that opens all Rotary meetings—remain important in the texture of Rotarians' lives, the shared values the rituals represent are no longer germane to the vast bulk of the population: "One nation . . . indivisible" (the "under God" was added in the mid-1950s) has become one nation infinitely divided.

To say that social organization has become particalized is not the same as saying that organization itself has disappeared. The drive to belong, the desire for membership, is a core ethic—as powerful now as it was five hundred years ago, and as it will be five hundred years hence. Membership hasn't gone away, and it won't. What has changed are the clusters around which we group ourselves. What has changed are the ways we direct our desire to belong.

In an age saturated with media choices, the choices we make from among them form our media communes, and the seven media communes themselves become a more powerful predictor of affinity among their members than whether they jointly attended one of the Seven Sisters colleges or one of the seven Ivy League schools, or even whether they live within seven houses of each other.

The long-term loyalty and relationships of corporate life—fraternities of colleagues—have been replaced by the short-term loyalty and relationships of the deal—a succession of fraternities of strangers. Foreknowledge of one another vanishes, replaced by an exchange of résumés. Ingratiation periods are done away with under the pressure of compressed and miniaturized time. Instead of the old rules of social behavior that required us to build relationships based on a reciprocal self-disclosure of information, we build them instead on a systematic sharing of information in the service of the deal at hand. And when the deal is done, we all walk away.

As protection against the rent, against the emotional cold, against loneliness—and in fulfillment of the drive for belonging that their splintered families never provided—Generation X'ers group themselves into cohabiting affinity groups and television networks, always desperate to spot a curve, give them the hit series that celebrate their new social organization: *Cheers, Melrose Place, Seinfeld, Friends* and its many imitators in the cohabiting affinity group prime-time sector: *Champs, Buddies, Partners, Good Company, My Guys,* and *Pursuit of Happiness,* to scratch the surface of the 1995–96 TV viewing season.

Faced, in short, with the primitive need to belong, we more and more belong today in the most primitive way: not to family, not to fraternal organizations, not to work-related groups, but to tribes. And thus it is only by marketing to tribes that you can penetrate the full dimensionality of people's lives. It is only by penetrating that dimensionality that you can create the one-on-one contact that is necessary in a demand-based economy.

Tribalizing the Customers

Why are consumers willing to pay twice as much for Iams puppy chow as they will pay for Purina puppy chow? Because Iams markets its dog food not through supermarkets—a mass intersection where many tribes cross and mingle—but primarily through veterinarian offices and upscale pet stores, places where the specific tribe of dog lovers is at its most concerned and vulnerable. Iams goes to great pains to be present and highly visible at the most central event of the tribe of dog lovers—the Westminster Dog Show held annually in New York's Madison Square Garden. What can seem campy about the Westminster show to those outside the tribe is, in fact, the most profound sort of ritual and ceremony for those within it. And ritual and ceremony are the mother's milk of tribes. Winston cigarettes has achieved the same sort of bonding with the tribe of race-car enthusiasts through its sponsorship of NASCAR racing, another event steeped in ceremony, ritual, and icons in the form of goods bearing the NASCAR logo. Happily for Winston, NASCAR also historically has attracted the group most likely to smoke cigarettes: young, white, low-educated males.

Why are Harley-Davidson motorcycles such a great marketing story? Because while the *Mad Max* trilogy of movies took cycles to the max, and the aquatic hogs of Kevin Costner's unintentionally bathetic *Waterworld* put them over the top, Harley-Davidson figured out how to put motorcycles in middle- and upper-middle-class garages. How? By a process of tribal initiation and reinforcement so elegantly simple that a gross of Harvard MBAs couldn't have thought of it in a hundred years.

Buy a Harley and you become, on purchase, a member of the Harley-Davidson Club: initiation. The clubs meet every Saturday at the dealership, where you can buy Harley-Davidson gear loaded with the company's logo and head off on day trips with other club members. The rides themselves provide weekly reinforcement of the experience of owning a Harley. Out of the random universe of motorcycle owners, the rides create a fraternity of strangers. And the Harley cycles themselves, as well as the clothing and accessories marked with the Harley logo, create a set of moveable icons that enforce the ritual. Every year, Harley sponsors a summer get-together in Sturgis, South Dakota. Some 280,000 people showed up for the fiftieth anniversary celebration—nearly all of them riding Harleys, nearly all decked out in Harley logos and icons. It is exactly such reinforcements of ritual that turn a fraternity of strangers into a literal tribe. Just ask the good people of western South Dakota.

A sign, we were once told by an Oxford don, points to something beyond itself; a symbol assumes the properties of what the sign is pointing to; and an allegory is symbols systematically moving through a narrative. Harley's annual gathering in Sturgis is an allegory of tribalism, a symbolic narrative of a new culture of hunters and gatherers.

Great ideas deserve copying, which is why the Saturn car people have copied Harley's marketing approach almost to the letter.

Defending the Cave Persons

Why is an Army vet just an ex-GI, while a Marine never forgets his "Semper Fi"? For the same reason the Bloods and Crips are among America's most successful social organizations. Both are built around the social structure of tribes. Like Harley-Davidson, both use initiation rituals, disciplined reinforcement, icons—medals in the Marine's case; tattoos and "tagging," or graffiti, for the gangs—and closing ceremonies to make the tribal values the values of their members.

The Army has its initiation rituals and reinforcement as well. A soldier who did his basic training at the Army's Fort Dix may never forget those days; if he stays in the military long enough, he will accumulate a salad of medals for his chest. And if he or she is a high-ranking officer, at retirement there will be a closing ceremony worthy of a Roman emperor. But a Leatherneck who has completed successfully six weeks at Parris Island, South Carolina, is a Leatherneck forever; his survival of the initiation ritual is the eternal proof and measure of his manhood. An Eagle Scout may always treasure the time he spent accumulating the twenty-one merit badges that qualified him for scouting's highest honor. He may have learned lessons that will serve him well in life. But a Blood or a Crip—or any gang member who has sealed his covenant with the group in blood or in physical violence—is at some elemental level a gang member for life. Leonard Bernstein had it exactly right in *West Side Story*: "When you're a Jet, you're a Jet all the way / From your first cigarette to your last dying day."

Any organization, be it a tribe or a company, builds up "endotruths" and "exotruths" about itself. Endotruths are the ones known inside but not outside the microculture, the ones that drive deep to its beginnings and shape the internal understanding. Exotruths are the presumed truths about the tribe, the ones that determine its external value and reputation and cannot be shaken loose even by denying them. Collectively, the two truths explain why two organizations—the Army and the Marines, the *Chicago Tribune* and the *Miami Herald,* the American Cancer Society and the American Heart Association—can be in fundamentally the same business and yet have radically different cultures and be understood from outside in radically different ways. Tribes stamp us from within and without.

We called it other things—political correctness, equal rights and equal opportunity—but the battle over sexually integrating the military's service academies and such state-supported service schools as the Citadel and Virginia Military Institute was at heart a battle between tribalism and social values. Indeed, it remains an open question whether modifying the initiation and reinforcement rites of the schools to accommodate both sexes will allow the academies to train future leaders whose values are the values of the tribe. The U.S. Naval Academy, certainly, has compiled a fairly sordid record of cheating and illegal and extra-legal abuses since becoming coed. It remains an open question, too, whether a drill instructor who is part psychologist, part counselor, and part calisthenics leader—the new military model for an old military ogre—can finally prepare troops to go into battle without questioning their orders or whether troops will now have to conduct a colloquy before going over the top. The job of the DI has always been to prepare his charges to do the former.

We call it other things in the business world, too—human resources problems, most notably—but it is really the consequences of tribalism that produce many of the greatest diversity conflicts in corporations today. We were talking the other day with the head of an international computer company, a man worth hundreds of millions of dollars in his own right. Something had happened to him, he said, that had never happened before: He had been doing his weekly round of the offices, when a middle-ranking employee had stopped him to say that the company needed advertisements that talked to Christians about the role of computers in their lives. The CEO encouraged open communication; it was part of the company's ethic. Still, he wanted to know, where did that come from?

The answer, we said, was that racial and sexual animosities within a corporation have become secondary to tribal animosities. He had an evangelical tribe within his employees, and its need to be true to its own values—evangelizing, in this case—was greater than its need to mesh with the values of the corporation as a whole. What's more, if he directed an advertisement explicitly to born-again Christians, he would quickly discover that he also had an atheist tribe under his roof (cybergeeks with a strong predilection toward the *Mother Jones* media commune), and probably a paramilitary one as well.

Therein lies one of the great dilemmas of management today. The temptation is to succumb to the demands of individual tribes within the workplace—to advertise computers to evangelicals, in this case— but to do so inevitably encourages other tribes to make their demands known, because it is in the nature of microcultures to seek to capture all the control, all the access they can. Finally, the business itself becomes the captive of the collective tribes that make up its workforce. It is only by fusing these competing tribal ethics along with the individual realities they represent to a single corporate goal and a clearly defined set of values that corporations can survive.

The Hunt, Not the Hunter

In primitive tribes, hunters aren't ostracized for failing to bring back the kill. They are ostracized for failing to perform the hunt properly. In Victorian society, children who violated the mores of the tribe—children, that is, who misbehaved in a society that placed enormous value on proper behavior—were "sent to Coventry," a lovely Victorian expression for the awful punishment of being locked in a closet. So it is still with today's neo-tribes, and so it is that pseudo-intellectuals actively pursue an entry in *Who's Who*, while real intellectuals flee from such exposure. Why? Because it is in the culture of the tribe of pseudo-intellectuals to want recognition— recognition is the validation of their pursuit—while it is in the tribal culture of real intellectuals to be eternal outsiders.

About one in 10,000 male births and one in 15,000 female births produces a truly smart child, a child that by all the psychometrics available—and they are now quite good—can be called something close to a genius. Nobody knows why smart children are born in such small proportions or why males are favored over females. It's simply a fact of life, and of life's imperfect equality. Virtually everyone wants such a child, because intelligence is the most highly prized of all human commodities today, but virtually no parent is prepared for the consequences of such a gift. The rules of such exceptional intelligence are very simple for children: Never acknowledge it, not even to yourself, and never flaunt it in front of others. Yet very smart children almost inevitably know they are very smart, and from an early age. They understand things before other children even begin to grasp the question, and they are too smart to miss that fact. Other children see it, too, and begin to organize their own tribes in defense against such intelligence.

Thus is born what is known as the "dilemma of the genuinely talented individual." And thus, too, arises the fundamental ethic of the tribe of true intellectuals: never pursue celebrity and never care what others think about you. To hunt recognition is to do the hunt wrong, and to do the hunt wrong is to be ostracized, to risk being sent to Coventry. Miss that ethic, and you have missed what lies at the heart of the tribe. Miss what lies at the heart of the tribe, and you have missed the tribe altogether. (In case you haven't guessed, true intellectuals are to Mensa, the IQ club, what true cigar aficionados are to a Phillies Blunt.)

Tribal instincts count. So do the icons that tribes rally around and advertise their affiliations with—from the sports team jackets of the "real men" tribe to the prim dresses with high necks of the "Eagle Forum" tribe. Read those instincts and icons right, and you can begin to penetrate the full dimensionality of tribal members' lives. Read them wrong, and you can hire Ed McMahon to deliver your message personally to their doors, and no one will be home. To market today, you have to go where people are, and where they are is where their tribe meets, their ceremonial ground.

Not long ago, Rockport, the shoe company, asked us to be consultants on the marketing plan for a new shoe the company was preparing to launch. The target audience went as follows: "Men 40–49; $75,000 or more in annual income; more than likely have children and very involved with family; own a dog; have a four-wheel drive vehicle." So far, so good. The psychographics, roughly the Robert Redford/Sundance tribe, were neatly lined up in a row, and it's a great group to market to. The only problem was that the shoe itself was designed for the cybergeek tribe: low weight, low static, low design—a shoe not for mountain trails or sidling up to the bar at Jackson Hole, but for long hallways lit with overhead flourescents. That's not a bad demographic to market to, either: Data-pigs need footwear, too. But the balls weren't the same color.

Right tribe, wrong shoe, we told Rockport. Or wrong tribe, right shoe. Take your pick. We haven't been asked back since.

White Man Speak with Forked Tongue

Lastly, how did American Express manage to shoot itself in the foot? It seemingly had the perfect theme with its advertising message "Membership Has Its Privileges." As MCI did with its "Friends and Family" calling program, American Express tied itself to the new tribalism. It promised members who joined the tribe something special for belonging. And . . . it never delivered. Privileges? What privileges? The only one we could ever find was that an American Express card gave you the privilege of membership in American Express. As with tribalism, so with everything else about marketing: When consumers own the marketing equation, they can demand authenticity. American Express didn't deliver on it. Visa, which understands about risk management, has been cleaning American Express's clock ever since.

5

Right Speech: Downward Nobility

Why was "privilege" the wrong word for American Express to use in its "Membership Has Its Privileges" advertising slogan? In part because of the context of what American Express was offering. There were no extraordinary privileges built into the implicit contract; there was only the circular, internal "privilege" of membership.

But "privilege" was the wrong word in a more critical and absolute sense as well. "Privilege" implies exclusion when it is inclusion people are searching for. Worse, "privilege" implies conspicuous consumption when it is inconspicuous consumption, stealth wealth, and downward nobility that are helping to drive the dynamic of the marketplace today. Not only had American Express's advertising copywriters not crossed the 500-year delta, they hadn't even come within sight of it.

What do you find when you cross the delta?

• **That work can be fun again.**
Most of America has given up on work as a source of satisfaction, but people who know the difference know that work on the other side of

the delta can be enormously satisfying. Shed the notion that any loyalty is to be given or received in a business relationship, realize that you are a freelancer moving from deal to deal even when you are in someone else's employ, and understand that there is only one person you are working for: yourself. You're the boss. You're the only person in charge of the only career you can control: your own. That may be scary. If you have been taught to be primarily defensive, it may even be debilitating. But this isn't servitude, this is freedom.

- **That it's okay to waste time.**
  Avoid the activity trap. Manage choices out of your life, not into it. In the storm of information washing over you, realize that only a tiny fraction of it is germane to your own goals and that it is that tiny fraction on which you absolutely have to concentrate. Take a nap, catch an afternoon matinee. Conserve energy and you'll have more of it for the things that really matter. You're the boss; you'll make sure you get the job done on time. That's freedom, too.

- **That the fifteen minutes of fame we have all been promised isn't worth the chase.**
  Ask the movie celebrities being dogged by paparazzi or the instant celebs raised high by the media only to be dropped like dirty laundry: Fame is nothing but grief. What is more, fame so easily achieved is equally fame diminished in worth. Meanwhile, privacy ascends in value as it grows ever more scarce.

- **And most important for the discussion at hand, that materialism is neither good or bad.**
  Materialism just is.

Therein lie the roots of downward nobility.

The simple fact is that we have to buy stuff. We have to own. Some of the things we buy are necessities. Some—a significant part in upper-income families—is for dialogue. We're compelled to communicate, and consumption is communication about our wants and needs. But on the other side of the delta, people aren't trapped by their possessions. They don't let the ownership of things and the meaning of the things they own dominate their own sense of self-fulfillment, self-worth, or self-control. On the other side of the delta, people accept materialism and consumption for what they are: involuntary responses, like breathing and providing the body with food and drink. And the further simple fact is that a lot of people are already there.

The rise of so-called "peasant foods"—the fajita phenomenon, dim sum, feta, and hummus—was made possible not just by the collapse of culinary borders. More important was the fact that in a rising era of downward nobility, the financial ability to eat every night at Lutece in New York, Charlie Trotter's in Chicago, or Masa's in San Francisco would no longer impel the necessity to do so. "Trends are bottom-up, fads top-down," John Naisbitt wrote in his 1982 bestseller *Megatrends*. In that, John Naisbitt couldn't have been more right.

Why does Calvin Klein sit so securely atop the fashion world? Because Klein's minimalist style is in perfect harmony with the stealth-wealth ethic of downward nobility. It isn't denial that downward nobility drives to, it's quietness, taste, and discretion.

Downward nobility led to Nike's creation of the "cross-trainer" shoe, because it is not a multiplicity of objects that people want today—a multiplicity of shoes, in Nike's case. Instead, just as the Marines want a few good men, people want a few good things. Downward nobility was also, in part, behind Kellogg's decision to stop promoting its cereal as a fount of health and instead promote it as part of the practical management of wellness. Chest thumping is out. Like stealth wealth, stealth health is in.

Chest thumping is out in product promotion, too. Speak with a whisper in an era of downward nobility, and you'll be heard as a roar. Instead of shouting from the rooftops, adopt the Tiffany model. There is nothing loud about the famous blue box that all Tiffany products leave the store in, but that box says everything about its contents that many women want to hear.

Historically, the most intimate question one American male could ask another was how much money he made. People would jerry-rig wealth to create status. They would deck themselves out in status-laden objects to let people know that they made a bundle. But they would talk about abusive parents, homosexual experiences when they were fourteen, psychotic siblings, or the peculiarities of their own children's sex lives before they would reveal a true word about their income or net worth. Today, people can still fake it. The question "How much do you make?" can still bring a conversation to a cold, dead stop. But faking it no longer accretes power, and the question of wealth itself has become largely immaterial.

If you want status, walk into a room and announce that, amidst the ambient chaos of our times, you're a happy person. If you want status, announce that you've been a happily married man for twenty-five years. Everyone knows what you went through to achieve that. Everyone knows that there were days—perhaps weeks or months—when you and your spouse could barely stand the sight of each other. What society has always treasured is what is scarce. The old status objects are all over the place, begging to be bought. Satisfaction and domestic contentment have rarity, and rarity, as always, has the greatest value.

We should point out—and welfare reformers should take note—that a minimal level of income appears absolutely necessary to achieve the satisfaction we are describing. In all our research, we have never found a single demographic below the poverty line that was ready to declare itself happy with its lot. But we've also seen no research to suggest that the richest Americans have the greatest purchase on happiness or satisfaction either. Rather, the ones most likely to have achieved satisfaction—the ones most likely to have internalized that they don't have to overspend their capability in order to achieve very high levels of social and self-esteem—are people who are living ordinary lives extraordinarily. Therein, as we wrote earlier, lies the true democratization of status. Therein lies another freedom writ large.

How do you create and position products with downward nobility in mind? Three rules:

- **Value, not embarrassment.**

  Gulfstream Aerospace faced a classic problem in downward nobility: creating a justification for a business jet in an era of stealth wealth and, not entirely coincidental, stockholder revolt against extravagant executive perks. Its production solution was to both diversify and globalize the manufacturing of the plane by including in it parts made by a former Soviet airframe maker as well as other pieces from around the world. Why? To hold its cost down and to increase sales potential in nations where domestic content is either a de facto or de jure element of doing business.

To market the plane, Gulfstream focused not on its luxuriousness, but on the value of a CEO's time. It wasn't up to Gulfstream to argue that a Michael Eisner, who earned $233 million from the Walt Disney Company from 1991 through 1995 according to *Forbes* magazine, might be overpaid. Neither Gulfstream nor any other source outside of Disney and its shareholders can affect that. Instead, Gulfstream pointed out that the time of an executive who is paid an average of $46.6 million annually is valued at $1.48 a second, and thus every hour that executive waits in an airport for a commercial flight costs the company something on the order of $5,320. Given the average annual travel time of a CEO, you don't have to run numbers like that out long before a corporate jet made thriftily from an international assemblage of parts seems inconspicuous consumption of the most humble sort.

• **Collection, not consumption.**
Stop thinking of your customers as a mass market and start thinking of them as a mass of individual collectors. You will understand far better where they are coming from and what they want.

In the era of downward nobility, people will still spend to consume; they will even overspend. But they won't overspend to keep up with the Joneses; they will overspend to keep up with their category, whatever that category may be. What does that mean? It means that to keep up with the Joneses you have to overspend across categories—on cars, on houses, on clothes, on vacation, on lawn services and country clubs. The Joneses are extraordinarily demanding competition, and it is keeping up with them that has driven the dynamic of conspicuous consumption through at least the last two generations. Keeping up with category status is something else entirely.

Study after study has shown that opinion leaders know they are just that. What is equally true today is that virtually everyone is an opinion leader in some category of his or her life. It might be gardening, flower arranging, bread making, automobiles, or international affairs. The category doesn't matter. What matters is that more and more people will underspend in other categories to allow themselves to overspend in the category they perceive themselves to be leaders in. If that category happens to be rock 'n' roll, they might go without a new car to own a $4,000 Alembic bass guitar. Like collectors everywhere, they want to maximize the intelligence of their purchases in the categories in which they have specialized knowledge and expertise. But in the era of downward nobility, they will equally minimize their purchases elsewhere so they aren't trapped by their possessions.

It's worth repeating: People don't want things today. They want the specialized ownership of a few good things. To penetrate the full dimensionality of their lives, you have to offer substance, authenticity, quality at the absolute bleeding edge of your category.

• **Remember the underclass.**
It is in the underclass that category-status leaders are most often found. We don't necessarily mean the literal underclass, although many fashion trends begin in the ghetto. We don't mean an entirely figurative underclass either. Most of the people who make up the bleeding edge of computer users are not wealthy. Most of those who are on the bleeding edge of car design are not wealthy either. Like other status leaders, they will underspend their income elsewhere to stay at the bleeding edge in their category, and because they form the vanguard of early adopters of any new product—and thus are the gateway to the mainstream—to abandon them is to lose both them and finally the mainstream itself.

IBM, to cite one example, abandoned the cybergeeks and lost them and then its leadership in the personal-computer field. Apple did the same for less reason, because of all companies, Apple should have known the geeks inside and out. Chevrolet abandoned the auto status leaders, too, when it dumped the Chevy 409, and not a single rock 'n' roll hit since has been written about a Chevy. Who else forgot about the underclass in their flight to the mainstream? Converse All-Stars, which were once every child's dream of a sports shoe. Spalding golf clubs, which saw an oddball driver named the Big Bertha, originally used only by a relative few who wanted to be at the bleeding edge of golf technology, turn Calloway into a dominant force in the golf equipment industry.

Nothing is harder for a company to do than keep up with this underclass. Because category-status leaders form such a small part of the total market and because they are so demanding of innovation, keeping up with them is extraordinarily expensive. The profits roll in only when you use mass media to make the transition to the mid and finally mass markets, and then the bottom line positively swells. But if you abandon the category-status leaders, they won't be there when you go back to refresh your product line. If they are not there, they won't be able to send a message to the people who look to them in this time of inconspicuous consumption for the few good things they want.

No company, we should add, has been more effective at balancing the needs of early adopters and the mass market than Levi Strauss. It always talks to category-status leaders first, and it never rushes to the mass market without first assuring those leaders that they—and Levi's—are still cool, cool, cool.

A final note on downward nobility—a project we are personally involved in. In late summer of 1997, Gateway 2000 expects to roll out a new personal computer it is calling the BMF in development. What will the BMF have? Multiple languages, two screens, and a Windows capability that will allow a user to drag his mouse across and between both screens to access all the windows in both virtually simultaneously. And that's just for starters. The price tag? A pro-jected—and whopping—$15,000. At best the company might sell 10,000 units, for a gross of $150 million. No, Gateway is not likely to make much money out of the BMF itself, although it won't go broke on it either. Yes, people in the computer industry are even more likely to have a good laugh over the BMF than they had over Gateway's Destination, a personal computer with an average unit price of $4,700 that was rolled out in the spring of 1996. But category status leaders watch and wait, and when they see what they want, they pounce.

About a month after Destination was introduced, Gateway poured about $4 million into a flight of three national television ads devoted to it, and the company jumped from an average of 52 calls a day about the product to about 150 calls a day. With a conversion rate of about one in seven, that meant Gateway was selling some twenty-one systems a day—twenty-one systems at nearly $5,000 each—and sell-ing them *over the phone*. But a rising tide also lifts all ships. Total calls about all Gateway products jumped after the Destination ads from

800 to 14,500 a day, with a conversion rate of about one sale for every five calls, and an average selling price around $3,200. Just as Destination did, BMF will tell category status leaders that Gateway cares about what they care about, that the top of its multi-media line is for them and them alone, that if they are looking for only one good thing to consume this year, this is exactly what it should be. And it will tell those who look to status category leaders that this is where the leaders themselves are looking. And that, in the long run, will be worth every penny to Gateway 2000.

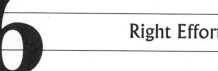

6 Right Effort: Risk Management

Snapple iced tea, as bottled-tea lovers know, has an almost endless variety of flavors—seventy-two at last count. Lay each variation end to end, and they would stretch almost from the great tea fields of the Himalayan foothills to the top of Mount Everest itself. This panoply of tastes, Snapple executives long thought, was their product's greatest marketing strength. In fact, it was Snapple's greatest strength only if the company managed its customers' choice for them. Why? Because in a time-crunched world, no one has the raw minutes to sort through seventy-two flavors. Lunch would be over by the time you made a selection; the supermarket would be closing, the vital organs dehydrated and shutting down.

How could Snapple get around the problem? How could it offer an immense variety without turning a multitude of choices into a chaos of choices? We made this suggestion: Come up with a simple shelf set of eight choices. Four would always be the same so that Snapple would offer customers the pleasure of familiarity. Four would be changed every week so that Snapple could continuously refresh and renew its product line and so that customers could work their way out

215

on a limb—mango-raspberry flavored or peach-papaya flavored?—if they so chose. In effect, Snapple would come into harmony with the ambient cultural schizophrenia of our times: It would have one foot in the comfort world and one in the anxiety world. Even more important, Snapple would be managing the risk that its customers might make a mistake. And in a Chaos Age, nothing is more important than that.

The rise of the demand-based economy handed the keys of the marketing equation to consumers. The particalization of social organization created the imperative of tribal marketing. Downward nobility impels marketing to status category leaders. But the very nature of chaos requires businesses to manage their customers' risk, because in a world no longer governed by reason, a world from which loyalty has been banished, a world from which the old assumptions of logic and economics have been shaken loose, you are always exposed to risk. Risk, quite simply, is an endemic part of the ambiance of the Chaos Age. One other factor needs to be mentioned as well: In an age in which raw intelligence is the most prized commodity, being thought stupid is the greatest fear. Making customers feel stupid is the worst sin a business can commit.

The *Washington Post*'s advertising slogan—"If you don't get it, you don't get it"—plays directly to risk management and the fear of being left behind. Subscribe to this newspaper, the slogan says; read it carefully; parse its columnists for meaning; or someday soon you will be sitting at a dinner party, the subject of Burundi will appear on the table, and you won't know a Hutu from a hoot owl or a Tutsi from a tootsie. You will, in short, be thought dumb. You will be exiled from the tribe of political cognoscenti, and in Washington, D.C., if nowhere else on Earth, life won't be worth living.

Risk management also lies behind a new marketing campaign put together by Hatbrands, which owns Stetson and a large number of other hat companies. How do you sell a product at the close of the twentieth century whose historical purpose has been to keep the sun off the heads of cowboys? For one thing, in an age driving toward individualism in fashion and in lifestyle, you tie your product to the perceived rugged individualism of the Old American West. (It is not for nothing that Marlboro, the cowboy's cigarette brand, now operates 750 stores in Europe, selling everything from jeans to the very hats we are describing.) But Hatbrands also created a connection between the wearing of hats and the management of the risk that exposure to ultraviolet rays would be injurious to a customer's health. Stetson hats, it should be noted, have become so commonplace in downtown Manhattan that it might look like home, home on the range if there weren't so many cabs.

How do you manage risk for a customer? Not by eliminating failure in your production processes as the so-called "quality movement" would have you do—customers aren't fools; they know that mistakes get made—but by learning to say "I'm sorry" about your mistakes and fixing them on a timely and unquestioning basis.

"Zero-fault" is a lovely chimera that blinds you to the world as it is. "Fault tolerance"—the capacity of any system to absorb the bad that inevitably happens—is right in line with the reality of the Chaos Age, when the bad can arrive from any angle, when circumstances can shift so quickly and can so thoroughly undermine your plans and pronouncements that sometimes all you can do is throw up your hands and invoke the "painters on Friday" rule. (As in "I never said we'd meet our third-quarter earnings goals/there was no problem with halving the accounting staff/the Justice Department wouldn't dare prosecute." I said, "'The painters are coming on Friday.'") A sustainable company is like a sustainable society—best measured by its capacity to withstand the bad, not generate the good.

You manage risk not by pretending it doesn't exist, but by offering authenticity. You manage it by being the best at the bottom price to minimize the risk that customers will pay too much. Or you manage it by being the best choice for the people most knowledgeable about your category, which is never the cheapest, to minimize the risk that what your customers pay for will not assure their continuation as category leaders. You manage it by offering not just guarantees, but proof that your guarantees have meaning.

Not long ago, a freak afternoon thunderstorm launched a lightning bolt that struck a tree near one of our houses, snaked through the ground, and blew out a telephone transformer that, in turn, sent a surge through our phone line and fried our 28.8 Global Village

TelePort Platinum modem. (We admit it—we had neglected to run our phone lines through a surge protector.)

We called Global Village as soon as the phone was safe to touch again, because our modem was still under warranty. By 10:00 A.M. the next morning, Federal Express had delivered a brand-new 28.8 TelePort Platinum to our front door. And thus Global Village provided the proof of its guarantee. It managed the risk that we would be cut off for any significant period of time from faxes, e-mail, and the ether of cyberspace. And it built a customer relationship that will be both binding and multiplying. Just ask us what kind of modem you should select for interfacing with *your* home computer.

How do you manage risk in more specific terms? Let's look now at a variety of companies.

Editors, Brokers, Intermediaries, and Intimidators

What Gateway 2000 does is simultaneously simple and ingenious. By allowing customers to select the components they want to fit their particular needs, Gateway personalizes computing systems. It individualizes them to fit an age of individual realities. But more important, Gateway serves as a component editor for the consumer. From the swirling universe of computer parts—a chaos of choices—it selects the ones it deems best. Further, it assures that those parts will work together, that they will interface, and thus it serves as a risk intermediary, as well as a component editor, for the customer.

Anyone with a solid knowledge of computers could do what Gateway does on his or her own, and many do, but Gateway crunches the time necessary to achieve a personalized system and it packages the system under a single guarantee that it stands four-square behind. Thus it once again reduces risk and crunches time when failures surface. But Gateway does one other thing as well: It produces machines at the extremes of possibility for the core computer enthusiast—the early adopters—so that the middle of the market will know that it can operate at the edge of the unknown and therefore can operate at the center of what's possible. Just as Porsche did with its line of racing cars, Gateway creates risk insurance for its customers by pushing the edge of the envelope—by testing what does and does not work—so that the center of the envelope will be buffered and protected by the experience.

Thanks to its Olympic Sponsorship Program, the U.S. Olympic Committee has become a risk manager as well. The corporate donations the sponsorship program brought in gave the Olympic Committee the financial firepower to become, in essence, the broker of amateur sports in America and their risk intermediary on behalf of their consumers—sports fans. Prior to the mid–1980s, Olympics-related amateur sports had been operated under the aegis of separate national governing organizations (NGO's)—one for swimming, one for gymnastics, one for track and field, and so on. By collecting money from the sponsorship programs and then dispensing it back to the NGO's, the Olympic Committee assumed the locus of power in amateur sports. The result has been a more smooth-running and consistent operation, even in an increasingly litigious environment, a standardization of eligibility requirements, and—witness the 1996 Summer Olympics in Atlanta—generally greater success for U.S. athletes.

Charles Schwab Brokerage Services is a literal broker, a company that facilitates the buying and selling of stocks, but first and foremost, Schwab is a risk broker. Charles Schwab began life as a discount firm offering most of the usual array of stocks-and-bonds services at such rock-bottom prices that it was regarded as a significant threat by the rest of the industry. But what Charles Schwab—the man, not the company named after him—gradually came to understand was that consumers no longer necessarily wanted pure investment knowledge from their brokers, knowledge that required time to digest and a willingness to grapple with. Instead, Schwab discovered, consumers wanted a commitment to do things in a narrow way well enough that they could simply rely on the service. And thus Schwab redirected his business toward a family of mutual funds and mutual-fund services that would allow consumers to feel comfortable that their money was being managed well. In other words, his company became a risk intermediary, where the risk is not knowing enough to make an intelligent decision.

What sets Charles Schwab apart from Fidelity and the other mutual-fund-and-services families is its reliance on a single human presence, on Charles Schwab himself. And what sets Schwab apart is not the perception that he is able to anticipate moves in the stock market—until he stepped down, Fidelity's Peter Lynch of the Magellan Fund had that field all to himself—but rather the perception that Schwab actively seeks to understand and respond to the needs of consumers who are too busily engaged in their own entrepreneurships and nanopreneurships to manage their own money. Like Wendy's Dave Thomas, Charles Schwab stands up for consumers.

What other companies have capitalized on the role of risk intermediary? Service Master, for one. Service Master is in reality a family of companies mostly with better-known names: Terminex, ChemLawn, True Green, and Merry Maids, as well as a lesser known home-repair company and another company that insures home appliances. Each of the companies under the Service Master umbrella has a similar purpose: to manage for a continuing fee a particular household dilemma on behalf of the consumer.

In the case of Merry Maids, Service Master manages the risk that a maid might steal at the same time that it gives back to consumers the time they would otherwise expend to privately secure a maid and to handle the paperwork involved in tax obligations. ChemLawn manages the risk that the chemicals used on a lawn might be harmful to the environment or the household, or might be the wrong chemicals to achieve the desired result. Terminex manages the similar risk that chemicals used within the household might be toxic to family or pets, or ineffective at killing roaches or silverfish. Individually, each of the brands in the Service Master portfolio stands for the capacity to master a particular household service. Collectively, Service Master itself stands as the risk backstop—the promise to a consumer that she or he will not be taken advantage of. It is, in fact, a truly brilliant business concept.

Visa is another name that deserves special mention, in part for the very ingeniousness of the name itself. Born of the Latin for "to see," a visa is admission, a ticket, endorsement, an entry pass redolent of travel to exotic locales. But Visa deserves even more special mention for the way it has used negative advertising to reinforce the message of risk mediation. What is the whole gist of Visa ad campaigns? That if you don't have a Visa card you will be denied entry, you will lose access to what matters to you the most and thus will be unable to perform as an adult in this world. And the campaign works so extraordinarily well that at the bottom end of the economy, people are willing to put down a deposit equal to the card's credit limit in order to secure a Visa card and assure their personal efficacy.

• • •

And then there's the case of the Walt Disney Corporation. Historically, Disney's function as a risk intermediary has always been to occupy the center. A Disney movie was a promise that the subject matter would neither be too risqué to offend the children nor too Ingmar Bergmanesque to tax the adults. No *Seventh Seal* for the company a mouse built. Disney's theme parks offer much the same risk mediation. In exchange for a considerable entry fee, parents are assured that the rides will be fun and colorful, though never death-defying; the lines, though often long, will never be onerous; and the educational element at such places as Orlando's Epcot Center—which was never built as the experimental prototypical city of tomorrow that Walt Disney envisioned—will be Culture Lite.

Today, though, there is serious question whether Disney intends to continue occupying the center. On its film-making side, Disney has been drifting toward the mainstream Hollywood obsession with edge issues. What remains to be seen is whether the rest of the Disney enterprise will follow its moviemakers out of the middle and, if it does, what role the company can still fulfill as a risk intermediary, because the company must continue to fulfill that role in some way. The tendency of any good person looking at strategy is to want to do just what Disney's filmmakers have done—push the envelope; say, yeah, but I'd like to do this, too. Chaos theory, on the other hand, teaches that the essence of strategy sometimes lies more in the things you tell yourself you won't do than in the things you promise yourself you will do. In the still center is the dance.

Finally, there is the issue of managing your own risk in the Chaos Age, because, as we said earlier, in the Chaos Age you are never without risk.

Dances with Wolves

One of the things we like to do best is simply talk with highly successful people and listen to their life stories. And one of the things we are always most struck by is how the most highly successful among them—the happiest, the most satisfied, the most centered and in control—were given the gift of danger at a very early age. Yes, the *gift*.

They were born to teenage mothers, not to parents who waited to have children until they could afford to send them to private schools, clothe them in Shetland wools, and assure that all their summer camping experiences would be meaningful ones. They were forced to fend on their own as children, because there were no nannies to follow them around, chattering in Spanish. They got into fights, because fighting is in the nature of boys, at least, and the fights taught them that if they followed a feint with the left, they were likely to get clobbered by a roundhouse right.

Surprisingly often, their parents drank too much, were too crazy, and rarely came to their baseball games, swim meets, school plays, or scout gatherings. If they were boys, they stole cars in surprisingly high numbers, because there is something irresistible to a curious fourteen-year-old about a car with the keys left in it—and in those days drivers often couldn't be bothered to take the keys out of the ignition. If they were girls, they shoplifted occasionally—candy, cosmetics, what used to quaintly be called notions—because there were no exit scanners, no magnetic tags to be demagnetized at checkout. Was it a more moral time? Probably not. Was it better training for the world as it is? Undoubtedly so.

What the highly successful people we love talking with learned to do was cope with danger. They didn't *learn* enlightened anxiety; they internalized it as a basic survival skill, because it was only through enlightened anxiety that they could keep themselves out of harm's way: the long arm of the law, the sudden slap of an inebriated father, a psychotic mother. They didn't learn that life is a series of oxymoronic coincidences; they internalized that, too, because that is in the nature of a childhood left alone to grow in its own chaotic fashion. They didn't learn to cope with irrationality; they practiced it in the fiber of their existences. And that is why they are successful today.

What does risk management mean at a personal level? That the only way to manage risk is to embrace it. That the only way to cope with risk is to swim in it, dance with it, let it happen. A victim says that the world is at fault for exposing me to this risk. A thrivalist—a person who not just survives but thrives—says that every risk is an opportunity. More about that, too, in our chapter titled "Right Concentration: The Disaster Agenda."

7

Right Livelihood: Public Privacy

How will the future be shaped in the Chaos Age? By the collision and fusion of seeming opposites, by paradoxical and disharmonious conjunctions. But what can appear to be oxymoronic about the future is often just a matter of making accommodations with reality. So it is with the simultaneous drives toward connectivity and privacy, toward what we call public privacy.

Societal turning points breed dissidents and discontents. Take the Luddites who rose up in Nottingham, England, in 1811. (Take them *please*, a British industrialist of the early nineteenth century might have added.) Operating mostly at night and mostly masked, Luddites destroyed factory machinery in Nottingham and neighboring districts—and later throughout the shires of York, Lancaster, Derby, and Leicester—to protest the dismissal of handicraftsmen and artisans and the rise of shoddy merchandise brought on by the Industrial Revolution. The hangings and deportations that followed a mass trial in York in 1813—probably including the real man behind the invented "King Ludd" for whom the group was named—brought a temporary end to the movement, but it flared again in 1816, spreading through the whole of Great Britain until rising prosperity and repressive legislation finally capped the violence.

We have no doubt that a convergence of societal shifts of the magnitude we are now experiencing will bring about far greater dislocation, produce far more dissidents, and lead sadly to far more violence. Indeed, we already have witnessed more than enough of the latter. The Unabomber's self-styled "manifesto" was a screed against technology, pollution, and much else, but collectively it was a rant against the totality of reality, written by someone—Ted Kaczynski or otherwise—whose own highly individualized view of reality had splintered off from the main.

Almost certainly, it seems, the April 19, 1995, bombing of the federal building in Oklahoma City that left 169 people dead was carried out by a paramilitary group or members of such a group whose collective view of reality had been fed by a highly segmented, deeply interconnected media commune. Indeed one of the most oxymoronic parts of the oxymoronic future that has already arrived is that connectivity leads to individuation. The more people are brought together through high technology, the more they create separate realities.

The very rich who want to escape connectivity can head to low-tech compounds. We expect to see many more of those, especially among the "old rich," for whom paradigm shifts are almost always threatening. Those whose highly segmented views of reality have led them to see a conspiracy wherever one or two are gathered can head, as Ted Kaczynski did, to the deep valleys and high ridges of the northern American Rockies, although it is worth noting that however primitive their cabins might be, most are likely to be wired for cyberspace. (Check out the bulletin boards and chat rooms of the Internet for everything you always wanted to know about paranoia but were afraid to ask.) Religious millennialists can disconnect from the present tense as they wait for the Second Coming and eternity. (Look for an odd and exponentially growing intersection in Idaho and Montana of the heavily armed and the heavy in prayer.) For most of us, though, connectivity is not an optional course. Indeed, for most of us connectivity is a deeply treasured value.

We accept the permanent sway of the Hawthorne Effect—this

state of being under unending survey and examination—because the Hawthorne Effect is one of the prices we pay for the ability to exercise our freedoms to know, to go, to do, and to be. We just want to be paid for the information we surrender about ourselves, because that information represents our own intellectual property and we now control the market equation.

We accept that connectivity works both ways—that access necessarily sacrifices a portion of our privacy—because we realize, consciously or otherwise, that connectivity has also democratized information. For the first time in the history of mankind, access to information is no longer a privilege based on birth, race, sex, or economic means. But to be willing to sacrifice a portion of our privacy in the name of connectivity is not to be willing to sacrifice it all. Privacy is a deeply held value, and the rarer it becomes, the more it grows in worth.

How then do we satisfy both the impulse toward connectivity and the imperative of privacy? How do we accommodate the reality of the Age of Access?

In part, by the New Civility we mentioned earlier. In small ways, by the cyber-equivalents of "please" and "thank you." In larger ways, by recognizing that the memory of men and machines is finite, that time has become compressed and miniaturized, and that no currency has greater value than that of personal energy. What will be the worst breaches of etiquette in the New Civility? Useless, infinitely replicated e-mail. Information that is not germane to the issue at hand. Response delays. Show-off communications. Messages that flaunt the hardware and software used to create and send them—a cyber-violation of downward nobility. Anything that hogs memory, that wastes time, that requires us to expend our own energy in ways not directly linked with outcome. The New Civility will be part of a larger new social contract built not on artificial distinctions but on simple respect, because only by respecting each other can we each be free to pursue our individual destinies.

How else will we satisfy both connectivity and privacy? By hiring someone to manage the task for us. Here's a prediction you can take to the bank: Within a decade, privacy management will be one of America's great growth service industries. In less than a decade, there will be no greater status tool than having someone manage your privacy for you, because there will be no greater proof of your worth than that the flood of connectivity directed toward you is beyond your capacity to control yourself. Build *that* and they will come. But remember as you're building that a privacy manager in the Age of Access has three distinct functions to fulfill.

The Privacy Sheriff

When we wrote that a high-ranking executive in a technologically astute company receives an average of something like two hundred e-mail messages a day, we were speaking from personal experience. How many e-mail messages a day Steven Spielberg receives is probably beyond our comprehension. How many e-mail messages Intel CEO Andy Grove gets daily is probably beyond Steven Spielberg's comprehension, but if industry CEO standards mean anything, Grove has at least four and possibly five people who do nothing but handle his schedule, and at least half of their time is e-mail time.

As with Andy Grove today, so with Steven Spielberg tomorrow. And as with us today, so with nearly everyone tomorrow. Connectivity and a willingness to share in it is nothing less than the price of entry into the world of affairs, and connectivity breeds connectivity as surely as a warren of rabbits multiplies itself. That will be the privacy sheriff's first job: to serve as bodyguard and gatekeeper, to provide a central point of entry for all the connectivity links to you, and to sort through the communication received there according to whatever instructions you create. Think of it as call blocking, call forwarding, and call paging for the cyber-age. Once Andy Grove realizes how cheap the service is compared to the four or five people now performing the same function for him, even he might be interested.

But being a bodyguard will be the lesser part of a privacy sheriff's job. More important than the protection he offers for in-coming information will be the control he (or she or it) exercises over outflow. Everyone wants the information, and the more they can afford and need privacy management, the more they will want it. Against this constant demand, it will be the privacy sheriff's job to make sure that only what clients want to go out actually goes out.

What kind of information might that include? Video-rental preferences for one thing. Congress rushed the Video Privacy Act to law in 1988 after an enterprising reporter dug into the records of then-Supreme Court nominee Robert Bork's favorite video outlet. (Judge Bork's tastes, it turned out, ran toward John Wayne movies.) But if video stores can no longer disclose rental records without the consent of the customer or a court order, it's only public pressure that keeps them from selling lists of its customers categorized by the types of movies they favor. Let them be sold, the new privacy ethic will hold, but include the customers in the information transaction, and include them as well in transactions that reveal their age, house value, salary, family structure, or any other pertinent information. And note that a privacy sheriff who lets any of these items slip out without client approval is going to be turning in his (or her or its) badge.

The Privacy Editor

Think of all the information trying to reach you in any given day as the gloriously disarranged manuscript of *Look Homeward, Angel* that Thomas Wolfe delivered to the office of Maxwell Perkins, his great editor at Charles Scribner's Sons (and editor to Ernest Hemingway and F. Scott Fitzgerald as well). Now think of your privacy editor as Maxwell Perkins himself as he begins to read and sort through Wolfe's colossal—and brilliant—pile. The privacy editor's job isn't only to delete, although that is part of it, because everything has a space in which it has to fit. His or her job is also to arrange, to create as Perkins did the reality of the book from the raw material of genius.

Think of your privacy editor next as the editor of a great American daily—the *Los Angeles Times*, the *New York Times*, the *Washington Post*, the *Wall Street Journal*, the *Philadelphia Inquirer* or *Baltimore Sun* or *Chicago Tribune*, it doesn't matter which one. The time is late afternoon. The place is the daily editorial conference. The task at hand is to decide what goes where—above the fold or below the fold on the front page, inside the "A" section, on the front of "Metro" or "Living" or buried back by the classifieds. What stays and what gets spiked. What the banner is and what the front-page teasers are. That, too, is part of a privacy editor's job. That, too, is the daily business of arranging reality.

Last, think of your privacy editor not as an information specialist, but as a knowledge specialist, someone whose job is to convert into knowledge the sea of information made available by connectivity—whose job, that is, is to make the information germane to your interests and needs.

The Elias Sports Bureau, to cite one example, can tell you almost anything anyone could ever want to know about any baseball player. It has crunched more numbers than any other service; it has created more permutations and combinations of statistics than there are angels that can be fit on the head of a pin. And every bit of it is all utterly worthless—unless, that is, you happen to be deeply interested in baseball. Then it is pure gold. If baseball happens to be a part of your individual reality, then your privacy editor will have the Elias figures waiting for you and, if the privacy editor is good, the figures will be infinitely malleable. If gardening is also a central part of the reality you have created for yourself, the Rodale Press's gardening books and guides will also be waiting. Exhaustive figures on every battle of the Civil War will be waiting if that's what you want.

In effect, NewsPage, the on-line business news service, does this by scanning some six hundred publications and providing subscribers with digested news based on a menu of more than eight hundred business topics. Others news services do this as well. What your privacy editor will do is pull all such news services together, leach out all the white noise between them, and allow you to change the parameters of your daily information load as situational needs demand. Your editor will give you not all the news that's fit to print, but all the news that fits the moment. And by fitting news and information to situational needs and aficionado lifestyles, your editor will turn both to knowledge.

If your privacy editor is very good, he (or she or it) will even anticipate the input you want and need. Imagine coming home in the evening and having waiting for you a listing and description of the five television shows, scanned from five hundred satellite channels, that you are most likely to watch based on your past viewing behavior and attitudes. In a world of miniaturized time, anticipation will be right livelihood.

The Privacy Agent

The privacy agent's job is both the simplest and most complex of the triad of tasks that make up privacy management. It is to make sure you get paid for the information you give up about yourself and to make sure you get paid the most for giving up the information you least want to surrender.

We confess that we don't begin to know how such an arrangement would work—whether each information transaction would be billed separately or whether information would be given up longitudinally on a continuing-contract basis. Nor do we know how much a privacy agent could command, or whether payment would be on a flat-fee or commission basis. We are only certain that privacy management is coming and coming soon, because if a company like TRW can convert itself from a business that dealt in automobile after-market parts to one that did defense contracting work to, virtually overnight, one that became the dominant force in credit management, it or its peers can just as easily change again overnight into a privacy manager.

Build the dominant force in privacy management and Andy Grove might even send *you* an e-mail. Our advice: Instruct your privacy editor to patch it straight through to you.

8

Right Mindfulness: The Energy Model

Here's a screwy idea for you: To create a New Age album, we'll import a musical form that harks back to Pope Gregory I, who reigned from 590 to 604 A.D. What's more, in an era obsessed with celebrity, we'll have the album sung by a group no one has ever heard of—the Benedictine Monks of Santo Domingo de Silos. Just for good measure, now that Latin is almost dead and gone even from the Catholic mass, we'll have the songs performed in Latin, and we'll give them such catchy titles as "Mandatum novum do vobis" and "Occuli omnium." Could it ever work? Obviously, yes. Angel Record's *Chant* is one of the best-selling New Age albums in history.

Why did it work? Because in New Age music, words themselves aren't important. Indeed, words are an impediment. To the extent that the lyrics are intelligible, they impel an intellectual response—they demand to be listened to. By keeping the words in Latin and thus untranslatable for virtually all listeners, they become an integral part of the music, inseparable from and equally soothing with it. As for the music, the sharper the variation in the melodies, the more demanding it, too, becomes. New Age music has to work subliminally. It is both entertainment and therapy for people on whom too much demand is already placed. Finally, New Age music is less about music at all than it is about energy—its amassing and its conservation—and it is that new currency value of energy that *Chant* tapped into so successfully.

In the same spirit of energy conservation, Avis has been developing what it calls the "Rapid Rover Return" policy, a constellation of ideas all meant to minimize the loss of energy at one of the places where time and stress intersect most dramatically—airports. At its test facility at Newark International Airport in New Jersey, and now at other selected locations around the country, Avis has started giving out airline flight information at the car-return facility. The information won't make the flights depart any faster, they won't prevent backups in the major air-traffic corridors, but they will allow passengers even before they arrive at the terminal to begin planning their use of time while they wait for takeoff. That, in turn, will reduce the stress of their travel experience. Soon the company will be installing "countdown clocks" in Avis courtesy buses to tell passengers exactly how soon the bus will be departing for the terminal: 4:59, 4:58, 4:57, etc. Again, the clocks won't save time, but they will reduce the impact of stress upon time by allowing passengers to use their time more effectively.

Instead of having customers pull their rental cars into a barren, macadamized lot, Avis also is considering making its return areas more like a botanical garden or arboretum, depending on the climate. The plants themselves would give a small gift of energy, and they would recognize in a quiet way a very loud fact of many business travelers' lives: that airline travel is draining enough these days without having to extend the misery to the rental-car provider.

Why such emphasis on energy conservation? Because as the rate of change accelerated, time itself became compressed and miniaturized. All the studies kept telling us that we had more and more discretionary time, but all our intuition and experience told us far more forcefully that we had less control over the time we did have, less capacity to manage it effectively. It was under the pressure of the miniaturization of time that the family vacation shrank from a two-week getaway at the lake or shore to a one-week dash to the

Caribbean to a succession of weekend bed-and-breakfast getaways to, today for many couples, three uninterrupted hours out for dinner. (The latter, by the way, has dramatically changed the dynamic of expectations that many people bring to dining out—a fact largely missed by the restaurant industry.)

The compression of time is only part of the equation. As the rate of change accelerated, change itself accreted. It assumed density and weight. It gained mass, and as it did so, stress gained mass with it. Again, anyone who has been operating in the world for any period of time knows it intuitively.

Three decades ago, an aspiring junior executive was required to learn perhaps one new thing a year—a new skill, a new system of calculating, a new way of conducting the affairs of whatever business was at hand. Today, under the dual impacts of the speed and mass of change, that same aspiring junior executive at the same point in his or her job trajectory might have to learn one new thing a day. Change arrives too quickly, it piles up too high to do otherwise without being entirely left behind. By 2010, it is entirely conceivable that that same person at the same career point might have to learn one new thing an *hour* because to survive and thrive, businesses, like ecosystems, will have to be subtly changing with their environment, subtly becoming different day by day, hour by hour, minute by minute. There will be no other way to keep up.

Collectively, though, time and stress only explain one side of the equation of the modern condition. Time by itself can be managed— by a day planner, an appointments secretary. More than anything else, time management is a matter of saying no and meaning it. As for stress, there is an entire subset of the pharmaceutical industry— Valium, most notably—devoted to nothing but keeping it in check, which is another reason why the "War on Drugs" is fundamentally unwinnable. America is not a nation with pockets of addiction; we are an addicted nation. But as time and stress converged and fused, what they finally had the greatest impact on was energy demand, and energy loss is not so easily treated.

Which has the greater value today—money or human energy? It depends, of course, on your position in life. Inside the ghetto, below the poverty line, gung ho and just starting a job, the issue is money straight and simple. You can't eat it, but you can't live without it. Beyond the ghetto, though, past the marginal neighborhoods and the group houses of youthful strivers, money is often far easier to come by than the freedom from time compression and stress that allows you to enjoy it.

In the 1950s, mobility—social, professional, and residential—was the dominant objective. By the 1970s, the dominant objective had become exploration and experimentation—newness for newness's sake. Today, the dominant objective is conservation of energy and the second-most dominant objective is the accrual of more energy. What has the most value is what is most scarce, and what is most scarce today for many of us is our own energy.

What does the energy model teach us? That managing choices about where you invest your energy, including managing choices *out* of your lives, is the single most important survival skill in business today. What's needed today is less attention than "distention"—not inattention, but the refusal to involve yourself with issues that finally have no relevance to you. Think about your daily life; you'll find dozens of such issues. Learning to swim with chaos requires the recognition that in the Chaos Age you have to operate from self-interest. Self-interest means focusing only on that which you can affect directly. Practice distention, and you'll manage enormous numbers of choices out of your life. We've learned to do it; so can you.

What else does the energy model teach? That the greatest gift you can give an employee or even a loved one is not the one with the greatest monetary value, but the one that gives that person the greatest control over the intersection of time and stress: the gift, that is, of energy. The time chits Avis is now experimenting with are just such a gift, but there are many more ways to say thank you. Perhaps the greatest evolutionary question facing mankind today is not environmental or genetic, but whether as change accelerates and changes mass we have the energy to adapt along with it. At what point does change overwhelm us? At what point do the circuits shut down? At what point do we brown out? Black out?

Finally, the energy model teaches that one of the most profound questions facing businesses and corporations today is not the nurturing and preservation of its physical or capital resources, but the nurturing and preservation of its human-energy resources. Lose those and you have lost for good.

Two Steps Forward, One Step Back

In its December 11, 1995, issue, *U.S. News & World Report* published one of the more interesting survey statistics we have seen in recent years. Among other questions, surveyors asked a nationwide sampling of adult Americans whether they would prefer more free time even if it entails a loss of salary or a higher salary even if it entails putting more time in on the job. Slightly more than half of those polled opted for more time, while only a little more than a third favored more money. Half of all those polled also said they had taken steps over the past five years to simplify their lives, including a move to less hectic communities and jobs and refusal to accept promotions. Significantly, although not surprisingly, those most willing to give up salary for time and those who had most actively sought to scale back the pace of their lives were those with the highest salaries and those who had climbed the highest on the corporate totem pole. Put another way, the more successful respondents had been in the workplace, the more the currency value of time and energy eclipsed the currency value of money. How then do you run a business or any system in which authority and income accrue with age, but the desire to expend the energy necessary to exercise that authority and thus justify that income decreases with age?

One way is to use early retirement to force people out the door at the moment their focus switches from the accrual of income to the accrual of energy. Indeed, early retirement has become a nearly universal solution in an era of corporate retrenching, but it was around long before the downsizers took hold. Early in one of our careers, we went to work for a toy company. Not long after we got there, a key salesman who had been with the company for thirty-two years was forced to take early retirement. He wasn't the national sales manager, but he had a large and important territory, and he had been building up his contacts for over three decades. Before the salesman left, the eager young person who was to take his job spent three weeks traveling his route with him—in theory, meeting everyone that mattered and learning everything the job entailed. And not surprisingly, within a relatively short time after that, the eager new salesman's network dissolved virtually in its entirety, and the company tumbled precipitously in revenues.

In effect, in throwing out the older worker, the company had thrown out his intellectual property—his knowledge of the peculiarities of the buyers he called on, his long history with the product lines, his word and bond—along with him. Multiplied nationwide, that discarding of intellectual property represents a resource loss of staggering proportions.

How else do businesses deal with the waning energy of their senior executives? By creating side positions, empty roles within the organization, sinecures, all in an effort to create a justification for continued employment. It's a better solution if it can be done so that the employee's dignity stays intact—no easy task—because it keeps the intellectual property in-house. But it almost always fosters resentment among younger workers who expend greater energy and exercise greater real authority for less pay.

How *can* it be done? Is there a better way? We suggest using the equations of the energy model. Recognize that after age fifty many workers are, in fact, willing to trade income for energy. Realize that as most workers get older, energy becomes more important than money, more important than time—no one wants to live to be ninety and be old the whole time, and no one goes to his or her grave wishing he or she had spent more time at the office. Realize, too, that the intellectual property every seasoned worker carries within is among the business's most important assets.

And how can that be done when politically correct management rules require that everybody be treated the same—that an equal expenditure of time at an equal level of servitude must be met with equal salary and other considerations regardless of race, sex, or age? By changing those management rules to recognize that in a world based on energy, compensation itself should be based on energy expended, not time delivered.

Granted, managing political correctness while you make the change might prove in the short run far more difficult than the problem you are making the change to solve. It's even possible—should the matter ever be adjudicated and rise to the top of the system—that a majority of justices of the U.S. Supreme Court might not agree that energy is a fair equity divider. If the justices worked a fuller schedule and had fewer eager clerks at their beck and call, the principle would almost certainly be more meaningful to them. But in the long run, striking deals with older workers based on energy, not time, will meet them where they are living at that point in their lives. It will preserve their intellectual property for the good of the whole and preserve their dignity in the bargain. In so doing, it will penetrate the full dimensionality of their beings. Doing so is as important in employee relationships as it is in customer relationships.

9

Right Concentration: The Disaster Agenda

What is the probability today of someone's being involved sometime during his or her adult life in a significant crime—being robbed; being in a bank or a liquor store when it is robbed; being shot or shot at or seeing someone else being shot; attending a concert in a park when a bomb goes off; being in or walking past a building when it is blown up; being in an airplane when it is hijacked or having one of your top executives kidnapped; having your business vandalized by infohuns, infopirates, infomaniacs? Fifty percent? Seventy-five percent? We put it at a clean 100 percent, a sure thing, a mortal lock. Why? Because in a chaos-based world, we will all be subjected eventually to participation in chaotic events. Why? Because even if you are not robbed or shot at or bombed or vandalized during your adult life, even if you somehow escape the mortal lock, the only way to survive in a chaos-based world is to be 100 percent prepared for all those things to happen. Ducking for cover and planning for disaster aren't just exercises for the nuclear generation. Today, they are exercises in sustained reality—and for corporations more so than any other single entity.

A final why? Because as governments fade into immateriality and corporations emerge as the lords of a new, borderless world order, the media attention previously reserved for governmental disasters is being refocused to corporate disasters. And when those disasters strike, media focus can accelerate out of control in moments.

Ask Exxon about the Exxon *Valdez*. Ask ValuJet about its May 11, 1996, crash in the Florida Everglades or TWA about Flight 800. Ask the World Trade Center. Ask Union Carbide about Bhopal or General Public Utilities about Three Mile Island. Ask the United States Olympic Committee, which was conducting a beautiful summer Olympics in a nearly impossible city until a bomb went off in Centennial Park a little after one in the morning at a concert being attended by some 30,000 people.

How do you plan for the inevitability of disaster? By taking the blinders off. By seeing the world as it is. By counting on the certainty of uncertainty, not the certainty of certainty. Not by trying to wish the bad away, but by acknowledging that things are going to happen soon to you and your business—things that by all your current reasoning schemes are anything but reasonable. Here's an exercise that we have clients do: Take out a sheet of paper. Write down the ten worst things that could happen to your business in the next five hundred days, the next five hundred weeks, and then start acting as if they will happen, because in a chaos world they or something very similar will.

Here's another exercise—one in scenario planning—that we go through regularly with clients as diverse as the Royal Dutch/Shell Group; Brown & Root; the Edison Electric Institute; and automakers, international camera companies, Japanese banks, textile-fiber companies, Italian and Latin American petrochemical firms, multinational pharmaceutical companies, computer manufacturers, a Canadian energy company, and other corporations that would prefer their names remain confidential. Take a management strategy you have developed, pinpoint the key decisions factors, and then run them through the maelstrom of business and political environmental forces that could affect those decision factors—not just the most likely ones, not just the most benign ones, but the most unlikely and the most disastrous as well: the Saudi government falls to Islamic militants; pharmaceutical prices are capped by a newly belligerent Congress and White House; your chief designer goes to work for your chief competitor; your plant on the Columbia River is discovered to have been leaking chemicals that are blamed for a huge salmon kill, and the doomed fish, flopping in pools at the base of picturesque rapids, make for excellent TV news footage. (We've laid all this out in the template below.)

As the key decision factors get skewed and splintered by environmental forces, develop a scenario logic for each factor. From these, create actual scenarios. Now consider the strategy implications of each scenario, feed those back into the key decision factors, and fold those back into management strategy. Now disaster may come—now it will come—and now you are prepared for it.

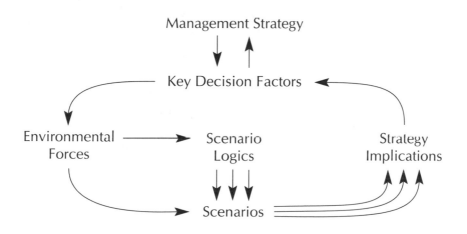

How else can you prepare for disaster? By asking the right questions, starting with the question just below:

Where Are Your Moats?

Castles weren't built with moats because the princes, lords, and thanes who inhabited them thought the moats would be picturesque. Castle walls weren't built thick and crenellated, capped with walkways, and cut through with thin slits in the expectation that seven hundred years later the structure would become a tourist trap. The drawbridge wasn't kept up except on market days to prove that the winch worked. The moats kept ladders away from the walls, which made the walls harder to scale. The crenellated tops of the walls—

from the old Latin *crena* for "notch"—provided both protection for soldiers as they raced along the walkways and openings for, among other things, pouring burning liquids on enemies who happened to breach the moat. Those splayed, slit windows were for archers—easy to fire out of, hard to fire into. The drawbridge was kept up because a prince or lord couldn't wire his wealth daily to a safe bank in London or Geneva. His jewels, his crowns, his gold and silver were stored in the strongest, innermost part of the central tower of the castle—the keep—and it was his existence in the castle, his possession of it, that entitled him to the lands that surrounded the walls and the taxes imposed upon his vassals and serfs.

Do this exercise, too. Write down where your own business's moats are, where and how fortified your castle walls are, where the intellectual property of your company—its secrets, its private systems—is stored, who has the key and how many keys there are. If you can't provide answers for any one of those questions, you are not prepared for or protected against disaster. If you don't even know whether the drawbridge is up or down, or who is in control of raising or lowering it, then trust us: You soon will be overwhelmed. In an open-systems world, a world without borders, the Huns and Visigoths can arrive from any direction, at roughly the speed of light.

Thrival Skills

Here's another way you can prepare for disaster, another way you can learn to swim with chaos instead of letting chaos overwhelm you: Think clearly about the skills that are necessary to get you across the delta, the skills that will help you survive and thrive on the delta's far side, and make sure that you, individually, and your business, collectively, are actively pursuing their mastery.

What were the skills necessary to thrive a century ago? Farming, probably—about 43 percent of the total U.S. labor force was directly involved with farming in 1890. How to make tools from scratch. How to sew. How to deliver a calf or a baby. How to pound nails. Enough engineering to keep a wall from falling down or a roof from collapsing. How to separate the wheat from the chaff, literally. How to behave in church. How to hunt, fish, saddle a horse. What thrival skills had been added by fifty years ago? How to behave in a crowd in a nation and world becoming increasingly urbanized. How to show up to work on time in a nation and world becoming increasingly industrialized. How to say, "Yes, sir" and "Thank you, ma'am," and "Please." Manufactured tools and factory-made clothes were readily available, but you still had to know how to pound nails.

What do you need to know today? What are the thrival skills that will sustain you tomorrow?

- **How to communicate.**
  Even for people living on the streets, the single most important skill to thrive is understanding how to communicate within the bureaucracy.

- **How to connect.**
  It is only by connecting that you can exercise your freedom to know, to go, to do, and to be.

- **How to anticipate.**
  It is only by constantly anticipating risks that you can master them.

- **How to do nothing.**
  The best thing to do when you are lost is wait to be found.

- **Permanent flexibility.**
  The capacity to move in different directions simultaneously, to be constantly different while still focusing on constant outcomes, to live in mystery and doubt without irritably searching after fact and reason—what John Keats called "negative capability"—because the facts don't matter and there is no reason. The ability in a world in which borders of all sorts are collapsing to move easily among different people, different cultures, different mind-sets.

- **Most important, intelligence.**
  The ability to learn a new language every day, because as distinctions between national tongues die out, a new vocabulary is being born at a staggering rate—already roughly a third of the words in any standard dictionary are less than twenty years old. A familiarity with psychology, chemistry, biology, physics, genetics, cybernetics, with scientific theory in general, because it is in the sciences that the greatest

number of ideas are being born—and ideas are the raw ore of the information economy. The capacity to access complicated problems very quickly in real time, because the world won't wait for an answer.

Assemble those skills under a single corporate roof, and your business will be ready. But will you be?

Personality Engineering

Is it possible to engineer a personality with which to cross the delta? We contend that it is, and we offer ourselves as examples, not because we set out in any way to do that, not because getting where we are has always been pretty or straight or even right, but only because circumstance has prepared us. In our example, you might be able to find your own story.

Like the highly successful executives we wrote about earlier, we, too, were given the gift of risk at an early age: by the quirks of personalities that left us outside the herd, by dysfunctional families—drugs, alcohol, neurosis, psychosis—that meant we were never not in danger in the place we should have felt most safe. In the frequent misery of that, we learned to embrace risk to survive; we learned to rely on ourselves; we learned that the only way to become a victim was to let yourself succumb to victimhood. One of our journeys to Alcoholics Anonymous is a trip we wouldn't wish on anyone, but at AA, we learned that it is important to bring your body and trust your mind to follow. Frankly, we've learned in a slow, groping way the same thing about faith.

We arrived separately at our passion for sacred sites, for places that allow us to see the world from the periphery—through the eyes of a Rastafarian prophet who uses a satellite beam system to transport images of himself over the Jamaican mountain he lives on top of, through the eyes of a Montana cowboy who has taught us about the dance at the still center—because it is only at the periphery that you can truly see the world clearly for what it is, that you can escape the illusion of reality and meet reality face-to-face. Our advice: Find your own sacred site, not ours, a place where you can sit on the edge and look back to the center. There is no greater clarity to be found anywhere.

We arrived separately, too, at our passion for real disguise, for slipping into the stream of life and letting it take us where it will—panhandling, wrangling, harder places, worse situations. There is surprisingly much to be learned in a junkie hangout at two in the morning, a lesson in chaos theory and in real reality that the business schools never teach. But don't imitate us. Find your own real disguises, escape your own cognition, and you'll find your true self.

We're more proud to say that between us we have nearly fifty years of marriage and with one wife each. If loyalty is not an obligation, true loyalty can occur. We freely own to having been lucky beyond our wildest dreams, but we have opened ourselves to luck. We've let it come to us, and we've been ready to take advantage when it did. You can do that, too. Notwithstanding the experience of the Trojans, the old saw has it just right: Never look a gift horse in the mouth.

Maybe our greatest gift has been our work. As we wrote earlier, we have been paid large sums to simply listen: to Nobel physicists, to CEOs of multibillion-dollar multinationals, to heads of global charities. We're not going to turn over the keys to our trade to you, but the operative principle is the same: Listen, escape your own white noise, and you'll be astounded by what you will hear.

Remember what we learned in AA: Bring your body and your mind will follow.

Renewal

Finally, some very practical advice on preparing to cross the delta, an annual ritual of renewal that we have been doing for a number of years. Try to remember the date of the first day you ever had an adult job, mark it on your calendar, and every year on that date, write down the five things that made a difference in the success of your enterprise or career in the year just past, the five things that will make a difference in the year ahead, and the five things that you expect to make a difference in the year after that. And from that exercise, define the things that you have to change immediately—the things you have to renew or alter at a personal and corporate level—and the things that you have to be preparing to change in the near future.

Why? Because if you don't continually renew your vision of what the world is and how you can manage your way through it, if you don't continually renew the vision of what your company exists for, who its competitors are, how it makes what it does, how it communicates with its people and the world at large, you will only become more and more efficient at doing the wrong thing. Change will overwhelm you, and disaster will follow as sure as night follows day.

A last irony of the Chaos Age: It is only by concentrating on the inevitability of disaster that you can free yourself to pursue the fruits of possibility.

New Rules for a Chaos World

PART V

How do you survive and prosper in a world in which change has been so rapid and has accumulated such mass; a world in which change has arrived like a river system rushing at flood tide? You survive and prosper—you thrive—by focusing, settling, and simplifying. Amidst the ambient chaos of our times, you thrive by sticking to basic principles.

We have divided those principles below into five categories, but don't think of them as functioning separately. All these principles, all these categories, are part of a single continuum. Each reinforces, augments, and strengthens the others. To practice one is, in effect, to begin to practice all. Remember: To enter a web is to come in touch not with a single point, but with the whole of its creation.

The Wisdom of Planning

Stop planning around chains of causality.

A five-year plan that relies on causal projections is a five-year trap. The acceleration of the rate of change means that you will be wedding yourself to assumptions that are obsolete the moment you make them, banking on givens that are anything but, and thus planning for a future that will never happen. There really is no certainty.

Microsoft is a wonderful company with a wonderful record—arguably the most powerful company in the world as we write. But the only certainty Microsoft can safely count on is that the primacy of its MS/DOS system will hold for, at best, another five hundred days. The only certainty it can count on is that while owner Bill Gates twirls the gadgets in his $30 million home, a dozen individual entrepreneurs in a dozen little basement workshops around the world are working on operating systems that will revolutionize home computing. That is not off-the-cuff future-mongering, by the way. It is fact pure and simple, as sure as the rising sun, as bankable as the turning tide. And this is also fact pure and simple: One of those dozen entrepreneurs will succeed.

Start planning around the certainty of uncertainty.

Instead of counting on the certainty of certainty, count on its uncertainty. List the five worst things that could happen to your company and your career, assume that each of them will, and then develop a scenario to deal with each circumstance, to turn each to opportunity. (See below about the necessity of gathering information constantly.) When the worst arrives, it will arrive with such blinding speed that you will have to be prepared to deal it before it gets there.

Forget process.

You can play at ball or you can play ball, and the difference is absolutely fundamental. Those who play at ball think about the process. They worry whether their models are right; they exhaust energy on a causal relation that doesn't exist. People who play at ball tend to "glossofacilia"—the use of very large words to explain very small phenomena—because their natural reaction to a world of radical change is to complexify it, in language and in life. People who play ball are the ball, the game, the thing itself. Another of the ironies of an age that so empowers the individual is that to succeed, you must submerge individual identity into whatever you do.

Perhaps the saddest consulting job we ever had was handling communications for the company that had insured the Pan Am Boeing 747 jet that was blown up by a terrorist bomb over Lockerbie, Scotland, on December 21, 1988. Among the 270 people killed, eleven of them Scots on the ground, were 38 Syracuse University students and many U.S. military personnel returning home for the holidays. The sorrow, the anger, the horror echoed across the globe. There are models for dealing with these situations; in our case, there was precedent—we had consulted on other airline disasters, although nothing as shocking as this. There were protocols we had to follow. And we succeeded, for our clients and their clients, and most particularly for the parents of the dead students and soldiers. But we didn't succeed because we "handled" the parents. We succeeded because we "became" the parents, because we have children of our own, because we felt their anguish and thus understood their needs. Don't do. Be.

Focus on outcome.

Jim McCann built 1-800-FLOWERS into the greatest florist company in the world not by following a twelve-step program to get there, but by determining from the outset that that is what his company would be. In effect, McCann pursued complicated simplicity. In a world of immense complexities—a world in which disharmonies constantly converge and the future is built paradox by paradox—he succeeded by keeping the end point clear and simple. The critical issue in planning today is not how to get there. The critical issue is where you want to be. As we said earlier, it is as true of individuals as it is of businesses.

The Wisdom of Preparing

Learn to conserve energy.

Think of your professional and personal lives as the control room for a power grid. With each new activity, each new demand on your time and decision-making capacity, a new light bulb flashes on the grid. "Overload in new accounting practices!" "Overload in children's schedules!" "Overload in peer relationships!" In a chaos world, a world in which time is becoming compressed and miniaturized, you have to decide which power sectors are worth operating at peak performance, which you can brown-out, and which you can fade to black altogether. Learn to manage your choices—including managing out choices you choose not to engage in—or the choices will manage you. Waste time. Take naps. There is not enough energy to go around. Ever.

Learn to accept responsibility.

The corollary of a rise in the value of intuition, of the new regency of self-reliance, of the advent of a deal-based world, is self-responsibility. No one will choose your path for you. You must choose it for yourself. And keep choosing it over and over. Constancy creates success is the old rule. Constant reinvention is the new one. Ralph Waldo Emerson had this one right: "A foolish consistency is the hobgoblin of little minds, adored by little statesmen and philosophers and divines. With consistency a great soul has simply nothing to do. He may as well concern himself with his shadow on the wall."

Gather information constantly.

When life is a continuous pursuit, when the need for decision-making arises in rapid and unpredictable bursts, education becomes a continuous necessity. You cannot possibly anticipate enough knowledge. All you can do is gather data constantly in the hope that it will one day inform an important outcome. Cause and effect still exist, but there is no time to parse them and nothing to be gained by doing so.

Gather experience constantly.

Think of the five levels of sales expertise: the unconscious incompetent, who doesn't know what he's doing and doesn't know that he doesn't know; the conscious incompetent, who still doesn't know what she's doing, but has figured out that she doesn't know; the unconscious competent, who knows what he is doing, but can't repeat his success; the conscious competent, who knows what she's doing and can repeat it; and the unconscious conscious competent, who knows what he is doing so well and is so able to repeat that he never has to think about it. It is the fifth level you want to get to, and it is only by going through the other four that you get there. Experience is a poor teacher, but it can be a great trainer.

Practice intelligent disobedience.

In an age of reason, it was reasonable to follow rules because the rules worked out for the good of everybody. Today, not only do the rules not work out for the good of individuals, they don't work out for the good of the whole either. Break them.

Get out of the box.

Try this exercise: Take a sheet of paper and list all the tenets that you have adhered to in your professional life. Be thorough: loyalty, working the chain of command, the value of precedent, collegiality, career building, whatever they happen to be. Next, write down at least one example of why each didn't work: The chain of command didn't respond when you proposed an auto vacuum that would plug into the car's cigarette lighter; you attached your career star to this senior vice president rather than that one only months before your would-be champion walked to the competition. Now—carefully observing local fire codes and conditions, and all admonitions never to play with matches—take the list outside, set it on fire, and watch it blacken and shrivel into nothingness. Yes, you will continue to attempt to be reasonable; yes, you will continue to try to impose reasonable solutions on an irrational world. You will continue to hunger for a career. These things are not to be avoided or even rued: It is useful for a prisoner to remember the scrape and drag of shackles. But until you expunge everything that holds you where you are, you cannot move on to where you need to be.

We admit to a certain excessive fondness in this regard, and not only through our panhandling, our "real disguises," our pursuit of sacred spots. To get out of the box, we also collect art by schizophrenics, religious visionaries, prisoners, the certifiably insane and the not-so-certifiably whacko, outsiders of every sort. To be perfectly honest, one of us has been in prison himself—a youthful indiscretion while crewing on an oceangoing research vessel that worked the waters between South America and the Florida coast. Our lives are not perfect, far from it, and no life experience is replicable. But the point is not to imitate in any event. The point is simply to escape, to see the world differently, by whatever means, so that you can see it clearly.

One more stab at Ralph Waldo Emerson, because a century and a half ago he saw with crystalline clarity what it would take to succeed in the world now forming just ahead: "Whoso would be a man, must be a nonconformist. . . . Nothing is at last sacred but the integrity of our own mind."

Listen to your own life.

In listening to it, recognize that most of the things that have truly changed your life have been the fruition not of elaborate plotting but of coincidental accidents.

How did you meet and come to marry your spouse? Probably not by plotting and, unless you're Indian or African, probably not by parental arrangement and an exchange of dowries. One of us has been married for more than twenty years to the woman who refused his invitation to the high school prom. The other met his wife because he signed up for a course called "The Rhetoric of Freudian Psychology" at the University of California at Berkeley—for no reason other than that he loved the title and desperately wanted to avoid entering the real world—and because she happened to have signed up for the same course and was wearing a really terrific white angora sweater on the first day of the semester.

How did you do your last deal? By sitting down months earlier and saying, On this day all these random forces are going to come together, all these variables are going to somehow interact in my favor, and gold will gush from the spigots? Unlikely in the extreme because even if you had said that, you couldn't have controlled the variables, and the more you tried to, the more the variables would have controlled you.

How did you find faith if you have it? By reading six pages of the Bible each night and saying grace before supper? By poring over the Torah? The Koran? Or through a full-goose, bells-and-whistles encounter? Chances are it's the latter. The God of the Age of Reason, the one who revealed Himself through the rational order of His creation, gets harder and harder to find amidst the ambient chaos.

The truth is that any life is proof that reason and linear time don't apply, and they don't apply most dramatically in the things that matter most. The new model isn't planning. The new model for the oxymoronic future that lies ahead is opportunity. It is responding to coincidental accidents—accepting events as they occur, not as you want them to occur. The new model is letting it happen and having within you the set of values that gives you the confidence to make a choice. Bring your intuition and opportunity will follow. And always keep your eyes open. In order to depart from the logical models of the Renaissance, you have to recognize where you have been. In order to recognize where you have been, you have to see where you are going. Chaos liberates. Particle logic empowers the individual.

Try a little happiness.

We veer here, we know, toward what might seem the terminably corny, but the simple reality is that there is a rising epidemic of happiness in the work world and that, while only those who take a vow of poverty can be truly happy in an impoverished state, it is a happiness largely unrelated to economic status. Perhaps one in five of us has learned to accept this transitory world as it is, and in the end it is the person who does that, who doesn't ask the world to be more or different than it can be, who will find the greatest contentment. What confers the greater status today? To conspicuously consume, to announce your success with your possessions? Or simply to walk into a room and announce by word and deed that you are a happy, contented person? The fact is, it's not even close. As Warren Buffet once said, the only good thing about having money is that it stops you from having to chase it.

Bye-bye, Beamer. Hello, beaming.

The Wisdom of Managing

Control risks, not behavior.

In a world in which success depends upon being innovative, managers have to accept that their most valuable employees are going to be their most creatively disobedient ones. Think of yourself as refereeing a basketball game. Your job is to manage risks for players and spectators: to make sure the game gets finished in a reasonable time, to protect players against flagrant fouls. Call every infraction, every bump, every extra half-step, and the game will be played according to the book—and the stands will be empty by half-time. Call only the ones that matter, and the self-interest and creativity of the players will assure the beauty of the whole. Remember: Controlling risks lets intuition blossom below you. Micromanaging employees drives off those most likely to come up with the innovative ideas that can create new revenue streams.

Build unrules into the structure.

Then hold employees accountable for their performance. What does it matter if your star employee wants to go to a movie during the workday so long as she gets back the time at night? What does it matter if she files the report from her laptop while staring at the sunrise from the top of Mount Kilimanjaro so long as the report—the *great* report—does get filed and the job does get done. Okay, Kilimanjaro is extreme, but unrules recognize the growing merger of work and leisure. More than that, unrules recognize that the most creative, most productive employees are going to break whatever rules are imposed. In a chaos environment, that's exactly why they are the most valuable players. Instead of disciplining by rules, discipline by motives that are consistent with the employees' greatest self-interest. Then employees will be disciplining themselves.

Open up communication, but control the communication process.

Textron was one of the first American corporations to understand that well-protected lines of communication stunt growth instead of encouraging it. Back in the 1970s—long before Volvo had come up with its team-managed assembly lines and IBM had devised its team-based service delivery systems—Textron realized that its rigid vertical communication structure would never provide it with the productivity or innovation gains necessary to propel the company to the top. And so it simply abolished walls within the office space. The experiment didn't address the corporate hierarchy per se, but it did provide a physical environment that encouraged people to communicate without a pretext for the communication. The result? Within four years, this open-communication environment told the company that it needed to change again, and the recognition of the need to change is the beginning of wisdom.

Like unrules, opening up communication recognizes an existing reality: In the Age of Access, anyone can get through to anyone. How then do you prevent communication from becoming the whole business of the organization? Not by squelching e-mail, but by building process into organizational communications. Not by trying to forbid involvement in a decision stream, but by spelling out clearly the decision points at which different actors may get involved in it. Not by subverting the four new freedoms of the access age, in short, but by managing around them.

Embrace change.

Because without embracing change, you cannot embrace chaos. What is the engine behind the astounding profits at General Electric? Not lightbulbs. Not even jet engines. The driving force is GE Capital. General Electric makes oodles not because it produces general electronics, but because it sells money. General Motors and Ford have done the same thing through their financing wings, GMAC and Ford Credit. Even as their proportionate share of the global auto market decreased, they were making the purchase of a car, virtually any car by any manufacturer, a fiduciary relationship that lasts nearly the life of the car. In doing so, they were climbing into bed with their customers in the most direct way.

That is what successful companies do: They learn to penetrate the full dimensionality of their customers' lives. They structure themselves so that they are prepared to change as the dimensionality of their customers' lives changes. Successful companies are different every single day because the environment of the marketplace is different every single day. And successful employees will have to learn to do the same.

Institutionalize diversity.

Not because the U.S. government tells you to, not because your office black caucus or female caucus or disabled caucus demands it, but because the greater the diversity of your senior staff, the more capable you will be to respond instantaneously to chaotic circumstances. The problem with twenty white men making decisions in a conference room isn't that the tenets of affirmative action are being snubbed; the problem, at least as judged by the balance sheet, is that twenty white men collectively have a truncated perspective, a narrow band of cognition. Collectively, they have a low diversity IQ, a foreshortened ability to see the world through multiple perspectives. An organization that wants to see the world differently every single day has to be built around people who see the world differently from each other every single day. The test of employment shouldn't be skin color or sex, graduate schools or clubs. The more diversity of interests and focuses, the better. The only test should be whether employees share the organization's core business values. If they don't, they are wrebels—rebellious workers who seek to wreck an organization's value system. And if they are wrebels, they must be gone, whatever their race, sex, or cultural heritage.

Surrender control.

Nothing is harder to do, and nothing is more essential to organizing successfully in a chaos world. If you can predict what your subordinates are doing at any given moment, they are doing the wrong thing. If you can say where a project will be tomorrow, it is going in the wrong direction. In a rational world, confusion in the parts meant confusion in the whole. In a chaos world, confusion in the parts is the only way to build certainty in the whole. General Electric gets another mention here: Of all major U.S. corporate players that have been around long enough to have a deep history, it is the only one that is close to getting this right. Yielding power creates power that matters. That is the lovely paradox of chaos-driven organization.

Surrendering control can even create beautiful music. The Orpheus Chamber Orchestra was founded in New York City in 1972 by a small cadre of young musicians determined to perform without the autocratic presence of a conductor. Interpretation and phrasing would be decided democratically; the concertmaster for any particular piece would be elected by the orchestra voting as a whole.

As James Traub noted in an August 1996 *New Yorker* article on the group, such utopianism was soon tempered by the realities of orchestral life and, later, by the growing international prominence of the group. An executive committee of musicians was established and, eventually, a nonperforming executive director. Feelings were hurt; some of the original members left. But without a conductor the orchestra remains to this day, and in the absence of a maestro, the members have learned to listen to one another, not the insistent tap of a baton. They have developed an intense trust in each other, a deep responsibility not just to their own parts, but to the piece as a whole. And in doing all that, they have learned to produce extraordinary music. "It is as if," Traub writes, "the process that Orpheus uses to achieve a sense of common purpose reproduces itself in the harmony of the music."

Yielding power creates power that matters.

The Wisdom of Sitting at the Top

Don't watch the stock.

In the chaos of the market, the circumstances that will move share price around are beyond your control. The more you try to exercise control, the more you will be chasing the wrong goals and the more energy you will be investing in the pursuit of unattainable ends.

Treat each customer as an individual market.

Do this for one very simple reason: Each customer is treating himself or herself that way. If institutional loyalty is a thing of the past, if each individual is married to an individual agenda, if each person is creating an individual reality, then the moral is clear: You have to go where each individual is. Forget those elaborate census-tract breakdowns; forget the cute consumer typologies. Today, you might as well search for a mass performed entirely in Latin as search for a mass market. Brand loyalty is dead and gone. Customer loyalty is alive and well. In the particalized marketplace, the building of customer loyalty—one customer at a time—will be a fundamental part of the building of any successful product and any successful company. Remember: All manufacturing is really service.

What does that mean in the everyday world of business? Two examples: The telecommunications giant MCI is considering instituting an annuity phone bill that would guarantee customers free phone service as of age sixty-five if they have been MCI customers for a still-to-be-determined number of years prior to that time. Doing so would penetrate to the core of an aging population's fear of being penniless in retirement. In a world short on loyalties, this would be a loyalty contract struck one-on-one with each customer. The Calico Corner collection of some two hundred fabric stores nationwide, meanwhile, has been creating separate spaces in its stores where kids can use a doll house–like configuration to experiment with colors and textures they might like for their own rooms. As all women and very few men know, fabric shopping can entail up to three hours in the store. Involving children in the process solves a very real management problem for mothers. It allows them to concentrate on the hard work at hand. And it turns the drudgery of fabric selection into a shared experience. Instead of forcing customers to conform to it, Calico Corner is conforming to its customers, and thus, at a minimal cost, it is building maximal shopping loyalty.

Invest in innovation paths.

As the window closes on the length of time it takes a product to reach total adoption, the need to constantly reintroduce new products becomes ever greater. Early adopters have no patience, and once you lose the slim market of early adopters, you lose the larger market of confirmers. And once you lose the larger market of confirmers, you have lost altogether. To stay on the innovation path in children's television, the Nickelodeon cable-TV channel formed an advisory panel of two hundred kids, each provided with a computer that shares a common server. Nickelodeon provides panel members with early tapes of television programming, test-marketing concepts, test advertising, and tests of promotional programs such as the Clean Up America campaign. In return for keeping Nickelodeon ahead of the curve, the children have the ego satisfaction of serving as arbiters of taste for their generation.

Think in the future, act in the present.

Hire IQ and be prepared to pay for it.

If the Renaissance is over, it follows that the day of the Renaissance man—able to do a little of everything well—is over, too.

He'll be sorely missed; no one was more charming at a company cock-tail outing. But the information economy rewards intelligence, not cocktail chatter, which is why the raw power to process problems is the most highly paid skill in the world today.

Let IQ solve the problem it was hired to solve.

Remember that IQ comes in many shapes and sizes not measured by the Stanford-Binet test or confirmed by the Educational Testing Service. The Chicago Bulls' Michael Jordan is not a book-trained physicist, but he has solved a problem in the physics of space that no machine could be built to replicate—and solved it so spectacularly that he is perhaps the most easily recognized individual in the world today. Indeed, in one of the more intriguing quirks of the information economy, a serious legal argument recently has arisen as to whether "signature" athletic moves such as Jordan's glide to the basket are copyrightable as intellectual property. The economic valuation of individualism is only in its infancy.

Own ideas, not property.

Ideas are portable; property is fixed. Ideas are supple; property can't bend. It's the intellectual content in a software system or a bundle of titanium-alloyed steel, a clothing line or a line of frozen foods, that gives them value and creates the largest marginal price stretches. It's the intellectual content that counts in the moviemaking process, too. DreamWorks—the movie studio founded by Steven Spielberg, David Geffen, and Jeffrey Katzenberg—owns almost nothing. Production work is outsourced. What DreamWorks "owns" instead are the best minds for analyzing the interests of consumers of television, movies, and interactive media—interests that change with the flicker of the latest psychological, sexual, or social fad—and the best creative minds in production and programming for responding to those inter-ests. In the old days, a studio's power rose in direct proportion to its capacity to control the production process. DreamWorks knows that the future belongs to studios that own moviegoers, not the hardware of moviemaking.

Control average costs by controlling specific costs.

In the particle corporation, it makes no more sense to impose across-the-board cost-control policies than it does to impose across-the-board personnel policies. In the pursuit of uniformity, you will be choking the diversity necessary to survive. Instead, control the specific cost of the most variable expenses, and the average will take care of itself.

Be attuned to the points of distinction in your category.

Then focus on them. The dangerously competitive pricing that characterizes any industry group in a supersaturated marketplace too often leads businesses to treat their defining products as commodities: If all accounting firms are alike, so the thinking goes, then all that distinguishes them is the hourly rates they charge. But what's true of oranges and pork bellies is not true of accounting firms—or soft drinks or computers or publishing houses. To win individual consumers, you have to know what individuates your product. You have to reinforce it constantly, and you have to be constantly aware that within that category what makes your product unique for consumers is often razor-thin.

The difference between Coke and Pepsi is finally so infinitesimal that a Martian would never get it, but that difference is worth an extra $29 billion in equity to the Coca-Cola Company. The difference between movie theaters solely as a venue for watching movies is not that great either. What has allowed Cineplex Odeon to grow to the point where it now manages more than 2,000 theaters and has been able to invent and enforce the $8 movie ticket is its concentration not on what shows on the screen, but on what is sold in the lobby. Food is Cineplex Odeon's point of distinction, because the company understands what customers want in a movie snack bar and it concentrates on assuring that a theater is a comfortable consumption enterprise as well as a comfortable theater enterprise.

It is not products per se that consumers want. Products are everywhere, generally at deep discounts. In a world starved for scarcity, uniqueness gains value. And it is only by focusing on points of distinction that you can produce uniqueness within your category. No company understands this better than Mont Blanc Pens. A pen is, in effect, a self-powered, single-colored, portable word-processing system worth about nineteen cents—which is to say that a nineteen-cent Bic will do the job. How then does Mont Blanc manage to extend the value of the base product a thousand times? By concentrating on its points of distinction. By crowning its self-powered word-processing instruments with a snow cap. And by merchandising them in environments that suggest exclusivity and specialness. With a Mont Blanc, a customer doesn't buy just a pen; a customer buys self-definition—at roughly .2 percent the cost of self-defining herself with, say, a new Mercedes-Benz. A Mont Blanc is noblesse oblige for a world of downward nobility.

When buying a company, don't mistake ideas for the people who have them.

Test No. 1: Is the idea so caught up in the personality of a single person that the idea disappears when that person goes away? Test No. 2: Even if the idea is not caught up in a single personality, will the human infrastructure that supports it survive corporate mixing? In fact, the landscape is littered with examples that failed both tests. From the outside, AT&T's purchase of Seattle-based McCaw Cellular seemed a can't-miss deal. AT&T wanted to break into cellular phones, and McCaw was a high-flying little company with spectacular cost control. So AT&T parted with a couple of billion dollars and put Craig O. McCaw on its board. And what happened? Turned out, McCaw Cellular *was* Craig O. McCaw, and after taking one quick look around the AT&T boardroom, McCaw took his billions of dollars and left to build satellites.

IBM provides another example. Big Blue thought it had pulled off a major coup when it purchased the Rolm Corporation in 1984 for $1.5 billion. Eight years later, Big Blue was begging Siemens A.G. to take the bulk of Rolm off its hands for $1.15 billion. Why? Because Rolm was the hot shop in the development of electronic switching and its highly paid engineers believed heart and soul in the future of generic telecommunications. And because IBM believed, at heart, in the telephone as a front-end device for a computer.

The bottom line: You can find synchronicity of vision, even synchronicity of goals, but if the values are not the same, the companies won't be the same color when they meet. And if the color isn't the same, they cannot merge.

Never assume that acquiring a company is going to expand market share.

Customer relationships are proprietary to the value system impressed in the company you are buying, which means that the reason for its market share is not the same as the reason for your market share. If the company is a "Wall flower"—a corporation seeking owners—its values have been shaped not by long-term ambitions, but by the short-term ambition to be acquired. And if you fail to understand that, you fail to understand at a fundamental level what you are acquiring.

Just because it works doesn't mean it's broken.

Another cautionary tale for would-be company acquirers. The genius of Warren Buffet's Berkshire Hathaway isn't in what companies it purchases so much as it is in the fact that when Buffet does purchase a company, he adds value to the management of the treasury function and leaves the rest of the outfit alone.

Among Berkshire Hathaway's holdings is Kirby Vacuum Cleaner. On paper, everything about Kirby is wrong. Its salesmen still go door-to-door and throw dirt on the floor. The drive motor of the machine hasn't changed since 1945. Why not change the operation? Because that drive motor happens to power the greatest vacuum cleaner in the history of the planet and because, for this particular machine, going door-to-door works. Kirby mints money, and Warren Buffet leaves it alone to do that.

A corollary, by the way, is this: Everything that works can't be made to work better. The Schlegel Corporation owns the global monopoly on weather-stripping and door-sealing systems for vehicles. Just about every car that's manufactured gets $18 worth of Schlegel seals; a great many new houses get around $140 in Schlegel weather stripping. And all the genius in the world isn't going to improve that seal or make the installation go faster. Happily, London-based BTR realized that when it bought the company in 1988. To change either product—Kirby vacuums or Shlegel's door seals and weather stripping—would be to turn the imperative of innovation into the dead weight of innovation.

Think of new money brought to any business in terms of subatomic physics—as elemental breeding matter, as capital quarks. Unruly quarks produce excessive governance, excessive capital, or excessive expectations. Venal quarks undermine the basic philosophy of the recipient company by requiring it to behave like the capital source. Both are, in essence, pagan capital, because they destabilize the value structure that brought the recipient company success in the first place. Fluid quarks, by contrast, immediately engage and sustain progress, because they merge seamlessly with those values. And social quarks add social magnificence to the basic philosophy that underlies the recipient company's values.

Keep in mind, too, the country doctor who stopped to draw a drink of water from the well before going inside to see the ailing farmer. As he leaned over to grab the bucket, the doctor lost his balance and fell to his death in the abyss. As Warren Buffet has repeatedly shown, the challenge is to tend to the sick and leave the well alone.

Stick to the core business and reinforce it constantly.

Tampax, the company that invented the tampon, was in a quandary: For years it had owned 30 percent of the feminine protection market, but both its stock and its prospects were seen as weak, because tampons could never serve more than roughly 50 percent of the population and the product itself was subject to duplication. To broaden its base, Tampax made some acquisitions, changed its name to Tambrands, and launched a line of household products. And with that, Tampax/Tambrands turned a quandary into a genuine problem. Not surprisingly, people resisted cleaning their houses with products they inevitably associated with the handling of female menstrual blood. Tambrands Band-Aids worked just fine, but somehow it seemed like wearing a tampon on your finger.

Driven to its senses, the company shed the acquired companies and returned to its core business, feminine hygiene. The new strategy was to position the company as the global source of knowledge on female reproduction. To add value to its customers' lives, Tambrands began providing practical, simple advice on such complex subjects as teenage sexuality, but even here, the company fell short, because it went cheap. Publicly, Tampax was still all about freedom—with a tampon in place, a woman could go anywhere, do anything. To find the private and more meaningful message, customers mostly had to come to the package. And thus Tambrands failed to build the sort of relationship that creates a consistent predisposition to purchase.

There's a corollary here, too: Settle for adequate performance. The only thing wrong with having 30 percent of a market that includes 50 percent of the people on the planet is that Wall Street thinks it's wrong. And Wall Street could screw up a one-horse funeral.

Stick to core values, too.

Thomas Edison had dumped more than $40,000 into experiments on incandescent lightbulbs before he finally got one to glow for more than forty hours, on October 21, 1879. Never one to let a lit bulb lie, Edison almost immediately conceived the idea of illuminating a whole city, of putting his new lightbulbs in everyone's homes. For backing, he went where people went in those days—to J. P. Morgan, who turned him down flat. Undaunted, Edison sold everything he had, built a little dynamo at the foot of Wall Street, and set out to create a power grid that would serve a single square mile of Manhattan.

The work was tedious—wires had to be laid in the ground. And it was dangerous: Edison's dynamo plant ran on the DC motor he had invented, which meant that the current was continuous flow. In wet weather, horses that trod the streets over Edison's wires got electrocuted with shocking regularity. But the day finally came when he was ready to demonstrate his construction, and to do that he went to the living room of the same J. P. Morgan, whose mansion conveniently fell into the power grid. Let us set the scene: Edison turns the lights on. Morgan says, aha, here's the $3 million you wanted. I'll take my third of the company. And Edison says, no, that was then, this is now. And now, I'm offering 1 percent of the company for $10 million. Out of that moment—out of Thomas Alva Edison's chutzpah and J. P. Morgan's $10 million—was born General Electric. Out of it, too, was born GE's decision nearly a century later to roll the dice on manufacturing jet engines and its decision to take a huge—and ultimately hugely profitable—flyer on the AC turbine engine and still later its decision to diversify into even more hugely profitable GE Capital, a move as wholly consistent with the company's values as it was inconsistent with its traditional enterprises.

Boldness has begotten boldness at GE, because smart top brass have hired people of similar values to keep the corporate culture continuous, just as tight cost controls have begotten tight cost controls at other corporations because their smart brass understood intuitively or consciously that core values are not to be tampered with.

One codicil needs to be added here: Stick to core values so long as the rules of business life don't shift completely beneath your feet. Eddie Hutton—the E.F. Hutton of E.F. Hutton and Company—was in his own way a bolder figure than Thomas Edison. He'd gone west at the turn of the century because his father-in-law, who held a seat on the New York Stock Exchange, didn't want his family scandalized by Hutton's philandering. There he purchased a private telegraph line that ran from San Francisco to New York, continued partying and philandering, and soon was dominating NYSE transactions in California gold and agricultural stocks. When the San Francisco earthquake hit in 1906, Hutton sent a colleague across the Bay in a rickety boat to take over the Oakland office of Western Union and short the market in California gold stocks before the rest of the world became aware of the full extent of the calamity wrought by the quake. Hutton made a fortune on the enterprise, and for nearly eighty years thereafter the company that bore his name continued to grow in his image. No brokerage house on Earth was a happier fit for brilliant, entrepreneurial, party-loving, philandering money men. And then, in the mid–1980s, the regulatory climate changed under the feet of the brokerage business, and E. F. Hutton and Company was as doomed as the dodo. For better or worse—and in Hutton's case, after a long and fabulous ride, it was finally for worse—you are your corporate culture.

Build change, not difference.

Think of the model of a newspaper. Its contents change every day, because the news and the advertisements and classified ad lineage change every day. But if the process that produced it was different every day—if the production, editorial, advertising, and human relations departments bumped against each other daily in new and unpredictable ways—the newspaper would never get published. It is the same with corporations. As the need for innovation rises, as the time span between product introduction and total adoption shrinks, as daily change becomes not an anomaly but a given, engineering and manufacturing—and manufacturing and marketing—end up touching one another constantly. The challenge isn't to stifle the touching—this isn't some corporate form of sexual harassment. The touching has to happen. The challenge is to make the touching predictable, to find the process that best makes it work and to repeat that process over and over again.

Build the structure right, and change recedes into the white noise of everyday corporate life. Do that—create change without difference—and the business becomes extraordinarily flexible.

And perhaps the hardest rule of all:

Remember, the customers have to spend the money.

Back in the 1992 Summer Olympics in Barcelona, the irrepressible Charles Barkley sought to add a little perspective to the "ugly American" stories that began circulating when the United States' first "Dream Team" of mostly professional basketball players—including Barkley—was clobbering other national teams by fifty and more points. Wait a minute, Barkley said, this is something we are good at. We *should* be beating up on these countries.

"Sir Charles" was absolutely right as far as he went, but there are two other things Americans do extraordinarily well—wage war (a subject we'll leave to the cultural anthropologists) and buy stuff. We Americans have turned consuming into an art form; we have even turned it into a critical form of dialogue. And as borders disappear, as connectivity communicates not just messages but wants and perceived needs, the American model of consumption is becoming the global model of consumption. The laments about the abysmal saving rates of Americans will soon become a planetary cry as well, and it will be just as meaningless then as it is now. The simple reality is that people don't chase money to accumulate it; they chase money to spend money. And everybody has a shopping list.

What does this mean for businesses? Stop worrying about whether the market is going to be interested in you. Worry instead about being interested in what the market wants, and worry about it one customer at a time. Successful companies don't sell what they want to make, and they don't make what the mass market wants or what the market in the abstract seems ready for. Successful companies know each customer, and they make what individual people want to buy. In the new particle economics, that is the most important lesson to remember.

And lastly, remember . . .

The Wisdom of Focus

What does that mean? Two things:

Settle.

Accept that it's a deal-based world. Forget about the old principles of social equity. What you get has no necessary relation to what anyone else gets. Industry comparables are useless. Salary benchmarks and bonus benchmarks are meaningless. What matters—all that matters—is what you can negotiate out of your employer and what your employer can negotiate out of you. Once the deal is done, neither side has any right to complain so long as the terms of the deal are lived up to. It's the Chaos Age, folks. Everyone is on his or her own.

Simplify.

The best insurance policy, the best car, the best personal computer today will not be the best insurance policy, the best car, the best personal computer tomorrow. The terms of the best deal you can make today will not be anything like the terms of the best deal you can make six months from now. The accelerating rate of change and the massive accumulation of change have overwhelmed surety. But so long as you focus simply on making the best car, assembling the best PC, offering the best insurance policy, making the best deal, you will be managing your business and yourself against moving benchmarks toward a fixed outcome. Bog down in process, obsess over the details, and you will not allow yourself to entertain new discoveries along the path. Ignore new discoveries, and the path itself will turn into a maze constantly doubling into itself. Keep your eye on the prize, and new discoveries will constantly reshape your path to where you want to be.

In 1988, Gateway 2000 spent $252,000 on marketing and managed $11 million in sales. Eight years later, the company was spending

$100 million in marketing, achieving more than $5 billion in sales, and directly employing 9,000 people. How? Because from the very first day, the company focused on a very simple motto: Our stores are our advertisements, and if people call, they will buy. Every adjustment that has been made since—in assembling, in marketing, in distribution—has been made in the pursuit of that end, in the pursuit of creating products and a reputation that will allow customers to pick up the phone, call the company, and feel good enough about the probable outcome that they will charge a $3,000 item on a credit card. And the result is a miracle.

Simplify your focus, and you become the guardian of the future, not the champion of the past. Simplify your focus, and you make the past—what you have learned, where you have been—coexist with the future, with where you are going.

The 500-Year Delta

PART VI

What lies ahead in the next five hundred days, the next five hundred weeks, five hundred months, five hundred years? Sorry, if we could see even ten minutes into the future with absolute clarity, we'd be at the racetrack right now, or on the phone with our broker. The only certainty in the Chaos Age really is uncertainty. For oracles, it's a bad epoch rising.

What do we *think* is going to happen in the next five hundred days, weeks, months, years? What have a collective five decades in the business of studying, observing, and calculating the current trend lines and projecting them into the future shown us? A great deal, not all of it rosy, far from all of it bad. Our kind of futurism is based rock-hard on the present tense. It's based not on divination, not on crystal balls or tea leaves, not on astral positions or on sorting the bones of sacrificed animals. Our futurism is based on digesting reality, on looking for its turning points, on looking backward into history to find the patterns of growth and change that will impel events through the present into what lies ahead, and on not being afraid to say what we see when we do all that.

We like to talk about clients who have taken our advice and used it to place themselves on the bleeding edge of their markets. For reasons we trust you will understand, we're less enchanted with mentioning clients who didn't like what we told them, clients who turned out to be content with their status quos, ones for whom the future wasn't someplace to rush into but rather a dark night to be resisted—clients, that is, who told us to get lost, who showed us the door, who said don't call us, we'll call you. We wish them all luck, and we don't claim to be 100 percent right in any event. But what we like to work for are companies that know the difference between eggs and bacon—that understand the hen is involved, but the pig is *committed*. That's what we're looking for: clients committed to facing the future, whatever it might entail for them. And that is what we give you here: the future unadorned, the future without attempts to pretty it up, the future that real time is driving toward.

We begin with the next five hundred days. Because we contend that five hundred years of logical, organizational, and economic structures are now in the process of being overturned—because we are convinced that we have arrived at one of those fulcrum points of history where everything that was tips over into everything that will be—we end with the conclusion of the epoch of chaos we see rising: the close of the twenty-fifth century. Shout at what we have to say. Revile us for it. If you think about it, too, we'll be happy to shoulder the abuse. Obviously, not everything we say is going to happen will happen to every individual, but in the aggregate, they all will happen to us all, and thus, individually you should presume they will happen to you or your descendants.

One footnote before we get underway. We were going to include in this section the following prediction: "Within the next five hundred days, civil-litigation issues, including sexual harassment, will be extended to the elementary school classroom." And then, just as we were finalizing the text for this book, Jonathan Prevette—a Lexington, North Carolina, first-grader—was briefly subjected to in-school suspension for kissing a female classmate on the cheek. The grounds for suspension: sexual harassment. The simple fact is that we are careening into the future at the speed of light.

Now, relax and enjoy the ride.

The Next Five Hundred Days

What will happen in the next five hundred days?

- Your most important employee will quit and go to work for your biggest competitor.

- You will have a joint venture with your biggest competitor.

- You will travel to a country whose existence you were not aware of five years ago, and you will find that it isn't any different than home.

- A member of your family will be a victim of a felony crime.

- A member of your family will be read his or her Miranda rights.

- A member of your family will appear on television.

- You and your spouse will discuss divorce.

- A member of your family will celebrate his or her one hundredth birthday.

- You will have to make a conscious decision for or against euthanasia in the care of a friend or family member.

- You will have to make a conscious decision about the use of bioenzymes to prolong your own life.

- You will have to make a conscious decision about the decriminalization of presently illegal drugs.

- Fat will be drug-controllable.

- Three of your organization's four best ideas will fail.

- You will be sued for being right.

- You will become intensely interested in a totally alien idea.

- A revolutionary PC chip will have entered the marketplace.

- A company not currently in your field will introduce a new product in your category, and it will be better than your product.

- There will be a major stock market crash.

- You will learn that one of your children is having sex at an age for which you are unprepared.

- You will learn that you are about to be fired.

- You will be offered another job, for a lot more money.

- You will actively pursue a career change.

- You will be deeply touched by a personal letter.

- Social chaos will have broken out in the inner cities of St. Louis, Cleveland, Phoenix, Los Angeles, Miami, and Boston.

- Central Detroit will show the worst wounds.

- Violence will have become the greatest killer in the United States.

- Global terrorism will make boarding an airplane a life-threatening decision.

- You will be paid to listen to advertising.

The Next Five Hundred Weeks

Lengthen your time frame out now by a factor of seven. What happens then?

- Your most important employee will also be working for your biggest competitor.

- Multinational corporations will have their own embassies.

- China will have the world's largest economy.

- The driving force of your corporate objectives will be participation in the subcontinent, particularly the Indian market.

- Yale will be bankrupt.

- Harvard will have branches on each continent.

- The capacity of major universities to distribute learning technologies on-line will have driven as many as a third of all currently extant four-year colleges and universities in the United States out of business.

- The National Football League will be the World Football League, and the Super Bowl truly will be just that.

- You will be in a career for which you never had any formal training.

- The underground cell-tissue market will have replaced drugs as the world's dominant criminal conspiracy.

- Previously illegal drugs will have been legalized, and they will have replaced abortion as the target of the political right wing.
- The dominant issue of the political left wing will be income bifurcation.
- There will be a new category in the Standard Industrial Code called "scarcity procurement."
- Market surplus will have replaced market share.
- Your individual value as an economic entity will exceed the value of the products businesses are trying to sell you.
- You will own the trade rights to your own life, and people will not be able to sell your name without paying you a commission.
- The pharmaceutical management of aging will have become a global mania.
- Five million Americans will be over one hundred years old, and 30 percent of the American labor force will be engaged in caring for the elderly.
- A third of the global population will be teenagers.
- Children will be routinely having sex before the age of ten.
- California will be a minority-white state.
- Canada no longer will exist as an independent nation.
- There will be a major border crisis over the ownership of New Mexico and Arizona, both of which Mexico has never formally ceded to the United States.
- Being unknown will be a status symbol.
- Forty percent of the world will have unsafe drinking water.
- The number of people testing positive for AIDS will top the 500 million mark globally, and communicable diseases and malnutrition will replace violence as the leading cause of death.
- A competency test will determine the right to vote.
- A computer operated by biomass will be fully functional.
- Consciousness will be downloadable, and the capacity to do so will arise from efforts to restore memory to Alzheimer's victims and the victims of strokes and head-trauma injuries.

- The rate of creation of new life-forms will exceed the rate of destruction of old life-forms.

- Three new sciences that we cannot today imagine will have been invented.

- There will be a holy war between Muslims and Christians.

- Japan will be a nuclear-weapons power.

- Germany will be a nuclear-weapons power.

- The attenuated death toll of the 1986 nuclear power plant meltdown at Chernobyl in the Ukraine will top the 5 million mark.

- There will be a bio-accident that will jeopardize the future of the world.

- The management of biotechnology, the supremacy of the international atomic agency, and the Treaty of the Seas will make the United Nations the most powerful force in managing global affairs.

- In the United States, airports and national parks will be privatized, and public-works projects will be undertaken by the private sector.

- The number-one problem facing companies will be corporate espionage.

Next, consider a set of hard facts and projections courtesy of the U.S. Census Bureau, the Social Security Administration, and the Bipartisan Commission on Entitlement and Tax Reform. (These statistics are gathered in persuasive form in Peter G. Peterson's book *Will America Grow Up Before It Grows Old?*)

- In 1995, 12.5 percent of Americans were age sixty-five or older. By the year 2040, as many as 24 percent of Americans will be sixty-five or older.

- While the number of Americans age sixty-five and older is expected to grow by as much as 129 percent between 1995 and 2040, the number of working-age Americans is expected to grow by 24 percent and the number of Americans under age twenty by

5 percent. By 2040, the number of Americans age eighty-five and older will roughly equal the number of Americans under age five.

- In 1995, there were 3.3 working Americans for each American covered by Social Security and Medicare, and payroll taxes for both consumed about 17 percent of workers' paychecks. By the year 2040, there will be 1.6 workers for each Social Security beneficiary, and under present formulations, payroll taxes for both will consume as much as 55 percent of workers' paychecks.

- In 1995, Social Security and Medicare together had an annual operating balance of $20 billion. Under present formulations, by 2040 Social Security and Medicare collectively will have an annual operating balance of greater than negative $3.2 trillion.

- In 1995, U.S. entitlement spending consumed about 12 percent of federal revenues. Under present formulations, by 2040 entitlement spending will exceed all federal revenues.

No wonder far more Americans under the age of thirty-five now think that UFOs exist than think that Social Security will exist by the time they retire.

What else, then, will begin to happen within the next five hundred weeks?

Whatever accommodations are reached to keep Social Security and Medicare afloat, the sum of the cost of entitlements plus the sum of the cost of debt service at all levels of the political hierarchy will still exceed the capacity of the federal government to pay. The political will to increase the effective tax base to meet existing federal obligations will be lacking. As the tax pressure grows, Generation X'ers will seize control of Congress from the aging remnants of the Baby Boom, and once they achieve a majority, they will determine that the only solution to the U.S. debt crisis is to print the U.S. debt out of existence.

As that happens, the power of global corporations that deal not solely in U.S. currency, but in a basket of multi-currencies will grow dramatically. "Units of owe"—currency units based on the actual ownership of corporate assets—will replace traditional currencies as the most accepted global transaction instruments. In effect, multinational corporations will then have the right to print their own money, and with that, national governments will cease to matter for the vast majority of their populations.

The Next Five Hundred Months

This time, stretch your perspective out another six-fold, to five hundred months. The Millennium has been cleared, the dust has settled. We're brushing up against the fourth decade of the twenty-first century. What does the world look like? For one thing, it's not just multinational corporations that are doing business in "units of owe." Once units of ownership are established in each person's personal portfolio, each person will in effect be printing his or her own currency, too. With the collapse of governments and their traditional role as the backer of national currencies, there will be no other choice. What else?

- Anyone who lives to be fifty will have a better than 80-20 chance of living to be one hundred.

- There will be term limits on life based on each individual's ability to pay for his or her own care.

- Reproduction will be taxed, and each person will be limited to the ownership of one child.

- It will take longer to get to the Los Angeles International Airport than it will to fly from Los Angeles to Tokyo.

- National parks will be restricted primarily to children and the elderly, and the right to visit them will be allocated on a societal time-share basis. The right to visit the rarest parks around the world will be sold at auction.

- Fusion power will be on-line.

- Most hydrocarbons will come from the ocean floor.

- A colony on the Moon will be engaged in the mining of rare Earth metals.

- We will know that we are not alone in the Universe.

- Cyber-components will be commonplace in humans.

- Genetic cosmetic surgery will be commonplace.

- Nonbiological pets will be commonplace.

- Life-form hatcheries will be one of the most important emerging industries globally, and the overriding philosophical question will be whether we are still the creatures of God's will in producing these new species.

- Zoos will contain prehuman hominids and other currently extinct species, and the main preoccupation of bioecologists will be maintaining recovered species and discovering why they vanished in the first place.

- Cloned dinosaurs will walk the planet again.

- Prophets, too, will walk the planet, and they will be greatly honored among men and women.

- The first cloned human life will have been created, using a surrogate mother, and whether cloned humans get to keep their memories—whether allowing them to do so gives them a fundamental cognitive advantage over non-cloned humans—will be a leading bioethical concern.

- The leading cause of death will be epidemics.

- A nuclear bomb will have been set off by a terrorist organization.

- The United States will no longer be a Caucasian-majority nation.

- The language formerly known as English will be the dominant language of the world.

The Next Five Hundred Years

Now, stretch your perspective to the maximum—five centuries, almost to the year 2500. What do we see? Nothing clearly. Probably no more than someone peering out at our own time from the purchase of the late fifteenth century could have seen. History is filled with fog, and never more so than when you try to look far forward. But history is filled with pointers, as well, with hints about where it wants to head. What do we find if we track those?

Much of what we have to say may seem radical. Some may seem

pure science fiction, and, we grant, it may prove to be that. But before you dismiss these predictions, think for a moment what someone born at the turn of the last century has lived through in less than one hundred years: the rise to universality of automobiles, the creation and universality of air travel, manned voyages to the Moon and unmanned voyages beyond the solar system, two world wars, the rise and collapse of the Soviet Union, organ transplants, in vitro fertilization, same-sex marriages, racial integration, the enfranchisement of women, computers, the Internet, television, and all that only barely scratches the surface. Then multiply that not just by five to get five centuries into the future, but by the acceleration of change as well.

Is it the greater vanity to predict that these things will happen, or to assume that they cannot?

- There will be fewer people alive than there are today.

- The world's population will be concentrated within two hundred miles of the equator.

- New York City will still be the most important city on Earth; because of its critical mass of talent, it will remain the one place on the planet most amenable to people who invent new ideas.

- Sustained by cyber-components, bio-enzymes, and genetic engineering, the average human life span will be eight hundred years.

- The average age of first marriage will be seventy-five years.

- The first person to have had more than one hundred marriages in his or her lifetime will be identified.

- The right to have children will be auctioned as a tax source.

- Memories will be based not on dates or any currently conventional understanding of time, but on process: college, careers, marriages—each will be a unit of time by which we will recall our experiences.

- Even minor crimes of violence will be met with permanent separation from society.

- Capital punishment will consist of artificially aging the criminal.

- There will be no money standard.

- The answer to the question "Where are you from?" will be "Earth."

- Risk aversion will be acute, and it will be inculcated at a very early age.

- The net IQ of the planet will rise exponentially, because only those capable of quickly evaluating risks will be able to avoid the dangers that would truncate their potential life spans and only those capable of being wildly and enthusiastically productive during their working years will have the resources to finance their longevity.

- Demattering will be possible, but the psychochemistry of the brain is so delicate that when you arrive where you are going and are re-formed, there will be no guarantee that you will be the same person you were when you left.

- The greatest terrorist threat will be disease.

- Driven by total connectivity and universal homophyly, the greatest threat to human life collectively will be a lack of genetic variation.

- A figure with the charismatic power of Christ or Buddha will walk the Earth once again. Instead of "What are we?" or "Why are we?" the question this figure will answer is "How are we?"

- The five things anyone can never have too much of will be unchanged from the time Aristotle first identified them: health, knowledge, self-esteem, friends, and love.

- And the one thing no one can live without will be the same as well: hope.

Afterword: The Age of Possibility

Twice before in this book we have asked you to find yourself in the scenarios we have created—the first of an uneasy sleeper, the second of that same uneasy sleeper's next day. Now we ask you to find yourself a last time, in a day just on the other side of tomorrow.

3:00 P.M.

A proposal sits on your desk. As head of the team that has created and is now finalizing it, you feel an immense responsibility for the proposal. The business it would generate is important to the company you work for. The success of the proposal is just as important to you. Having overseen it and having it be chosen as the winning submission will make you a player; it will establish your own market worth. Happily, the two goals in this case are in perfect congruence.

In some ways, the proposal should be an impossible task. The variables that affect the pricing are in constant fluctuation. The information platform upon which your team is basing its assumptions slips and slides in every direction, constantly reforms itself as new facts emerge, are entered into the equation, and alter its internal mechanics. But you have tools that have never before been available in the history of time.

The single edition of the *New York Times* lying in your briefcase contains within its pages more information than a cultured person living in Elizabethan England would have encountered in a lifetime, and it costs all of 60 cents on the newsstand. The Internet, the World Wide Web, the electronic data banks waiting for instant retrieval cost even less than that to access, and they contain within them more information than was held in all the libraries in all the world less than a century ago. And unlike those libraries, anyone can enter these. There is no test of race, of gender, of caste. No credentials need to be flashed to get through the door. The inability—physical or financial—to travel to their stacks is no discriminator. The stacks come to you.

Two offices down the hall from you, your information specialist is crawling through these data banks, searching for the critical elements that will make your proposal the winning one. She is black, Hispanic; white or Asian. She had a child too early; she grew up in the shadow of family violence in the inner city of Chicago, Los Angeles, Detroit, Philadelphia, New York, Houston; London, Madrid, Rome; Santiago or Rio de Janeiro. She grew up dirt poor on a farm in Mississippi or Minnesota. She grew up where schooling was only for the schooled—in Nairobi or Calcutta or Bangkok. But she had a computer and a modem and a phone line, and she taught herself to use them. And in so doing she opened a world for herself that never could have been opened otherwise. To be exact, she became a data hog. That she is your data hog is one of many things for which, at this moment, you are eternally grateful.

The proposal may succeed; it may fail. Other teams in other companies have their own data hogs, and this time they may be more good, more lucky than yours. At the last moment, you may make a decision on pricing or implementation that will be completely overwhelmed by circumstances it will be impossible to foresee. The world never waits. But so long as you have fully exercised your freedom to know, you will have done the right thing. So long as you have done that, you tell yourself, you have opened yourself to possibility, and beyond that, there can be no asking for more.

3:20.

A feeler came earlier today—couched, subtle, but a feeler all the same. You were on the phone with a professional peer in Berlin, in Sydney, in Johannesburg, planning the plenary session for a conference you are both helping put on, when she casually mentioned that a position similar to yours is opening up with her company. She never asked if you were interested, but the implication was there: "We're looking for someone like you."

What would it mean, you ask yourself now, to move across the ocean, the equator, halfway around the world? The answer, you are surprised to find: almost nothing. Perhaps there is a significant other to factor in. Perhaps children would have to be wrenched out of school, or an elderly parent left alone more than you would like. Those are personal decisions—each arrived at individually. But professionally, you realize, it no longer really matters where you are physically located. The currency you are paid in is backed less by the full faith and credit of the government whose name it bears than by the full faith and credit of the corporation you work for. The corporation itself will not succeed or fail because of the location of its headquarters; it is a little nation of its own. Borders themselves are infinitely permeable—less cultural discriminators than geographical conveniences.

There's still more than enough ambient horror around the globe to keep the all-news channels busy 24 hours a day. Life isn't any less risky. But this world you are living in has become one world—not because a supreme government declared it to be that but because connectivity made it so and because the individual governments that still divide the world on paper finally could not resist the will of the people or the reality of their lives. You are a citizen of that one world, a global person. You have the Freedom to Go, to open yourself to possibility anywhere on the planet, and beyond that there can be no asking for more.

3:37.

You have had a kind of internal feeler as well—not nearly so subtle. Lately an itch has been telling you it's time to leave this job. You like the work. You like your colleagues. It is not inconceivable that you could stay here another five or ten years, but it is also not inconceivable that you could leave the minute the proposal you are working on is finally ready for submittal, the minute it is finally accepted or rejected. It is not inconceivable, for that matter, that your significant other could do the same with his or her job, or that you and your significant other could do the same to each other.

This is not a world built on loyalty, you tell yourself, and you remind yourself of the downsides to this. It would be nice to know where you will be working, what career you will be in, who will be sharing your bed five, ten, twenty years down the road. Along with a loss of loyalty has come a loss of traditional community that no "virtual community" can readily make up for. Relationships are in flux.

But then you tell yourself something else: This is not a world constrained by loyalty, either. This is not a world in which loyalty requires repetition—yet another proposal team to head up next month, and the month after that, and the months endlessly after that until you are promoted and can elevate someone beneath you to do the job you are now doing. It is not a world in which loyalty requires attending to the corporate stations of the cross. Instead, it is a world in which loyalty is given by choice, not obligation; a world in which the greatest loyalty due is to oneself.

You could take your proposal-creating skills to a competitor in the same line of business. You could take them to a non-profit organization searching for grants. You could take your two best people with you and open up a consulting business specializing in such proposals, or you could take the product you are proposing to create, the service you are proposing your company to provide, and provide it yourself. Or you could flee this kind of work altogether and pursue your entrepreneurial skill, your intellectual passions wherever they might take you. Nothing holds you back but the reluctance to exercise your own Freedom to Do, and beyond that, there can be no asking for more.

4:00.

Finally, you. Not the professional you. Not you the significant other, you the parent, you the child. Not you the breadwinner or you the bread consumer. Just you. What is the reality of that person, you ask yourself? What is reality at all?

This is another answer you have come to understand only in recent months: that there is no mass reality anymore, that reality is anything you make it, that you construct the reality of each moment as you move through it. There is, in fact, no reality that binds you to this desk, this office, this business, to any single element of your life—no residue of race or class or gender that weights you down, no imposition of assumptions that limits you. There is only the Freedom to Be whatever you want to be and the ironclad necessity to exercise it. It is your office you are sitting in, not the corporation's; your life you are living and no one else's; your reality you are creating, utterly unshared.

Grab hold of it, and welcome to the Age of Possibility.

Glossary: A New Vocabulary of Change

Epochal transitions beget new language because old language is a box that confines thought and ultimately understanding. To escape the box means evolving beyond it. To escape means crawling out from under the accumulated weight of the symbols by which we communicate.

As the Renaissance flowered in England four and more centuries ago, William Shakespeare coined some 1,700 words in his plays and poems—nearly 15 percent of all the new words added to the English language between 1500 and 1650. Why? Partially, for the fun of it; partially, because he could invent and play with the language as no one before or since could. But there was a deeper reason. Although Shakespeare was often writing about mythologized history, he was seeing it through new eyes. Old eyes and old words were inadequate to his vision.

We lay no claim here to Shakespeare's facility with words. But the new epochal transition we are embarked upon both needs and demands a new language and a new linguistic elegance of its own. What follows is, of necessity, a work in progress. Many of the words and phrases are ours; others are borrowed from a wide range of sources. Add your own entries to it. Less important than the words and phrases themselves is the process of considering them. It is the process that takes us outside of the current box of language, and it is only outside of the box that we can begin to see the world not as we want it to be, but as it is.

With disclaimers, then, a glossary for the Age of Access:

Age of Access. The age we are already in, in which connectivity drives toward the access of everyone to everyone, everything to everything, and everything to everyone. The Age of Access impels new political and economic structures based on access, not scarcity. See *Connectivity*.

Alpha crimes. Crimes that become the leaders in their category. The bombing of Pan Am 103 over Lockerbie, Scotland, was the alpha crime of global terrorism, just as Charles Manson is the alpha criminal of mass murders.

Anthrolineage. The résumé of cultural experience that allows one, in a time-compressed world, to immediately discover identity with a short-term other.

Bionomics. Literally, the merger of biological and economic theory. In its more figurative sense, the merger of the world of the made and the world of the born. Bionomics will flourish as an academic discipline because as the two worlds merge, economic systems will assume the properties of biological ones.

Blue-chip ejaculation. The tendency of very large companies when confronted with massive amounts of change to ejaculate a single-point answer in a very large way. See *truncated perspective*.

Capital quarks. The subatomic structure of the elemental breeding matter of any business. Capital quarks come in four forms. Unruly quarks produce excessive governance, excessive streams of capital, or excessive expectations on the part of the capital market or supplier. Fluid quarks are capital that immediately engages and sustains progress. Venal quarks require the recipient organization to become like the capital source. Social quarks add social magnificence to the basic philosophical concept. See *pagan capital*.

Cityzen. Citizenship defined by the megacity one lives in, rather than by the national entity that happens to include that city.

Competitive uniphobia. A fixation on competitive situations that by their very nature are transitory. See *truncated perspective*.

Complicated simplicity. What's needed to survive and prosper in a chaos world in which reason no longer applies, in which you must focus on outcome, not process, and in which you must be, not do. "At the still point of the turning world. . . . there the dance is," T.S. Eliot wrote in Book I of his *Four Quartets*. "But neither arrest nor movement. And do not call it fixity."

Connectivity. The result of the fusion of computing and communications. First posited by Nobel laureate Arno Penzias. See *Age of Access*.

Convergence. The blending of culture and ideas into a single product.

Corporate Communalism. The tendency of executives within any corporation to group within their own think-sets, experience-sets, and product-sets. See *truncated perspective*.

Cryptocentrism. The tendency of media communes, tribes, and other micro-cultures to invent language that maintains in-group/out-of-group distinctions. Technobabble, gang "signing," and graffiti "tagging" are all examples of cryptocentrism.

Cultural schizophrenia. The modern condition born of a disconnection between attitudes and behaviors, between the world as it is presented and the world as we intuit it to be. Cultural schizophrenia occurs whenever society begins to reinvent its vision of how it will conduct affairs in the future.

Customer loyalty. The new imperative of marketing. As the marketplace approaches a supersaturation of products—as the power in the marketing equation shifts from product to consumer—brand loyalty disappears. To survive, manufacturers and retailers will have to create unique loyalty relationships with their customers, one customer at a time. See *marketing surplus*.

Disharmonious conjunctions. The organizing principle of a chaos world. Nothing can be planned. Nothing happens as part of a predictable chain of events. Decision making is driven by random convergences. See *oxymoronic future*.

Distention. Not inattention, but the refusal to involve oneself in issues that have no relevance over one's life. A necessary survival skill in a chaos-driven world.

Diversity IQ. A basic measure of the capacity to survive and prosper in the Age of Access. Diversity IQ is built on the ability to move freely and tolerantly among people of various races, cultures, backgrounds, and beliefs.

Downward nobility. The decline in the value of formerly status-laden items and the simultaneous growth in the status value of just being satisfied. Self-affirmation will come by underspending incomes and exercising independence as consumers and workers, not by depending upon objects to establish worth.

Ecomagnetics. The creeping tendency of all products to move toward the central values in the culture.

Endotruths. Truths that are known inside, but not outside a culture—whether it's a social, political, or economic organization, a tribe, or a media commune. Endotruths usually begin with the nature of the founder of the organization, and they explain why two companies in the same business often have startlingly different corporate cultures. See *exotruths*.

Enlightened anxiety. The path out of cultural schizophrenia. Anxiety cannot be erased because anxiety is a natural reaction to a world in extreme flux. Rather, it must be embraced and used.

Evilution. The transformation of evil from time to time and place to place and at differing rates of evolution, largely as determined by tribes and communes. For the *Mother Jones* media commune, Richard Nixon remains the embodiment of evil more than two decades after he resigned the presidency under the threat of impeachment. For the Republican cocktail party circuit, Nixon has passed from victim to embarrassment to redemption to radiant political authority. See *global pillory* and *media communalism*.

Exotruths. Presumed truths about a culture, whether they are in fact true or false. Exotruths are the myths that frame the social understanding of an organization. They determine its external value and cannot be disproved even by denying them. The exotruth of Coca-Cola is that the formula for Coke is kept in a safe deep in corporate headquarters; the *endotruth* (see above) is that virtually everybody who is anybody at Coca-Cola knows the formula by heart.

Fabulism. Short-term reasons why everything works or doesn't work. "Family values" or their absence are an example of fabulism in the political arena.

Fault tolerance. The capacity of any organization to tolerate calamitous events. Fault tolerance increases in direct relation to an organization's ability to say "thank you" and "I'm sorry."

Filocity. A capacity to come up to speed in alien cultures, to make cultural penetration and establish friendships. What Ferris Bueller had in such abundance in the movie named for him.

Flight impulse. The tendency of everyone between the ages of forty-five and fifty to seek a completely different lifestyle and actively plot their escape.

Fraternities of strangers. Ad hoc affinity groups created for finite periods to achieve specific ends. The new basis for social organization. See *tribal marketing*.

Futopia. Statements or ideas about how to live in the future that fail to make reference to or take into account the impending urban population explosion. All speculations about the future that do not factor in large urban crowds are futopic and, thus, futile.

Global pillory. Thanks to global access, global connectivity, and global media saturation, global pillory is where you go when you are globally bad. Nearly a decade after he was brought low by the law and despite extensive efforts to raise money for research into prostate cancer, which he suffers from, Michael Milken remains in global pillory, both famous and ostracized. See *alpha crimes*.

Glossofacilia. A tendency to use very large words to explain very small phenomena. Glossofacilia drives to complexify rather than simplify and is the natural instinct of reactionaries to an age of change.

Gosh. Contemporary definitions of God as our best friend. The prevalence of Gosh in Western, and particularly American, culture both affects and explains its inability to comprehend the roots of religious wars.

Herd crimes. Crimes that, once committed, are repeated communally, by everyone in the herd. Shoplifting is a herd crime of young teenagers; smoking marijuana was the herd crime of the counterculture of the late sixties and early seventies; padding expense accounts is the herd crime of junior executives.

Homophyly. The tendency of objects, when in close proximity, to assume the characteristics of each other. Based on genetic theory, homophyly is equally applicable to human behavior. It increases in direct relation to the increase in access and connectivity. MTV, for example, has created a global homophyly of musical tastes among young people, just as television, in general, and VCRs have created a global homophyly in wants and desires. The ultimate extension of homophyly is a global biological similarity that will threaten genetic variation.

Inconspicuous consumption. Defining simply your taste, not your life, by the items you consume. Part of the new economics built around individualism, not consumerism. See *downward nobility*.

Intelligent disobedience. What seeing-eye dogs are taught—essentially that they are to obey unless they have a better idea. Intelligent disobedience is already embedded in the corporate culture of companies like Microsoft. See *unrules*.

Instant history. Reinventions of history as a way of accounting for near-term behavior. The marketing of golfer Tiger Woods as a racial icon and Microsoft's introduction of Windows 95 were both examples of instant history at work, but no example better captures the spirit of instant history than the annual NFL Super Bowl. As ex–running back Duane Thomas once put it, "If it's so super, how come they're having one next year?"

Latent personalization. The unrealized capacity of a product or an idea to be taken personally. Clothing remains the highest per capita commodity expenditure among highly personalized products, but most products, from books to tractors, have a vast potential to be personalized. And in a world of splintering markets and individual realities, realizing latent personalization will become increasingly crucial to market success.

Loss followers. Substantive investment in products, without a prospect of recovering the investment, in order to catch up. The extraordinary concessions granted by the state of Alabama to attract a new Mercedes plant, the extraordinary expenditures undertaken by the city of Baltimore to attract the Cleveland Browns football team—rechristened the Baltimore Ravens—and Panasonic's heavy investment in a knockoff of the Sony Walkman are all examples of loss followers. In each case, the outlays were necessary to remain credible: as a state to relocate to, a city to invest in, an electronic product to consider purchasing.

Macronomia. The tendency of large organizations to experience feelings of normlessness and disgust with their own size. Macronomia drives corporations like IBM to partition their parts and decentralize their structures. The cellularity and decentralization, in turn, threaten value continuity in the whole. See *values-based management.*

Madonna syndrome. The capacity and willingness to remake oneself through the media whenever one wishes to and in whatever way one desires. In modern politics, Bill Clinton is the foremost practitioner and beneficiary of the Madonna syndrome.

Marketing surplus. A theory developed by McKinsey's David Court, which holds that success is determined not by market share, but by which one of the entities in any transaction—from raw-goods supplier through manufacturer, retailer, and consumer—holds the greatest amount of the surplus, or profit, made at each step of the process. As the market reaches saturation, marketing surplus moves to the consumer.

Media communalism. An affinity group in which members selectively manipulate their media lives to reinforce a singular worldview or set of values. See *truncated perspective.*

Media recluse. A person who, by dint of personal choice, divorces himself or herself from the media world.

Mediocracy. The hierarchy formed within microcultures on the basis of media appreciation for the individuals that make up the microculture. New York's Reverend Al Sharpton, to cite one example, has no political base, but has been anointed by the media as the mediocrat for his microculture. Because medio-crats tend to know one another, they are how microcultures communicate with one another.

Mental flexibility. The measure of a society's ability to accept change, and perhaps the largest single determinant of national macro-wealth in the future. A 1995 World Bank ranking of future economic potential, based in part on mental flexibility, placed Australia first in the world and the United States fifth.

Multiple you's. The capacity to re-create yourself as the situation demands. John Wayne, strong and silent whether he played a cowboy or a soldier, was the paradigm of a loyalty-based world. Tom Hanks shifting from idiot-savant (*Forrest Gump*) to AIDS victim (*Philadelphia*) to hero (*Apollo 13*) is the person-ality paradigm of a deal-based world.

Nanostalgia. The tendency to feel nostalgic over events, such as movies, that concluded only seconds ago. Krug champagne, for example, celebrates in its advertisements its capacity to deliver nanostalgic moments. *Instant history* (see above) takes advantage of nanostalgia by providing the throttle for such moments. Super Bowl replays are nanostalgic moments in the midst of an instant-history happening.

Non-sense. 1. What logic becomes as we cross the delta from reason to chaos. 2. The indefinable qualities of great brands that enable them to travel across and through time.

Nulture. The convergence of nerds and culture, and a powerful, growing force as a majority of the population actively seeks to assimilate and apply advanced technology.

On the bubble. As commonly used, a term of great respect. As it should be used, a term of great fear. To be "on the bubble" is to be so close to a trend that your future success is in imminent jeopardy. Why? Because trends move in ever more narrow bands, and the success you presently enjoy is likely to blind you to the changes you must embrace to succeed in the future. When you're on the bubble, it's time to blow your organization up.

Oxymoronic future. A future formed by the infinite repetition of *disharmonious conjunctions* (see above).

Pagan capital. Capital produced and delivered to a company with one set of values from a capital source with a different set of values. Whether in the form of direct investments or venture capital, pagan capital produces often huge dislocations in entrepreneurial companies, because the values that govern the capital are not commensurate with the values that created the success of the recipient organization. The great success of Warren Buffet's Berkshire Hathaway is directly related to the fact that the capital it delivers is never pagan. See *values-based management.*

Particle economics. The economic analogy of particle physics, which concerns itself with matter so small that it lacks magnitude yet still exerts attraction and has inertia. A central discipline as capital becomes ever more frictionless, ownership disappears as a measure of wealth, and money comes to lack intrinsic meaning.

Permanent flexibility. What all great companies and managers will have—the capacity to constantly remake themselves as different and randomly arising situations demand.

Privacy management. Critical in the Age of Access and one of the next great growth sectors. As connectivity spreads, privacy management will become the ultimate status tool.

Real disguise. Getting outside the box, adopting a disguise that allows you both to be yourself and to experience life or a situation from a different perspective. The standard work in the field remains John Howard Griffin's *Black Like Me.* See *diversity IQ.*

Shelf determinism. The capacity of products to transform themselves on the shelf without any physical changes—a characteristic of all great global brands. Tide, to cite one example, takes on different meanings for differing cultures, but however the culture defines "clean," Tide is its standard of excellence.

Sisbertizing. Named for the movie critics Siskel and Ebert, this is the process by which products and ideas are validated within particular microcultures by objective social critics anointed by the microculture to do so. Every microculture has its Sisberts, and it is crucial to appeal to them because, while advertising can create arousal among the microculture, only sisbertizing can create conviction.

Situal intimacy. Intimacy based on proximity, not deep association. The annual Bohemian Grove gathering in California—an exercise in shared nudity among the rich and powerful—is an example of the creation of situal intimacy, as is the U.S. Marine Corps' boot camp at Parris Island, South Carolina. Arthur Andersen institutionalized situal intimacy among its trainees by giving them free tickets and encouraging them to get drunk with each other. Situal intimacy can lead to *situational love* (see below).

Situational lifestyles. Deal-based, not loyalty-based lifestyles.

Situational love. Spasms of affection driven by circumstances that have no binding effect beyond the moment. The intensity of situational love grows in direct proportion to our incapacity to spend emotional capital in the course of our ordinary lives, and as the compression of time intersects with the acceleration of stress, the incapacity to spend such capital in the normal course of events grows exponentially. See *situal intimacy*.

Slinky theory. A theory of social history based on the premise that at any given moment society, like a Slinky toy, is either contracting toward consensus or expanding toward the exploration of end points.

Thrival skills. Skills that will allow individuals and businesses to not just survive but to thrive in the Age of Possibility.

Tribal marketing. The creation of affinity groups for commercial ends. Perhaps the most notable and successful contemporary example is Harley-Davidson, which has coupled the sale of motorcyles and peripherals to the creation of weekend motorcycle clubs and an entire way of life built around Harley-Davidson products. Tribal marketing works best when it is constantly reinforced with icons.

Truncated equilibrium. The theory that evolution occurs not as a succession of regularly repeated peaks and valleys, but in huge forward leaps followed by long plateaus. We are currently in the midst of one such leap.

Truncated perspective. What happens either individually or within corporations when communalism artificially limits the ability to see things whole.

Unrules. A form of corporate discipline built on the premise that in a chaos world the company with the fewest rules wins.

Value stacking. How generational values are transmitted. Each generation inherits a stack of values from its predecessors, and each value is subtly transformed as it is stacked and passed on. Value stacking is influenced by the acceleration in the rate of generational change.

Values-based management. Management based not on objectives, but on a finite number of incontrovertible beliefs never subject to a proof test. In a chaos-based world in which objectives are constantly overwhelmed by variables, values-based management assures that decisions ultimately arrange themselves to serve the good of the whole.

Vectron. An idea or product that pushes a company in a short-wave, relatively insignificant direction, yet is critical to the company's ability to operate on the bleeding fringe.

Wall flowers. Corporations seeking owners. In such companies, values are shaped not by the long-term future, but by the short-term ambition to be acquired by somebody else.

Wrebels. Employees who stray from the inherent values of an organization and thus seek to wreck its value system. If wrebels are important enough, they are sent to *global pillory* (see above).

Xerophilia. Not from the Greek root *xero*, meaning "dry," but from the company that turned its dry-copying procedure into a global trademark. The love of copying, and the ability of everything to be copied.

Index